Philosophy and the Arts

ROYAL INSTITUTE OF PHILOSOPHY SUPPLEMENT: 71

EDITED BY

Anthony O'Hear

CAMBRIDGE
UNIVERSITY PRESS

Shaftesbury Road, Cambridge CB2 8EA, United Kingdom

One Liberty Plaza, 20th Floor, New York, NY 10006, USA

477 Williamstown Road, Port Melbourne, VIC 3207, Australia

314–321, 3rd Floor, Plot 3, Splendor Forum, Jasola District Centre, New Delhi – 110025, India

103 Penang Road, #05–06/07, Visioncrest Commercial, Singapore 238467

Cambridge University Press is part of Cambridge University Press & Assessment, a department of the University of Cambridge.

We share the University's mission to contribute to society through the pursuit of education, learning and research at the highest international levels of excellence.

www.cambridge.org
Information on this title: www.cambridge.org/9781107661745

© The Royal Institute of Philosophy and the contributors 2013

A catalogue record for this publication is available from the British Library

ISBN   978-1-107-66174-5   Paperback

Contents

List of Contributors

Anthony O'Hear – Royal Institute of Philosophy

Matthew Kieran – Leeds University

Peter Kivy – Rutgers University, New Brunswick

Jerrold Levinson – University of Maryland

Anthony Savile – Kings College London

Paisley Livingston – Lingnan University

Martin Warner – University of Warwick

John Hyman – Queens College, Oxford

Mark Rowe – University of East Anglia

Robert Grant – University of Glasgow

Aaron Ridley – University of Southampton

Andy Hamilton – University of Durham

Preface

This volume contains papers based on the Royal Institute of Philosophy's annual lecture series given in London in 2010–1. In the series a group of distinguished aestheticians were asked to speak about different forms of art, highlighting where possible the distinctive ways in which each medium approached its subject matter, and also suggesting what each added to our aesthetic understanding more generally. So we had lectures on painting, sculpture, music, poetry and the cinema. To these medium-specific presentations there were more general discussions of artistic value, artistic truth, the value of performance and the problem of fakes, to round off what we hope will be a valuable and somewhat novel collection, of interest both to aestheticians and philosophers more generally.

The Royal Institute of Philosophy would like to thank the lecturers for their presentations, both oral and written, and also Adam Ferner for his work on copy-editing, proof-reading and indexing.

Anthony O'Hear

On Sculpture

ANTHONY O'HEAR

Is there anything significant in the fact that Aristotle, in explaining his conception of causation, takes the activity a sculptor as one of his key exemplars, his paradigm, if you like?[1] In this paper, I am going to see if, in using Aristotle's account of causation, we can illuminate the nature of sculpture and the approach sculptors take to their art.

Other artists make; poets make poems, painters make paintings, dancers make ballets, architects design buildings but sculptors *make* in an elemental, physical way.

They themselves wrestle with materials (*material* cause) – at least, that is our image of the sculptor, even if in some cases they actually have assistants to do some of the labouring for them. Sculptural materials are traditionally stone, particularly marble, and bronze and wood, hard and impermeable materials, weighty and endowed with presence, not easy to push around, in themselves inert and inanimate. It is this initial presence invested in the unformed material which the sculptor will enhance in the fully formed work, or at least he will if he is successful. In sculpture, the inert becomes animate, or if not actually animate, certainly worked through by mind, infused with life, meaning and finality by mind. Although Aristotle's example is of a sculptor working in bronze, maybe the paradigm sculptural case is the worker in stone. The typical sculptural instruments are chisel, hammer, knife, capable both of strength, necessarily so, but also delicacy.

He (Aristotle) would, of course, have known this well enough. Greek temples were virtual repositories of stone sculpture, not just inside, but outside, with magnificent statues of Athene, Zeus and other gods, and stunning friezes depicting mythological incidents, as part of the architecture. And there were, of course, the *kouroi*, those astonishing marble figures, often life-sized, their faces and figures human in a way Egyptian sculpture is not, but without the illusionistic smoothness and softness of Hellenistic sculpture. If we like to see works of art as material transformed – having a double

---

[1] cf Aristotle, *Metaphysics*, V.2; *Physics*, II.3; Thomas Aquinas, *Commentary on Aristotle's Physics, passim*. The scholastics made a great deal of the sculptor/sculpture example in their explanations of cause.

doi:10.1017/S1358246112000227   © The Royal Institute of Philosophy and the contributors 2013
Royal Institute of Philosophy Supplement **71** 2013   1

aspect in which the material cause is not disguised, factitiously made to look as if it is not what it is – the archaic kouros could be a paradigm case. (I'm going to come back to that, to the distinction between a sculpture and a waxwork, as it were.)

In working with stone there is risk and potential disaster, where one false blow could ruin the marble the sculptor has chosen. You can't stick bits of stone together without destroying their seamless quality. This 'hands-on' element makes working in stone akin to a high-wire act, particularly as when a block of good Carrara marble, say, is rare and expensive. But the worker in bronze and other metals will also get physically involved, forging his work, or, as is often the case, in a slightly less elemental way, moulding a figure in wax in preparation for the casting (the so-called *cire perdu* or lost wax method). In the 20th century, indeed, sculptors have increasingly gone back to working blacksmith-like, with heavy metal, forging and shaping iron, in paradigmatic craft fashion, as with stone sculpture, direct and at times hard physical labour undergirding artistic inspiration.

The physical moulding and shaping by the sculptor is the clearest image we have of *efficient* causation working on a *material* cause. We see before us the whole transformative process. But matter and efficient cause are by no means the whole story, in contrast to, say, an asteroid hitting the moon and causing a crater to appear.

In working with the material cause, the efficient cause (Polyclitus, the sculptor, in Aristotle's example) imposes *form* on the originally formless (*formal* cause). It may be objected here that the marble or molten metal or wood or wax is not completely formless. It is not *materia prima*; it is marble or wax or wood or molten metal; but it is not yet what we are talking about and what it will become, a sculpture. In particular, the unsculpted stone *is* unformed by human mind or hand, even if sometimes a sculptor will chose a piece of stone for the potential he sees in it, its potential to be a sculpture, or even in its veining and or its original conformation its potential to be the sculpture he wants to make (again a point I shall come back to). But even in these cases, it is the work of the mind of the sculptor to see the potential in the first place, to elicit the form that might have been there embryonically, and to work it up.

In thinking of formal causes, we are in the area of what John Hyman, in his paper in this volume, calls 'sense': where, in the case of a sculpture, a piece of physical matter becomes significant by virtue of how it looks. In a sculpture the matter (marble, bronze, or whatever) is to be seen as having an intended shape, as having a form if you like, and in some cases that form to be seen as having an intended reference to other things, such as the human body or a horse. Form or sense being intended is important here. Unlike Hamlet teasing Polonius about the shapes to be seen in clouds, in the case of sculptural form we are in what Robert Grant, in his paper in this volume, refers to as the tertiary realm, where (primary quality) matter with secondary qualities (shape, colour, etc.) is taken up into the realm of human significance and will, as meaning something to us, and intended to have that meaning by the sculptor.

That for which the sculptor's work is done (*final* cause) can be almost any human intention, from the most mundane to the most elevated, anything from a day's wage to the attempt to embody the serenity and majesty of the divine, and maybe sometimes both, as, for example, in *Le Beau Dieu* in the West Portal of Amiens Cathedral.

Of course, the day's wage is an external final cause, something in order to produce which the sculpture is made, whereas the attempt to embody the divine is internal to the structure and nature of the sculpture, inseparable from the form. Formal and final cause here come together, the final cause being that in the sculpture to which the formal cause is directed, the *outcome* to which the forming *process* is directed. Aristotle thought that they came together in the biological sphere too. The form of an organism was intrinsically related to its functioning, the heart the form it was to serve its function of pumping blood, a function and a form which were collectively the product of the designing intelligence. I am not going to get involved in the philosophy of biology here, save to say that I'm not convinced that Darwin has eliminated final causes from nature. The heart is still, even in the neo-Darwinian model, there because it pumps blood, in a sense then in order to pump blood. But still, in the biological case, we may have eliminated any notion of an intelligence guiding the process leading to the outcome, but clearly in the sculptural case, we know what the guiding intelligence is; it is that which guides the hand and the eye of the sculptor, which expresses itself in this activity (and note that in real life, as opposed to somewhat degenerate philosophy and even degenerate sculpture, the form emerges in the activity of sculpting, rather than being imposed as an external and already existing blueprint – sculpting by numbers, so to speak: it happens, but it is not the best case, where the intelligence and the matter and activity are all intimately conjoined). So in sculpture the efficient cause, in its production of formal and final causality, has to be seen as an intelligent artificer, the paradigm of the intelligent designer.

In considering *Le Beau Dieu* we go back to sculpture which is part of architecture, sculpture which is for the sake of some over-arching project or purpose. Looked at like this, sculpture of this sort is particularly apt for expressing the dialectic between the individual craftsman and the communal and in this case transcendent purpose. The individual work is not submerged in the whole, but is actually elevated by its role and position. Ruskin made a great deal of this aspect of Gothic sculpture, also maintaining that in Gothic work the individual craftsman was able to express his own soul: 'the principal admirableness of the Gothic schools of architecture (is) that they thus receive the results of the labour of inferior minds; and out of fragments full of imperfection, and betraying that imperfection in every, indulgently raise up a stately and unaccusable whole'.[2]

Underlying Ruskin's point here are two further considerations. First there is the value of the soul of the individual worker, which, in Ruskin's well-known view, is shredded in the division of labour, but he also thinks it is crushed when the worker has to work according to some pre-determined model of perfection – so, for Ruskin, perfection in a work of art can be a sign of weakness in the conception rather than its strength. Then secondly we should recognise our 'lost power and fallen soul', not as a state intensely and irredeemably painful, but as 'tending, in the end, to God's greater glory'. 'Do what you can', Ruskin says, 'and confess frankly what you are unable to do'. So we have his love of the weird and ill-shapen, even at times crudely and clumsily crafted, figures in the Gothic cathedrals – perhaps tending to God's glory in their contribution to the great churches in which they are placed, and in their manifestation of the individuality of the carver. But I think there may be another aspect to Ruskin's thinking here. Sculptors do not have the powers of Pygmalion, whose statue was made into the flesh and blood Galatea, nor should they pretend to such.

Sculptors are mortal men and women, lost and fallen into the material world. It would follow from looking at things in this way that we see the material cause transformed in their work, manual and mental – yes – but not alchemised into something else altogether, such as the flesh and blood of a living, breathing human being. Against the ambition of a Pygmalion, physical integrity of the material cause of the sculpture should be respected, maybe even in the manner of Michelangelo's *Rondanini Pieta*. Here the figures are still clearly part of the marble block from which they are hewn, which in a way emphasises both their vulnerability and the mother's poignant

---

[2]   This quotation and the phrases in the following paragraph are from John Ruskin's 'The Nature of then Gothic', in *The Stones of Venice,* in *The Works of John Ruskin,* edited by E.T. Cook and A.Wedderburn, George Allen, London 1903–12, vol 10, 190.

protectiveness of her now dead son. Even their faces can be seen as emerging from the marble, which, in contrast to classical and medieval sculpture was not painted – something which led to a concentration on the shape and material elements of the sculpture, elements which post-Michelangelo have taken on increasing importance in sculptural aesthetics. And perhaps in line with this shifting emphasis, Rodin was but one of many later sculptors who exploited the aesthetic possibilities opened up by having figures as it were emerging from the stone from and of which they were formed.

To go back to *Le Beau Dieu*, as the summit of the medieval spirit, so esteemed by Ruskin:

'Of the statue of Christ, itself, I will not speak at any length, as no sculpture would satisfy, or ought to satisfy, the hope of any loving soul that has learned to trust in Him'

so, no idolatry, no Pygmalion magic here, but

'at the time it was beyond what till then had been reached in sculptural tenderness; and was known, far and near as the 'Beau Dieu d'Amiens', yet understood... (as) no idol, only a letter or sign of the Living Spirit, which, however, was conceived by every worshipper as here meeting him at the temple gate (i.e. the Living Spirit, whose sign this stone is) ... the best single rendering of the idea (of the Lord of Hosts, the Lord of Virtues) ... to a well-taught disciple in the thirteenth century'

And he goes on point out that while, gathered round le Beau Dieu there are prophets who mourn, apostles who are persecuted, and disciples who are martyred, what we read in the stone before us is Christ, not as the crucified or the dead, but as 'the Incarnate Lord, the perfect Friend, the Prince of Peace on Earth, the Everlasting King in Heaven. This, according to Ruskin is the 'pure, joyful, beautiful lesson of Christianity', from which habitual contemplation of Christ's death must be a fall from faith. While 'every stone of the building is cemented with (Christ's) blood, and there was no furrow of its pillars that was not ploughed by His pain', what we have before us is the God of the Last Judgement: 'He holds the Book of the Eternal Law in is left hand; with is right He blesses – but He blesses on condition: "This do, and thou shalt live, this be and thou shalt live... (with) the further word 'This if thou do not, this thou art not, thou shalt die".' And for Ruskin this figure, and its weight of meaning, was seen daily by the people, 'simply, sternly for the great three hundred years of Christianity in her strength.'[3]

[3] All quotations from Chapter Four of Ruskin's *The Bible of Amiens* (1880–5), in Ruskin's *Work*, (*loc cit*), Vol 33, 147–8 and 169–70.

Anthony O'Hear

So, for Ruskin, this statue on a pillar in a gateway was a key sentence in a Bible, whose message could be read, clearer perhaps than writing which, for most of the medieval populace, could not be read... That sculpture *could* have this meaning is all part of its formal and final causation, that this statue is something with a meaning, a sense embodied in its matter, (formal cause) and there to be read in this way (as intended, as endowed with a purpose, a final cause). But note that, as Ruskin says, it is a symbol, a rendering of an idea (even if the 'best possible' rendering of this idea, best possible because the force comes from the aesthetic quality of the statue itself, in which severity and tenderness, divinity and humanity, majesty and vision are inextricably combined and articulated). It is not, though, an idol or a miraculous Galatea; it is still a stone (material cause) that someone has worked on (efficient cause).

I think we can say that the craftsman carver who did this – *soli Deo gloria*, perhaps, or maybe with an eye to his day's wage as well – has not so smoothed out the stone as to obliterate the statue's material provenance under an unnatural sheen (although it would have been painted), nor has he, in the manner of the Spanish baroque, tried to produce an object which, spookily, has the manifest properties of a live human being.

For me, precisely because of the stylisation, even simplification involved in the Amiens statue, its meaning is purer, more dignified and more forceful than a realistic work would be (which couldn't in any case, properly show forth the majesty of the Divine Judge – we would be distracted by the physical details so illusionistically crafted by the sculptors of the Spanish baroque, by Jesus's loin cloth or his hair style, or whatever).

Does it matter that we do not know the name of the Amiens sculptor? Are we (and Ruskin) fantasising about his spirit of service to a greater glory? I think not, or not entirely, which I think may come out by contrasting it with another work of genius, but this time one done by someone whose name we do know. What I have in mind here is Michelangelo's *David*. Even though this sculpture was, I believe, produced in order to play its part in an architectural complex (the Palazzo della Signoria, in Florence, the block of marble chosen some decades earlier for a statue of David having originally been destined for the façade of the Cathedral of Santa Maria del Fiore); even though all this, there is, I think, a sense here of self-assertion, or if not of assertion of the self of the artist, a sense that the statue itself is proud and assertive – of humanity? – in a way *Le Beau Dieu* is not, in a way a traditionally sculpted Buddha would not be. It would be very hard to see *David* as drawing our compulsions within, to a haven of inner peace, as opposed to asserting the physicality and humanity of this man.

So partly because of its very physicality, sculpture can subserve quite contrasting effects. But also because of its context – something we may overlook in seeing sculpture in a gallery, all jumbled up and taken out of context. Think of the Apollo in the Olympia pediment, to which Michelangelo might have been indirectly referring (not that he knew of this actual piece, but he certainly knew of the aesthetic underlying it). The Olympian Apollo is beautiful, the sort of beauty known (for obvious reasons) as Apollonine; out of context it is a human beauty, but here it is divine, definitely the divinity taming the human and the sub-human. But this itself shows us that focusing on Nietzsche's distinction between the Dionysian (music) and the Apollonine (plastic arts) might mislead; for, as we see in the *Laocoön*, we can also have the Dionysian in stone.

I've already mentioned that some people don't like this sort of Hellenistic sculpture, precisely because of its apparent aesthetic, of repudiating its material. Form here submerges matter, if you like. But maybe one can be too precious about the alleged purity of archaic Greek sculpture, if one thinks of the way the silken diaphanous fabric of the chiton is rendered in the 6th century Kore statues, the sisters of the Kouroi.

In practice in most sculpture there will be several final causes, several purposes for which the work is done; but as human work, it will have always have some final causality, and in having it, a sculptural object will be distinguished from a purely natural stone, however similar the two might be in appearance. We can appreciate this when we consider the prehistoric menhirs, standing stones, to be found all over Europe, put there by our pre-literate ancestors. A whole host of other questions, about form and meaning, will then come into play in determining our response to the sculptural object. In the case of the (thousands of) menhirs there are in Europe, we simply do not know their purpose; but we know that they are the products of intelligent design, with the full panoply of causation.

Even without understanding their final or even formal causes, menhirs and similar prehistoric stones do exemplify a fundamental aspect of sculpture, the way sculpture is spatial, and marks out space. Precisely because we do not know anything about their meanings or purposes, they allow us to focus on the nature of their spatiality, and, by extension, to delve into the nature of space itself. I think that the conclusions we might draw from these reflections could be drawn from considering natural objects in space; but this would be more difficult because natural objects are usually part of a continuous tract of space, and aren't so clearly self-standing, standing out against the rest of their environment. Objects we make, like tables or chairs, are not parts of a continuous nature, but we rarely look at them as they are in themselves, as opposed to as they are for our purposes, so like a feature of a natural landscape, they too are normally seen in their relation to other objects – all of which tends to make us look at space simply as a container, in which things are put, and in which they are related to us and to our purposes, or to other things in a wider environment; but there is another and more profound way of conceptualising space and our experience of space. In this more fundamental conception, space does not pre-exist objects. Indeed if there were not objects, there would be no space. Space and objects come into existence simultaneously, and we only forget this because in our experience there are always objects (and hence space) there already, and we tend to think of space as a kind of permanent, neutral background to the objects which we conceive as filling it.

I submit that when we see a menhir, because we know that it is not a natural part of a landscape, but something made or placed there, and because we do not see it in terms of our purposes, we see it as itself constituting a place, and not merely belonging to a place. Space here – its space or place – is not that in which the menhir is placed, but is brought into being by its presence. When we look at it, we see it as the centre of its world, both attracting us and our vision to it, and also articulating and constructing its own space around it, by which it comes into relation with other things and their places. If we question the container view of space, as I think we should on general philosophical grounds, then space arises only through the presence of the objects which come into existence, and which, by coming into existence and motion, define space and its hypothetical dimensions and limits. If there were no objects, and space were a container, how big would the container be? What would be (say) a mile or a metre within it? What would have to happen for the size of the container to be doubled or halved? I think that because these questions would have no meaning or answer, we should conclude that it is wrong to conceive of space as a container which is ontologically prior to the objects which we conceive as being 'in' space.

What I am suggesting is that certain types of sculptural object, because we see them as existing in and for themselves, and without any discernible purpose, can help us to experience the elementary nature of space. We sometimes experience sculpture as the centre of its own space, constructing its own space, gathering space around it, thickening it, so to speak, both tying things into its orbit and sending its own vibrations out beyond itself, to other things it connects with. (And maybe if we think of gravity as the curvature of space, brought about by the presence of physical objects, this experience or thought is not completely metaphorical or abstractly metaphysical.)

Something of what I am getting at is brought out by the following statement by Eduardo Chillida: 'Sculpture and music exist in the same harmonious and ever-developing space. The volume of musical sound fills the silence with tension; similarly there could be no volume in sculpture without the emptiness of space. In the void the form can continue to vibrate beyond its own limits; the space and the volume together, selecting from all the potential structures inherent in the form, build up its final shape. The rhythm is determined by the form and is renewed with it.'[4] The idea is of space or of a space being moulded, shaped, even brought into existence by the ebb and flow of the objects in it and their mutual relationships; as if objects bring their own space with them.

Chillida's own sculptures seem to me to be the best illustration of what I think he is getting at here. In his *Wind Combs* series (*Peine de Viento*), he produces work which encompasses, articulates and constructs its own space. These works, large and curved abstract iron forms, locked as they are into the rocky Atlantic headland of San Sebastian (Donostia), have the effect of focusing our attention not just on themselves, with their empty metallic curves drawing the lines of their own space, but they also humanise the wild environment of which they have become a part: humanise, but not domesticate. In fact, the opposite of domestication – they present us and our work and perception as being bound up in the wild, and in a way cast on its turbulence and in its eye, so to speak, a modern expression of the sublime.

> There is some notion,
> here, of the sea guffawing off reefs,
> to which we compose our daft music
> of comprehension. Rain front on rain front,
> then a sun-gash, clouds moody, the sea's mood
>
> turns from slate-black, to yellow ochre, to green.[5]

---

[4] Eduardo Chillida, quoted in Pierre Volboudt, *Chillida*, (trans. V. Menkes), Harry N. Abrams, New York, 1967, vii–ix.
[5] Geoffrey Hill, *Scenes From Comus* 1.4, Penguin, London, 2005, 4.

Anthony O'Hear

Traditionally Western sculpture has been raised up on an altar or a building or placed on a pedestal, and so not free standing in its own space, and this has in a way deprived it of its full expressive potentiality. In *The Burghers of Calais* it was Rodin's genius to take sculpture off its marble plinth, on to rough ground, so to speak, letting the burghers be on the same level as the public, and letting their own weightiness dominate their own space with an extraordinary psychological power. (In 1347, the burghers of Calais gave themselves and, as they believed, their lives up to Edward III of England, as the price of raising the siege of Calais. In Calais now the ensemble is ridiculously and against Rodin's intention placed on a stone pedestal.)

From the point of view of our fourfold causal analysis, Rodin is making full use of the material cause of his work to bring out the reluctance, the foreboding, the heaviness of the situation and of the weight of fate on the shoulders of the walking men – something which is made fully manifest only when we walk round the group, and see the figures as fully three dimensional. I think that this coiled up power, impression yielding expression, is very characteristic of sculpture from the first half of the twentieth century, which is often semi-abstract, so as to emphasise both the materiality of the material (material cause) and the way in which space is here made dense, dense with tension, releasing considerable psychological force. But, I would argue that in a way sculptors like Epstein and Gaudier-Brzeska, and later Henry Moore and Barbara Hepworth were following the path opened up by Rodin in works like *The Burghers of Calais* and *Balzac*.

Summing up a number of themes so far, Epstein wrote this:

> The unworked alabaster block lies in my studio for a year. I can conceive any number of works in it... I always try to get the whole feeling and expression of the work with regard to the material I am working in... with an isolated piece of stone they should regard the sculpture as primarily a block, and do no violence to it as a stone (MATERIAL CAUSE). There must be no exact imitation of nature to make one believe that one is seeing a translation of nature into another material. Imitation is no aim of sculpture proper, and a true piece of sculpture will always be the material worked into a shape. This shape is the important thing, not whether the eye is fooled by the representation, as at Madame Tussaud's waxworks... The work a sculptor is engaged in is continually in his mind (FORMAL CAUSE)... He sees it with his mind's eye, at any moment of the day or night... The vision of the work is there for analysis, as an

inescapable presence. The sculptor with his vision, planning, working, bringing his hands upon the willing and love-returning stone (EFFICIENT CAUSE), the creation of a work, the form embodying the idea, strange copulation of spirit and matter, the intellect dominating hammer and chisel – the conception that at last becomes a piece of sculpture.' (FINAL CAUSE).[6]

(In my discussion I have tended to think of final cause as internal to the sculptor, that effect to which the sculpture is directed, its achieved impression so to speak, that to which the form or sense is moving us, rather than more external aims, such as fame for the carver or his day's wage.)

Because we are so used to seeing sculpture either in two dimensional reproductions or as attached to a building, we tend to overlook its three-dimensionality (and conversely tend to underestimate the poverty of photographic reproductions).

Even in bas-relief, as with the horses in the Parthenon Frieze, there is the effect of the constantly changing light on the stone, and also of the viewer seeing it from different angles which again alters the way the light falls on the stone (to say nothing of the way this – then painted – marble would have looked so sharp in the Athenian light of its day). And one can also think of the extraordinarily delicate shadows cast by the wire and string pieces by sculptors such as Naum Gabo and, in certain phases, Barbara Hepworth, all part of the vibrant effects made possible by the sculptural three dimensionality of their constructions.

But I want to end by referring a work which may seem to go against the spirit of quite a lot of what I have said – but which, actually, in its own way seems to me to articulate its own space, in a way which is never still, which is never capturable in a two dimensional image, which has all the geometric potential of Chillida, but which at the same is intensely human, but elevating and dancerly, still, but never still. The point is that, like all sculpture, one has to see Canova's *The Three Graces* in three dimensions to appreciate it properly. (The Three Graces or Charities classically are akin to the Muses, daughters of Zeus, or perhaps of Dionysus and Aphrodite, Aglea goddess of splendour, Euphrosyne that of mirth and Thalia of good cheer: somewhat vague in origin and protean in significance, though clearly always invoking feminine grace, generosity and beauty) Here Canova has (in my view) exploited the three

[6] Jacob Epstein, *Let There Be Sculpture*, (Michael Joseph, London, 1942), 154–5.

Anthony O'Hear

dimensionality of the medium to the full, with ever changing complexity, perspective and emotional charge as one looks from different angles, a perfect expression of what Seneca spoke of as the 'giving, receiving, returning' motif of the Graces, by turns sensuous and humane and even, in a neo-Platonic sense, spiritual, akin to Botticelli's evocation of the Three Graces in his *Primavera* – a deeply affecting example of the power of sculpture, exploiting to the full its three dimensionality and its formal-expressive opportunity, even its spiritual potentiality, but not negating its materiality.

Royal Institute of Philosophy
editor@royalinstituepholosophy.org

For the Love of Art: Artistic Values and Appreciative Virtue

MATTHEW KIERAN

It is argued that instrumentalizing the value of art does an injustice to artistic appreciation and provides a hostage to fortune. Whilst aestheticism offers an intellectual bulwark against such an approach, it focuses on what is distinctive of art at the expense of broader artistic values. It is argued that artistic appreciation and creativity involve not just skills but excellences of character. The nature of particular artistic or appreciative virtues and vices are briefly explored, such as snobbery, aestheticism and creativity, in order to motivate a virtue theoretic approach. Artistic virtues are intrinsically valuable excellences of character that enable us to create or appreciate all sorts of things from everyday recipes to the finest achievements of humankind. Such an approach offers a new way to resist the age old temptation to instrumentalize the values of art.

Introduction

It is a commonplace to bestow a high value on art. We often look to works of art for pleasure, insight, emotional expression, solace or glorification. This is not to say that art plays the same roles in the lives of all. Nonetheless, engaging in appreciative or artistic activities of one sort or another is important to many. The mere fact that certain activities are significant for people bestows a certain kind of value on them. They are valuable just in virtue of people valuing them. Yet why activities matter makes a difference as to how and why we should value them. Train spotting or playing games, for example, matters to some, yet such activities do not have the same kind of value that pertain to artistic creation and appreciation. Why? Well at a minimum we might say that some pleasures are deeper than others. But that does not get us very far. After all, we might ask, what is it that makes the pleasures of art run deeper than the pleasures of many other activities (if indeed they do)?

doi:10.1017/S1358246112000197

Matthew Kieran

The Instrumentalization of Art

It is testimony to the presumption in favour of art that we have so many museums, concert halls and libraries. Indeed public taxation often subsidizes the collection and exhibition of works in buildings that amount to secular temples. It is, we might think, a mark of a civilized culture that it respects artistic achievement. It is also, we might think, the mark of a fair society that it seeks to cultivate appreciative capacities and access to art for all. Yet given the call on public resources what kind of justification can or should we give for the claims of art? On the one hand why give money for art rather than, say, the pleasures afforded by theme parks or through playing sport? On the other hand, why devote money to mere pleasures at all when we could give more to supporting people's health and well-being? Indeed, in times of financial austerity such questions seem particularly sharp.

The claims most commonly made on behalf of art, at least in the public sphere, emphasize further ends that art supposedly helps us to realize. In the U.K. the value of the arts, subsumed more generally under the cultural sector, is characterized from a public policy point of view in terms of socio-economic impact. Large claims are often made regarding the economic value of the creative industries or the creation of social capital and cohesion.[1]

Whilst there is much to be said in favour of such an approach (perhaps it is the only case that treasury departments are interested in), it is deeply problematic if it is the only case that is being made. Justifying art instrumentally, whether that be in economic, emotional or any other terms, threatens to lose sight of what is most significant about artistic creation and appreciation. It is to treat art as one practice amongst many, all of which can instrumentally lead to the same ends. Taking part in or following a particular sport, for example, may bring many of the same benefits. Football clearly can cultivate a sense of communal belonging, facilitate emotional expression and, given its

---

[1]   The U.K. Department for Culture, Media and Sport has consistently emphasized that the cultural and creative industries promote economic growth. See, for example, the DCMS report *Staying Ahead: The Economic Performance of the U.K. Creative Industries* (2007). The recent DCMS commissioned report by David O'Brien, *Measuring the Value of Culture* (2010) examines how the arts might adopt economic valuation techniques that mesh with H. M. Treasury (as is the case with health and the environment). This is far from a parochial concern. See, for example, the U.S.A's National Endowment for the Arts report *Time and Money: Using Federal Data to Measure the Value of Performing Arts Activities* (2011).

popularity, bring large economic benefits with it. It might be tempting to respond that sport hardly cultivates insight and perhaps insight is the instrumental benefit art best promotes. Close followers of sports might disagree. The interest in many sports centres on battles of wits, wills and psychological dramas more generally. Hence 'this beautiful game that is battle and sport and service and art'[2] might be said of many sports. No matter. If we are looking for uncontroversial insight why invest in art rather than history, psychology or documentaries? What framing matters in such instrumental terms occludes, as we shall see, is how we appreciate, seek to do justice to and admire artworks.

The instrumentalization strategy also provides a great hostage to fortune. Consider the 'Mozart Effect'. It has become something of a popular myth to hold that listening to Mozart (and certain kinds of classical music more generally) can make you smarter. Don Campbell's popular psychology and business is based on endorsing a strong version of the claim; namely that listening to classical music enhances mental functioning and improves a wide variety of disorders.[3] The idea took hold to such an extent that Zell Miller, the governor of Georgia (USA), set aside over $100,000 of the state budget in 1998 to provide every child with a classical music cd. Yet the original study initiating such a wave of enthusiasm was much more limited than popular uptake might suggest, only claiming to demonstrate that spatio-temporal abilities were *temporarily* enhanced after listening to Mozart (as measured by part of a standard I.Q. test).[4] It is even unclear that the music in the study is enhancing subjects' mental capacities as opposed to just setting a background mood enabling people to perform better. Indeed, the results of a range of meta-studies, conducted by Ellen Winner and colleagues at Project Zero, Harvard, show that many claims concerning art's capacity to improve our mental capacities remain unjustified.[5] Common assumptions about the instrumental benefits of art are often on shaky ground. If instrumentalism is the only public case made for art,

[2]   As spoken by the famous England cricket captain Douglas Jardine in Michael Pinchbeck's play *The Ashes*.
[3]   See Don Campbell, *The Mozart Effect* (New York: William Morrow Harper Collins, 1997) and products such as *The Mozart Effect – Music for Babies*.
[4]   Frances H. Rauscher, Gordon L. Shaw and Catherine N. Ky, 'Music and Spatial Task Performance', *Nature* 365 (14th October, 1993), 111.
[5]   See Ellen Winner and Lois Hetland (eds.), 'The Arts and Academic Achievement: What the Evidence Shows', *Journal of Aesthetic Education* 34 (2000).

then it could be that there is not much of a case after all (and perhaps most of the money spent on art should go to sport or health).

In what follows an alternative case is made for valuing art. Artistic value matters for appreciation (though this is not to say that is the only way it matters). Examining the plurality of artistic values and what is involved in appreciating them leads to the recognition that artistic appreciation is a skill. Yet it is also more than a *mere* skill. Why? Artistic appreciation depends upon certain motivations and dispositions. Art is tied up with intrinsically valuable dispositions to create or appreciate and these excellences are virtues of character. Appreciation and artistic creativity can also be undermined by what we might think of as appreciative vices (such as snobbery or sentimentality). Art is not just worthwhile because of what it is we appreciate. It is valuable because of the skills and character involved in appreciation.

Subjectivity, Objectivity and Appreciative Expertise

Pleasure is often a mark of a work's value as art. However the mere fact that someone takes pleasure in a work (or some group of people do) does not show that it is good as art. Thomas Kinkade's kitsch landscapes are extremely popular in the U.S. and Jeffrey Archer's novels remain bestsellers in the U.K. Yet no one would seriously make claims to artistic greatness on behalf of such works. This is not to deny that there is such a thing as guilty pleasures in art. It is just that the pleasures are guilty due to knowingly enjoying works more than their quality or value merits. The failure to take pleasure in some works can also reflect something about us rather than the work. I may battle through the first 300 pages of Proust's *In Search of Lost Time*, complain that nothing seems to happen and give up. This may just reflect where I am at as a reader rather than tell us something about the value of Proust's literature. The point is our appreciation can be naïve or sophisticated, better or worse. How so?

Artistic appreciation may be subjective in the sense that it is tied to our responses and mental states (e.g. that I feel pleasure when reading novels). Nonetheless it does not follow that there is no disputing tastes. Why? First, at least part of the point of criticism is to make claims about the nature and value of works. Reviews, testimony by friends or the verdict of the test of time point us toward works that, it is claimed, are worth engaging with. Of course, they may be mistaken. That is the point. Second, critics also often point us toward contexts or aspects of works that alter our experience of them (for better or worse). Imagine going to a free jazz concert and being frustrated by the discordant sound of the piano. A more musical friend points out that listening for the piece's harmonic qualities will be frustrating since the percussive nature of the piano is being foregrounded. Listening to the performance under a percussive aspect you might suddenly hear a previously unnoticed musical relationship between the piano and the drums. Much discussion about art is taken up with how to approach works in the most fruitful or appropriate ways. Third, as the music example suggests, our own experience shows that we can come to be better appreciators. When visiting galleries for the first time we may know little about what distinguishes expressionism, naturalism, classicism and baroque from medieval art. Lacking an understanding of context or an ability to appreciate various stylistic features we may consider medieval art to be artless. Yet with more background knowledge and greater experience we can come to see much more in works, at least good works, than we saw at first pass. We also sometimes revise our initial impression downwards, such as when experiencing a work again we get nothing more out of it than first time round and see its flaws more easily.

One model for the kind of objectivity presupposed is articulated by Hume's essay 'Of the Standard of Taste'.[6] Hume's idea is that artworks, like other kinds of objects, naturally give rise to certain kinds of responses in us. It is subjectivist in giving due recognition to the fact that what matters is our responses. Yet it affords an element of objectivity given what matters is how the object gives rise to our experiences. How so? First, someone's human nature can be defective or out of sorts. A colour blind person is a bad judge of colour just as someone with a fever may be unable to taste food. There is a huge range of sensory, emotional and cognitive deficits people can suffer from. Indeed, even being emotionally out of sorts might put someone in a bad position to appreciate artworks. In a state of suppressed rage someone might recognize the energetic nature of Matisse's *The Dance* without appreciating its serenity.

Nonetheless, as Hume recognized, it is not just a matter of possessing standard human nature in the relevant respects and being in an appropriate frame of mind. Appreciation can go also go awry because it is naïve. This is the lesson of Hume's wine tasting analogy when he refers to a story from *Don Quixote*.[7] Sancho's

[6] David Hume, 'Of the Standard of Taste', in his *Selected Essays* (Oxford: Oxford University Press, [1757]1993), 133–153.
[7] Op. cit. note 7, 141.

kinsmen arrive at a village and are invited to drink its wine. On tasting the wine, one kinsman notes that the flavour is marred by a hint of iron whilst the other claims to detect a leathery quality. Much amusement follows as the villagers poke fun at this apparent exposure of false sophistication. The villagers not only taste nothing wrong with the wine, Sancho's kinsmen can't even agree about the taste. Yet once the wine is finished, right down to the bottom of the barrel, what should be revealed but a rusty key bound to a leather thong. It is not that the villagers are radically mistaken about the nature of the wine. It is just that Sancho's kinsmen, who possess more refined pallettes, can discriminate more keenly amongst certain elements in the taste of the wine. Thus, as Hume suggests, appreciation and good judgement requires something like 'good sense, united to delicate sentiment, improved by practice, perfected by comparison, and cleared of all prejudice.'[8]

Artistic appreciation depends upon a wide range of perceptual capacities and cognitive-affective responses that are in principle open to refinement. It is also the case that a work's artistically relevant features depend upon relational properties that may not be directly perceivable. Identifying the relevant representational, expressive or cognitive features of a work of art depends on knowledge of the categories it belongs to and, hence, relies on a large stock of relational knowledge.[9] Without relevant background knowledge and experiences, viewers cannot always be expected to fully appreciate something as an Expressionist painting, a late Rubens or spot ironic allusions to earlier work. Expertise is required and more naïve viewers will often miss, misidentify or only loosely appreciate subtle yet aesthetically relevant features. Why? Good appreciation requires comparative experience, background knowledge, the refinement of certain capacities and, crucially, insulation against irrelevant factors. This is an achievement.[10]

[8]   Op. cit. note 7, 144.
[9]   This includes, for example, the art historical categories required to apprehend appreciatively relevant features such as a work's expressive and representational features. See Kendall Walton, 'Categories of Art', *Philosophical Review* **79** (1970), 334–367.
[10]   See Matthew Kieran, 'The Fragility of Aesthetic Knowledge: Aesthetic Psychology and Aesthetic Virtues' in Peter Goldie and Elisabeth Schellekens (eds), *The Aesthetic Mind: Philosophy and Psychology* (Oxford: Oxford University Press, 2011).

Artistic Skills and Values

A central aim of engaging with works as art is appreciation. But with respect to what? What features and values should we seek to refine our appreciation of? How should we judge the value of works?

Aestheticism focuses on what seems to be distinctive of art. Appreciating works as art is held to concern aesthetic features such as elegance, grace, beauty and the formal treatment of a theme.[11] Indeed, some hold that there are very general aesthetic criteria which govern the value of all works, such as how a work's lower level features combine to give a work its overall unity, complexity and intensity.[12] On this view to appreciate a work as art is not to appreciate it for any insight, knowledge or capacity to teach that it may afford. This is not to claim that the content of a work is irrelevant to its artistic value. It is just that a work's content is relevant *only* in so far as it indirectly impacts upon the work's aesthetic character. Thus, strictly speaking, whether or not Picasso's *Weeping Woman* conveys putative insights into the nature of vicious grief or *King Lear* shows us the folly of parental egoism is neither here nor there. The thematic content of such works is held to be relevant only in so far as the raw material of abiding human interest is artistically worked up into a coherent, unified and harmonious thematic exploration. Aestheticists can acknowledge that artworks may convey insight, but as such this is held to be irrelevant to a work's value as art. It is worth noting though that some aestheticists go so far as denying that artworks can convey worthwhile insights. Where we seek knowledge, justification is required. The aesthete's thought here is that works as art cannot provide justification for the claims they make.[13] We must look elsewhere, it is claimed, to history, science or actual human experience, to see whether grief really can be vicious or egoistic pride corrode familial relations.

Aestheticism is not without its attractions. It provides an answer to the problem of instrumentalization by conceiving of the value of art in distinctive terms i.e. its aesthetic aspect. It also gives an explanation,

---

[11]   See, for example, Peter Lamarque and Stein Olsen, *Truth, Fiction and Literature* (Oxford: Oxford University Press, 1997) and Nick Zangwill, 'Moderate Aesthetic Formalism', *Philosophical Quarterly* **50**, 201, (2000), 476–493.

[12]   Monroe Beardsley, *Aesthetics: Problems in the Philosophy of Criticism* (New York: Harcourt, Brace and World, 1958).

[13]   Jerome Stolnitz, 'On the Cognitive Triviality of Art', *British Journal of Aesthetics*, **32**, 3 (1992), 191–200.

amongst other things, as to how and why we can appreciate works we vehemently disagree with. Yet it is an overly narrow conception of artistic values that remains inadequate to how we appreciate art.

First, consider the fact that we often appreciate artworks due to how they engage and exercise our discriminatory skills or capacities.[14] Chardin's *Boy Playing Cards* might not look much at first. Yet it repays close visual attention. We have a wide on view of a boy seated at a card table, cards in hand. The whiteness of the cards, the cuffs of the boy's shirt and collar, set up certain triangular visual relationships. The effect is to heighten a sense of depth in the pictorial space whilst simultaneously foregrounding the canvas's flatness. It is a subtle demonstration of artistic skill that draws in and exercises the viewer's visual skills. Once we start to notice the whiteness of the collar, our eyes are drawn down toward the cuffs, which have a triangular relationship to the cards in the boy's hand. The cards in hand also have a triangular relationship to those laid out on the table. Finally, the cards laid out on the table and the cards in hand form the base points of a triangle, the apex of which is the card sitting at the very front tucked in a table drawer. This in turn serves to emphasise the flatness of the canvas, against the background structure of visual relationships which heighten the sense of pictorial depth. Chardin's painting flatters viewers with respect to their visual skills whilst simultaneously subtly flaunting its pictorial artistry. In doing so the painting speaks to a particular kind of appreciative engagement that draws on and cultivates skills (in this instance visual ones).

The point holds just as well for cognitive-affective skills as it does for sensory ones. Consider Picasso's *Weeping Woman* once more. It may be that we have never felt such a vicious form of grief nor seen others possessed by it. Yet we see the woman's finger's depicted as angularly slashing across her face, an acidic tear drop gouging the cheek. The deployment of such visual devices cultivates the viewer's ability to discriminate amongst a range of emotional states. We might, after all, now recognise viciousness in grief where we had been blind to the possibility before. Thus it is across a myriad of art forms from visual art to

[14] See Matthew Kieran, *Revealing Art* (London: Routledge, 2004), 138–147. The idea is that when Ernst Gombrich, in *Art and Illusion: A Study in the Psychology of Pictorial Representation* (London: Phaidon, 1960), focuses on appreciating visual schemas or James Wood, in *How Fiction Works* (London: Jonathan Cape, 2008), highlights fictional techniques which draw on seeing the world from another's point of view, we should think of these as the exercise of mental skills.

music or literature. We often appreciate works in terms of the exercise of discriminative capacities and skills, many of which are not concerned with aesthetic qualities whatsoever. Indeed it is through exercising them in appreciation that we come to cultivate and refine them.

Second, works as art often embody putative insights and solicit emotional responses us. Artworks can manifest attitudes and seek assent from us in so doing. Where an attitude is manifest, and deployed via artistic means, it is potentially up for evaluation in a way that can be directly relevant to a work's artistic value. Whether the attitudes sought are justified or not often should affect our appreciation and evaluation of works as art. Consider George Orwell's *1984*. The novel's literary power partly rests upon the dissection of totalitarianism as the pursuit of power for its own sake alongside the concomitant obliteration of individual intimacy. This is precisely what is so deeply horrifying when reading the novel. Now, as the aestheticist insists, part of the literary value does inhere in how the themes are explored. Winston's spiritual annihilation is a fittingly horrifying crescendo to the novel. It is the dramatic culmination of a psychological unease initiated from the very first opening lines:

> It was a bright cold day in April, and the clocks were striking thirteen. Winston Smith, his chin nuzzled into his breast in an effort to escape the vile wind, slipped quickly through the glass doors of Victory Mansions, though not quickly enough to prevent a swirl of gritty dust from entering along with him.[15]

Yet the novel is making truth claims (e.g. about the nature of totalitarianism) and seeks assent from the reader toward certain attitudes. We are supposed to be horrified at the prospect of such a state and this is justified. Why? The nature of totalitarianism, as the novel prescribes us to understand it, is such that it seeks to preclude autonomy, genuine intimacy and trust in others. If the novel were a misrepresentation of totalitarianism, the attitudes it seeks from the reader would not be justified. It would not be such a great novel. What makes the attitudes relevant to the novel's value as literature is that they are conveyed to us via literary means and are central to the novel's purposes. The reader might notice, for example, the irony that Winston's minor individual vices, the gin and Victory cigarettes, have been designated for him. We might pick up on how the Party is represented as being just as obsessed with controlling the physical (watching people's faces, compulsory exercises, gruelling work) as it is with controlling the mind (Doublethink, Thoughtcrime). The literary workings are designed to

[15] George Orwell, *1984* (London: Penguin, [1949] 1989), 3.

get us to apprehend, through prescribing and prompting our imaginative experiences, how and why totalitarianism works as it does. The artistry is designed to shape our attention and responses in ways that render the putative insights relevant to the work's value as art.[16]

The trouble with aestheticism is that it conflates the distinctiveness of art with the values of art. Beauty and aesthetic features more generally are relevant to artistic value, just not exclusively so. Yet we can and should appreciate many works in terms of the sensory, emotional or cognitive skills they call upon us to exercise. Moreover, we should appreciate many works in terms of the putative insights proffered and attitudes endorsed. Hence we are right to evaluate some works in terms of their profundity or depth and damn others for their callowness. If we are true to the myriad ways in which art works can be valuable, then we should recognize we often appreciate works in terms of their profundity, coherence, complexity, coherence, consistency, richness, depth and intelligibility. This is not to say that works cannot be good or great yet mistaken. After all, a work may be profound, yet mistaken, true to life or insightful, yet partial.

Given that insight and the appropriateness of solicited attitudes are often part of appreciation, it follows that the moral character of artworks is often relevant to artistic value. Yet it does not follow, as some have argued, that where a work commends that which should be morally condemned, this is automatically a defect in the work as art. Moralists would have us believe that failures in moral characterization or the solicitation of attitudes that are morally problematic *always* diminishes artistic value.[17] Whilst this may be true some of the time, it fails as a general claim. We commonly engage with works in order to suspend some of our moral commitments and explore different aspects of our intuitions and norms.[18] We appreciate the *Iliad*, *The Sagas of Icelanders* or Clint Eastwood Westerns partly because exploring honour codes involves attitudes and responses very different from ones we might sign up to in real life. Appreciating art

[16] See Berys Gaut, 'Art and Knowledge' in Jerrold Levinson (ed.), *The Oxford Handbook of Aesthetics* (Oxford: Oxford University Press, 2003), 436–450, and Matthew Kieran, *Revealing Art* (London: Routledge, 2004), 148–204.

[17] See Berys Gaut *Art, Emotion and Ethics* (Oxford: Clarendon Press, 2007) for defence of this claim and Noel Carroll, *Beyond Aesthetics* (Cambridge: Cambridge University Press, 2009), Part IV, for interrelated essays defending a more moderate moralism.

[18] See Matthew Kieran, 'Emotions, Art, and Immorality' in Peter Goldie (ed.), *The Oxford Handbook of the Philosophy of Emotions* (Oxford: Oxford University Press, 2010), 681–704.

works often involves a suspension of judgement. We allow some of our real life attitudes or values to be isolated, set aside or reconfigured. This is often a matter of bracketing off ways in which we normally would respond to imaginatively explore different ways of seeing, feeling, responding to and valuing the world. Our imaginative engagement with art works, as with imaginative dreams, fantasies and explorations, is much more complex than moralist critics allow. Whilst it is often the case that a work's morally good character contributes to its artistic value, nonetheless, at least sometimes, for principled reasons, the morally problematic character of a work can positively contribute to its artistic value.

Appreciative Vices and Virtues

Artistic appreciation involves the exercise of skill in apprehending aesthetic qualities, artistic originality, emotional expression, insight and moral understanding. Thus the development and refinement of artistic appreciation is an achievement. What kind of achievement? According to Hume we require something like delicacy of imagination, good sense, comparative experience, practice and freedom from prejudice. Why might this be? Experience is required in order to exercise and develop our discriminative skills. Comparative experiences enable us to compare and contrast different kinds of cases; if you want to know which beer to drink, best not to ask someone who has never drunk beer or only ever drunk Carlsberg. Freedom from prejudice and the dictates of fashion allows for the critical sympathy to appreciate what it is that an artist is trying to do. Delicacy of imagination may be required to pick up on subtle artistic devices, provide rich imaginative experiences and discrimination in our empathetic or sympathetic responses. Good sense might underwrite when it is appropriate to empathise, a grasp of what to take seriously in a work and what to consider irrelevant.

The importance of such requirements is reinforced if we recognize that appreciation and judgement often goes awry due to factors we are often unaware of. A host of recent experiments in psychology suggest that we are more susceptible to certain kinds of errors than we like to think. To take one example subjects at MIT were offered free cups of coffee in return for filling in a questionnaire.[19] After picking the

---

[19]   Marco Bertini, Eliie Ofek and Dan Ariely, 'The Impact of Add-On Features on Consumer Product Evaluations', *Journal of Consumer Research*, **36**, 1, (2009), 17–28.

coffee up, subjects were pointed toward a table with coffee additives (e.g. milk, sugar) alongside more unusual condiments (e.g. cloves, orange peel). After helping themselves to whatever they fancied to go with the coffee, subjects were then asked to fill out the survey. Questions asked included, amongst other things, how much subjects liked the coffee, whether they would buy it in future and how much they would be prepared to pay for it. Over the next few days the experimental set up altered the condiment containers. Sometimes the condiments were in elegant metal and glass containers, whilst at other times they were in jagged Styrofoam cups. The coffee served throughout was exactly the same. Subjects rated the coffee much better when the condiments were in nice containers than when they were in the nasty ones. The phenomenon the coffee experiment points to is not an isolated one and it keeps cropping up in matters of taste and artistic judgement.

In one experiment students at Cornell were asked to rate pairs of Impressionist paintings.[20] The images in each pair were by the same artist (e.g. Monet, Renoir, Degas), depicted very similar scenes and painted around the same time (within two years). The students tended to prefer the more commonly reproduced Impressionist paintings (e.g. in Cornell University art books) over the more rarely produced ones. This may seem unsurprising given the assumption that the more widely reproduced Impressionist paintings tend to be the better art works. All the students are doing, we might think, is picking out the better works. However, over a number of classes an experimental group was then exposed to all the images, with the more widely reproduced paintings in each pair being exposed far less often than the more widely reproduced ones (in a ratio of 1:4). When the course finished the students in this group were also asked to rate the image pairs. The result was that preference for the more widely reproduced works disappeared in the experimental group. The study concludes that mere exposure to works may explain our preferences much more than we like to think. Whilst the results are not at issue, the interpretation is controversial. It could be, for example, that it is not just exposure that is doing the work but, rather, that increased exposure leads to enhanced appreciation. Even the less widely reproduced works used in the study are pretty good. More generally, we might think that cost, social cache or frequent citation in certain contexts can be good indicators of quality. Nonetheless, the empirical studies are suggestive. It seems that

[20]   James Cutting, 'Gustave Caillebotte, French impressionism, and mere exposure', *Psychonomic Bulletin and Review* **10**, 2 (2003), 319–343.

sometimes we conflate the pleasures deriving from appreciation with pleasures derived from sources such as familiarity, cost or status. Indeed it is often much more opaque to us why we like what we do than is commonly presumed. This might tempt some toward scepticism about artistic appreciation. Yet it should be no surprise to learn that naïve appreciators are more susceptible than those with greater expertise to all sorts of aesthetically irrelevant causal factors.[21]

What Hume failed to emphasise is that it is not just skills and abilities that matter. What also matters is why we are motivated to appreciate the works we do and the subsequent kinds of considerations governing our appreciation and judgement. At this juncture it is worth reminding ourselves that only some reasons for artistic valuing count. The mere fact that a particular class likes something, that it is expensive, or popular, does not as such count towards a work's being valuable as art. This is not to deny that there may be all sorts of complex, indirect relations. In some cases that a particular group likes something or it is expensive may be some reason to think a work is good.[22] Rather, the point is, what *makes* a work good cannot consist in its costing a certain amount or possessing a certain social cache. Artistic appreciation and the art world are susceptible to exploitation for all sorts of social purposes. The assertion and maintenance of individual status within groups and in relation to other groups is a primary psychological drive. Indeed this is especially strong in societies where competition and self-expression are at a premium. Hence, to take one example, a key means for achieving social status is via snobbery and this is an appreciative vice that the aesthetic realm is particularly susceptible to.[23] Many people collect art in

[21] See Paul Hekkert and Piet C. W. van Wieringen, 'The impact of level of expertise on the evaluation of original and altered versions of post-impressionistic paintings' *Acta Psycholoigica*, **94**, 2 (1996), 117–131, and Marco A. Hann, S. Gerhard Dijkstra and Peter T. Dijkstra, 'Expert judgement versus public opinion', *Journal of Cultural Economics* **29**, (2005), 59–78.
[22] See Matthew Kieran, 'The Fragility of Aesthetic Knowledge: Aesthetic Psychology and Aesthetic Virtues' in Peter Goldie and Elisabeth Schellekens (eds), *The Aesthetic Mind: Philosophy and Psychology* (Oxford: Oxford University Press, 2011).
[23] Matthew Kieran, 'The Vice of Snobbery: Aesthetic Knowledge, Justification and Virtue in Art Appreciation'. *Philosophical Quarterly*, **60**, 239 (2010), 243–263. For more general virtue theoretic approaches see David M. Woodruff, 'A Virtue Theory of Aesthetics', *Journal of Aesthetic Education*, **35**, 3, (2001), 23–36, Peter Goldie, 'Virtues of Art and Human Well-Being', *Aristotelian Society Supplementary Volume*, **82**, 1, 175–195, Dominic McIver Lopes, 'Virtues of Art: Good Taste' *Aristotelian Society*

order to belong to and be picked out as a certain kind of 'superior' person. It is also clear that snobbery plays a strong role in art world fashions and artistic criticism. It is not uncommon to read reviews of novels being dismissed as genre fiction as opposed to literary fiction (a distinction that arose for commercial reasons in the 1970s). Why is this relevant?

At least some of Hume's characteristics make for good snobs (in the sense of being good at being snobbish) just as much as they make for good appreciators. Snobs are not always wrong and may often be right (perhaps the opera snob is right in claiming that musicals are an inferior art form). Nonetheless snobbish motivation explains how and why a snob's artistic judgement will tend to be unreliable in certain ways. Where the drive to appear superior causally enters into and figures in the wrong sort of roles in appreciation, then the snob will be open to error in a way a virtuous appreciator would not be. Hence the snob will tend to rate something highly just because doing so tends to bring social distinction with it, thereby judging the value of a work according to an inappropriate standard. The social standard will lead the snob astray in judging art wherever social distinction pulls away from tracking artistic value. Furthermore even where snobs get things right they will often lack the right kind of appreciative achievement. It is one thing to judge that a work is good, it is another to appreciate a work appropriately. We are interested in artistic judgements, whether a work is good or not, how good or bad it is, but much of the time because what we are really interested in is appreciation. Given that the snob is concerned with saying the right sort of things only in order to enhance his social status then he may be unconcerned with appreciation or concerned with it only in so far as doing so may achieve the desired social marking. Hence a snob might make good judgements based on acquiring lots of knowledge about art, yet if it does not feed into and amplify his appreciation then something is amiss.

Snobbery is far from the only artistic and appreciative vice. Whilst aestheticism fails to give due recognition to the values of art, in some cases it may constitute an appreciative vice. Where aestheticism is the psychological disposition to respond to works only in terms of narrowly aesthetic appreciation as characterized above, it constitutes an inappropriate standard for the appreciation of many kinds of art works. Following inappropriate standards may constitute a failing

Supplementary Volume, **82**, 1, 197–211, and Peter Goldie, 'Virtues of Art', *Philosophy Compass* **5**, 10, (2010), 830–9.

but it is not always a vice. After all, given where someone is coming from or the stage in aesthetic development doing so may be blameless. Yet where it constitutes a blameworthy aestheticisation of the emotional, cognitive and moral aspects of works, such a psychological disposition constitutes an appreciative vice. If anything like the above account of artistic values is on the right track, then aestheticism will tend toward the following kinds of appreciative errors.

Aestheticists will tend to over value some works where purely aesthetic criteria are applied to works that call for evaluation in cognitive or moral terms. To take an infamous example, Leni Riefenstahl's *Triumph of the Will* is an aesthetically appealing film of the Nuremberg rallies. The power of beauty is utilized to solicit admiration from us toward Hitler and the Third Reich. The psychological type of aestheticist just characterized will tend to savour and value the film highly, due to its aesthetic features. Yet, in line with the argument above, the moral character of the work is relevant to its artistic value. We ought not to respond as solicited and thus the film's value as art is marred. The aestheticist should be troubled in her responses to the film where she is not. Hence the aestheticisation of relevant moral aspects of the film leads her to over value it.

An aestheticist may also tend to under appreciate certain works for similar reasons. An aesthete's appreciation of Henry James's *Portrait of a Lady* would savour the quality of the writing, its allegorical nature and symbolic workings. However part of the point of the novel is bound up with the insight that life and art are not just a matter of aesthetic connoisseurship. Osmond is an arch collector of art, experiences and people. He reifies refined aesthetic appreciation. Nonetheless, Osmond's taste fails him because he is inclined to value aesthetic features in isolation from judgements of goodness. Ralph, the contrast to Osmond in the novel, professes to do so too; yet his coming to see that there is more to life and art than aesthetic connoisseurship marks the key difference. Thus Ralph comes to repent at having used Isobel for his own amusement, whereas Isobel is trapped in a marriage of her own making to Osmond who does not. Ironically the aestheticist may underappreciate such a work precisely because the insightfulness of the attitude explored is held to be beside the point. The point does not just apply to fine art but across a huge range of objects from furniture to architecture where functionality is important. A tendency to create and rate highly aesthetically appealing objects regardless of function is asking for trouble. Philippe Starck's iconic lemon squeezer may look supremely elegant but it is famously useless in fulfilling the function for which it was putatively designed. This is not to say that the philosophical position of aestheticism as such leads to appreciative vice. It is to say, however, that where someone is disposed to respond just to the narrowly aesthetically appreciable features of works, and where this is blame-worthy, it will constitute an appreciative vice where considerations of broader values are relevant to a work's value as art.

Appreciating the myriad motivations we have for appreciating art and how we can go awry is illuminating. We need to be aware of biases we may have and tendencies to confabulate for the purposes of self-aggrandizement. We need to ask ourselves whether we are striving to do justice to works and what our motivations in appreci-ation really are. Considering the role of motivation and character also promises to throw light on the excellences or virtue of character that may be required. Openness to experience is an important psycho-logical trait and one that is closely associated with artistic interest and creativity.[24] It is easy to see why. After all, receptivity to new experi-ences looks like it is an appreciative virtue given the requirement of comparative experience adduce above. It also looks like it is closely related to other appreciative virtues such as curiosity and humility. Curiosity construed as involving something like a disposition to seek out new experiences or explore new possibilities is presumably what often leads artists to develop new styles or techniques and leads appreciators to exciting new discoveries. A taxonomy of appreciative virtues is beyond the scope of this paper but it is worth spending some time on what is perhaps the master artistic virtue: creativity.

What it is to be creative in a minimal sense may be to possess or manifest a capacity to create something new and valuable in a given domain. Yet there is a richer sense in which creativity draws on excel-lence of character.[25] The psychological literature here is suggestive (and vast). One classic experiment took 72 creative writing students and randomly assigned (under certain restrictions) each subject to one of three groups.[26] Subjects in the control group were asked to

---

[24]   See Tomas Chamorro-Premuzic, Stian Reimers, Anne Hsu and Gorkan Ahmetoglu, 'Who art thou? Personality predictors of artistic prefer-ences in a large U.K. sample: The importance of openness', *British Journal of Psychology*, **100**, 3 (2009), 501–516.

[25]   For a more detailed elaboration see Matthew Kieran, 'Creativity as a Virtue of Character' in Scott Barry Kaufman and Elliot Samuel Paul (eds), *The Philosophy of Creativity* (Oxford: Oxford University Press, forthcoming).

[26]   Amabile, Teresa M. (1985), 'Motivation and Creativity: Effects of Motivational Orientation on Creative Writers,' *Journal of Personality and Social Psychology*, **48** (2): 393–99, and Mary Ann Collins and Teresa M.

write a basic poem on the theme of snow, read a John Irving short story, and then write a second poem identical in format to the first on the theme of laughter. Subjects in the two experimental groups followed the same procedure, except that after reading the short story they were asked to read and rank order a list of reasons for writing. The list for one group consisted of intrinsic motivations for writing (e.g. self-expression, insight, word play) whilst the list for the other consisted of extrinsic motivations (e.g. financial gain, social approval, prospects for graduate school). As judged by 12 poets the group primed with extrinsic motivations produced the least creative work at the end.

Whilst there are competing explanations as to what is going on, nonetheless the empirical work is suggestive. Assuming something like equivalence in artistic skills and mastery, intrinsic and extrinsic motivation seem to make a significant difference as to how creatively subjects performed. Intrinsic motivation is the desire to participate in some creative activity for its own sake. Extrinsic motivation, by contrast, is to be motivated to make something which realizes the values of art in so far as doing so instrumentally realizes some further aimed for end (e.g. social status or wealth). Art works can be created, collected and valued for their commodity value. It is no accident that we often refer to the movie or music industry and visual art works can be traded in pretty much the same way one might trade in stocks and shares. Collecting particular artists, knowing certain dealers and moving in some art world circles can also confer social status. It is not as if this is only true with respect to the 'high' end of the art world. Our discourse about and identification with particular kinds of art (e.g. indie music), down to extolling or condemning the merits of certain bands is replete with social signals and uses. The art world and its products can and often are used, amongst other things, in the service of social dynamics, networking, group recognition, in and out group identification, conformity and individualization. There are a myriad of external ends and values that the production and appreciation of art works can serve, and these can play a significant motivational role.

Extrinsic motivation often explains why someone identifies aims and goals that are taken to be the easiest to address in order to lead most directly to the realization of whatever the aimed for goal is.

Amabile (1999), 'Motivation and Creativity', in R. Sternberg (ed.), *Handbook of Creativity* (Cambridge: Cambridge University Press), 297–312.

Thus where creation is governed by extrinsic rather than intrinsic motivation, someone is far less likely to be creative. Why? Where the governing motivation is not directed toward the intrinsic values but contingent extrinsic ones, and where the extrinsic values pull away from the internal ones, extrinsic motivation will be inimical to creativity. This is what the term 'sell out' often denotes.

Of course this need not always be so, since in certain environments extrinsic motivations can enhance rather than undermine creativity. Intrinsic and extrinsic motivation can go hand in hand and recognition sometimes does track artistic achievement. It is just that intrinsic motivation pushes an artist to create valuable works even where the different kinds of motivations come apart. It is also an achievement of character. To remain true to what is worth making and why, despite the lack of recognition or status, is praiseworthy. Hence the admiration that is due to artists such as Van Gogh or Gauguin. It is also admirable to remain true to intrinsic motivations in spite of flattery and popularity. Where previous work has proved successful, dealers and audiences often want more of the same. Hence successful artists are often tempted to go on repeating variations on the same theme despite diminishing returns. It can take courage to remain true to the intrinsic motivations an artist has for creating art. Intrinsic motivation is an excellence of character that is both praiseworthy and explains why artists may be more robustly creative across a range of situations than they would otherwise be.

A Way Forward

An instrumentalized conception of the value of art does an injustice to the multiplicity of art forms and provides a hostage to fortune. Sport, conversation, study, gardening and mood enhancers might realize the instrumental ends supposedly promoted through art (and possibly much better). Aestheticism promises to resist an instrumentalized approach through focusing on the values distinctively realized through art. Yet the aesthete's conception of art leads to a false narrowing of the range of experiences and values artistic appreciation properly admits of. It is not just that skills are involved in artistic appreciation or that we should recognize a broad range of artistic values. Art exercises and cultivates valuable dispositions that include valuable excellences of character. Artistic courage or appreciative humility, curiosity and perseverance are feats of character worthy of praise and admiration. This is especially true given that it is all too easy to be prey to vices such as snobbery. Artistic virtues also explain how we can come to create and appreciate all sorts of things from everyday food recipes to the finest artistic achievements of humankind. If we start to consider the character involved in appreciating and making art, rather than just focusing on judging the value of artworks, we may come to see a more robust way of resisting the temptation to instrumentalize the arts.[27]

Leeds University
M.L.Kieran@leeds.ac.uk

[27] This is a version of my inaugural professorial lecture for the University of Leeds, Friday 12th November, 2010, and a public lecture in London for the Royal Institute of Philosophy, Friday 3rd December, 2010. Grateful acknowledgement is made to both audiences, including family, friends and esteemed colleagues, as well as the U.K. Arts and Humanities Research Council for funding research related to some of this work as part of the 'Method in Philosophical Aesthetics: The Challenge from the Sciences' project.

Authorial Intention and the Pure Musical Parameters

PETER KIVY

1. Introduction

Strictly speaking this is not an essay whose sole subject is music. For what I have to say here can be extrapolated to any other art that possesses the kinds of aesthetic properties that I am referring to, in music, as the 'pure musical parameters'. But I shall not attempt such an extrapolation here, and leave it to the reader. So for all intents and purposes, this *is* an essay on *music*, more particularly, absolute music, music alone, without text, title, program, dramatic setting, or any other extra-musical baggage.

How the topic (and title) of this essay came to be formulated is, I think, important for the reader to know. For it casts some light, I think, on why it should have come to seem an important topic to me and why, as well, it led me to believe that, so far as I know, no one in philosophy of art, at any rate, has attempted to deal with this aspect of authorial intent (although of course I could be wrong about that). So here is how it all happened.

In the July 2009 issue of the *British Journal of Aesthetics* there appeared a symposium consisting in a paper by Christopher Peacocke entitled 'The Perception of Music: Sources of Significance', four responses to Peacocke's paper, one of them by me, and brief rejoinders to these responses by Peacocke.[1] It is a problem, at least as I perceive it, in Peacocke's paper, my statement of the problem, and Peacocke's response to my statement that together have led me to the present reflections.

2. Posing the Problem

There is no need to delve deeply into Peacocke's complex paper. It will suffice to outline those parts of his argument that are essential to my purpose here.

[1]   *British Journal of Aesthetics*, **49** (2009). The other symposiasts besides Peacocke and myself were Paul F. Snowdon, Malcolm Budd, and Laurence Dreyfuss.

doi:10.1017/S1358246112000203   © The Royal Institute of Philosophy and the contributors 2013

Peter Kivy

Peacocke's goal is to explain how it is that we experience what might be called extra-musical qualities in music. 'We can experience music as sad, as exuberant, as sombre. We can experience it as expressing immensity, identification with the rest of humanity.' But, Peacocke continues, 'what it is for music to express these or anything else is easily asked; and it has proved extraordinarily difficult to answer satisfactorily.'[2]

The answer Peacocke offers to the question posed is, in a word, 'metaphor', or, more exactly, as he puts it, hearing 'metaphorically-as'. In brief, the proposal is that 'when a piece of music is perceived as expressing the property F, then some feature of the music, possibly a relational feature, is heard metaphorically-as F', as, for example, 'the rising passage and the progression in Josquin des Prez's setting of the lines "Caelestia, Terrestria, Nove replete laetitia"/"Fills heaven and earth

Example 1.

[2]   Christopher Peacocke, 'The Perception of Music: Sources of Significance,' *British Journal of Aesthetics*, **49** (2009), 257.

with new gladness" [in the motet, *Ave Maria*] can be heard metaphorically-as the gradual filling of a space with gladness.'[3]

The intricacies of Peacocke's proposal, and the complex argument he marshals to back it up are, as I have said, not relevant to my purposes here. What I am concerned with are the implications for our interpretation of *absolute music* if Peacocke's account, or one like it, is correct, of how we experience a passage of music's 'expressing the property F', when the property is an extra-musical one like 'the gradual filling of a space with gladness'. I will assume, then, that Peacocke's account, or something very like it *is* correct. My problem is with the consequences.

Here is the problem. The fact is that we *can* hear a passage of music, in Peacocke's terms, 'metaphorically-as' many *different* things. We *can*, for example, hear the passage from Josquin that Peacocke quotes as the gradual filling of a cup, as in the Twenty-third Psalm: 'my cup runneth over'. The question is: *Should* we hear it that way? Or, in general terms: Of the many possible Fs you can hear a passage of music metaphorically-as, *which*, if any, ought we to hear it metaphorically-as? What are the rules?

In musical settings of texts, as Peacocke makes clear, the answer is quite straightforward, to wit: 'The text fixes a proper subset of the metaphorical contents that *can* be heard in the music, and so *requires that* the music be heard in one kind of way rather than another.'[4] I take it that the meaning of 'can', here, is 'should', and that there is more or less general agreement as to how texts constrain our extra-musical interpretations: how, in Peacocke's terms, they constrain our hearing metaphorically-as (although even the presence of a text does not preclude off-the-wall interpretations). It is the *text* of Josquin's motet that, of course, compels us to hear in the music the filling of a space rather than the filling of a cup.

The problem – *my* problem – enters the picture when we turn our attention from texted music to absolute music. For in music without a text to put the brakes on runaway hearing metaphorically-as, it looks as if anything, or almost anything goes. There seem to be unnumbered extra-musical things you can hear a passage of absolute music metaphorically-as, that many, if not most listeners would find completely off the wall.

Peacocke himself, obviously not unaware of the problem, instances a famous, many would say *infamous* case in point, Susan McClary's interpretation of the written-out cembalo cadenza in the Fifth

---

3   Ibid., 260.
4   Ibid., 265; emphasis mine.

Peter Kivy

Brandenburg Concerto as expressing: 'The possibility of virtual social overthrow, and the violence implied by such overthrow...'[5] Peacocke remarks of this interpretation of Brandenburg 5: 'Some may smile at the specificity of the suggestion...',[6] and he is among the smilers, as am I. But what justification do we have for smiling – scoffing would be more like it – if whatever we are *able* to hear metaphorically-as 'in' the music *is*, *eo ipso*, 'in' the music? All things perceivable metaphorically-as are permissible: musically speaking, *esse est percipi*.

Now to be sure Peacocke is no more willing to embrace this radical conclusion than am I. For he writes: 'It is a fact that there are correct and incorrect, better and worse, ways of hearing a piece of music.'[7] And it is clear from other examples adduced that he thinks this dictum applies not merely to texted music, where the words can dictate what is the correct or better way, but in absolute music as well, where there is no such curb to our free fantasy, as, for example, and it is Peacocke's example, 'the trio section of a symphony'.[8]

Peacocke's way of dealing with the problem is to rely on what is sometimes referred to as the *principle of critical charity*, which enjoins us to choose that interpretation which makes of the work of art being interpreted a *better* work than it would be under any other interpretation on offer. And what that amounts to, for Peacocke, is this: 'To come to hear a piece of music better is to come to hear it as having a richer, more interesting or more significant metaphorical content than one succeeded in hearing in it previously.'[9]

The difficulty with this apparently *exclusive* reliance on the principle of critical charity, as I pointed out in my comments on Peacocke's paper, is that it is far too permissive either for Peacocke *or* for *me*. It will, for example, not license us to 'smile' at McClary's outlandish interpretation of the cembalo cadenza in Brandenburg 5 because she can quite plausibly insist that *her* interpretation gives the work, to use Peacocke's words, 'a richer, more interesting or more significant metaphorical content than one succeeded in

---

[5]   Susan McClary, 'The Blasphemy of Talking Politics during Bach Year', in R. Leppert and S. McClary (eds), *Music and Society: Politics of Performance and Reception* (Cambridge: Cambridge University Press, 1987), 4, quoted in Peacocke, 'The Perception of Music', 266.
[6]   Peacocke, 'The Perception of Music', 266.
[7]   Ibid., 274.
[8]   Ibid.
[9]   Ibid., 275.

hearing in it previously'. One certainly *can* hear it as McClary does. And if our only appeal is to the principle of critical charity, then we *should* do.

Now what I proposed, in my previous comments on Peacocke's paper, was appeal to authorial intent. This is not to say that I reject the principle of critical charity outright. But I take it to be not a sufficient condition principle: rather, a *ceteris paribus* one. And I take it, furthermore, that lack of authorial intent trumps it. In other words, the principle of critical charity says, with regard to absolute music, in part: of those ways you are able to hear the work or the passage that the composer *could have intended*, choose the one that makes of it the best work of art or the best passage.

Authorial intent does just what the principle of critical charity cannot by itself do: it can rule out off-the-wall ways of hearing metaphorically-as that both Peacocke and I would like to rule out. Thus, McClary's claim that the cembalo cadenza in Brandenburg 5 serves, to put it Peacocke's way, as metaphor for social overthrow and its ensuing violence through liberating the harpsichord from its 'subservient' role as mere accompanying continuo instrument and throwing it into an unexpected solo role, can be handily hung out to dry by simply adducing obvious facts that clearly show Bach could have had no such intention in the first place. Item. The two-manual harpsichord was in no need of 'liberation' from the humble role of accompanying continuo instrument, being the preeminent solo keyboard instrument outside of the church, for which Bach wrote many concerti and solo works, Domenico Scarlatti upwards of 500 sonatas. Item. The harpsichord in Brandenburg 5 hardly requires 'liberation' from the humble role of accompanying continuo instrument in the cadenza, being a solo instrument in the concerto right from the get-go. Item. Johann Sebastian Bach would have been just about the last composer in the world to have wanted to express social overthrow or violence in his works, having acquiesced completely in the professional and social role laid out for him from birth, devoting his entire life to the family business, namely organist, composer, and cantor in the service of the Lutheran communion. Conclusion. Even though we *can* hear the cembalo cadenza in Brandenburg 5 the way McClary suggests, we *shouldn't*, in the certain knowledge that Johann Sebastian Bach could not possibly have intended it to be heard that way.

Thus my challenge to Peacocke, if one wants to put it that way, was not to his suggestion that when we hear extra-musical 'content' in music we are hearing, the way he puts it, 'metaphorically-as'. As a matter of fact I am quite sympathetic with the suggestion. Rather,

Peter Kivy

my challenge to him was to back up his apparent claim that in music without a text to rule out errant instances of hearing metaphorically-as, off-the-wall hearings such as McClary's of the cembalo cadenza in Brandenburg 5, the job can be done without appeal to authorial intention but solely through the principle of critical charity.

And this brings me to Peacocke's response to my challenge, which I want now to critically examine. But before I do I want to make clear that the reason I cast a critical eye on it is not to try to initiate one of those boring philosophical disputes over minutiae. Rather, by implication, and not, I believe, by intent, Peacocke has, in his remarks, uncovered an issue in philosophy of art that has not, as far as I know, been dealt with seriously, if indeed at all. That being said, on now to Peacocke's response.

3. Peacocke's Riposte

The basic thesis of Peacocke's response to my worry is concisely stated at the outset: '...I do not think', Peacocke writes, 'that authorial intention that a piece of music be heard a certain way is a necessary condition of the correctness of hearing it that way.'[10] And he adduces as a case in point a very well known musical example, the thematic relationship between the subject of the fugue that begins the first movement of Beethoven's String Quartet in C-sharp Minor, Op. 131, and the main theme of the finale, that enters at bar 21.

Peacocke writes of this example: 'The heard relationship between the two [themes] is, in context, emotionally significant.' As he hears the emotional significance, the 'unalleviated sadness in the first movement...has been completely overcome in the final movement as a whole....'[11]

Note well – and we are now homing in on the main point of this exercise – that there are *two* relationships between these two themes: an emotional one and a purely musical one. And the purely musical relationship between the two themes, although Peacocke does not name it, is a well-known one, a familiar technique in the composer's bag of tricks. The theme of the finale is, in fact, a palpable if not perfect *inversion* of the fugue subject, preserving almost in tact both its intervallic structure and note values, although in a faster

---

[10]   Christopher Peacocke, 'What Is the Role of Authorial Intention in Determining the Correct Way to Hear a Piece of Music?', *British Journal of Aesthetics*, **49** (2009), 304.
[11]   Ibid., 305.

tempo. And, indeed, Beethoven all but 'tells' us, musically, that the theme of the finale is an inversion of the fugue subject by twice quoting its opening three notes directly after the first entrance of the finale theme (mm. 30–31 and 34–35). As Joseph Kerman describes the musical relationship between the finale theme and the subject of the fugue: 'Without duplicating the original fugue subject, this [finale] theme retraces its line, performs a sort of inversion or transformation upon it....'[12]

Example 2.

[12]   Joseph Kerman, *The Beethoven Quartets* (New York: Alfred A. Knopf, 1967), 343.

    Peacocke avers, quite rightly, that: 'No doubt Beethoven was in fact completely aware of the relationship between the two...themes, and the effect is fully intentional.' But he then proposes the following thought experiment: 'suppose' Beethoven 'had not been so aware, and suppose that including the second of the two...themes simply struck him as the best way of offering something that the resolution and energy succeeds in overcoming.' Under such a supposition Peacocke then asks, rhetorically: 'Does it follow that we should not hear the second theme as reminiscent of the fugue theme in the first movement, and that we should not hear the whole [last] movement as defeating the sadness and passivity expressed in the first movement?' His answer, of course, is in the negative. 'In such a case', he writes, 'it seems to me that the correct way to hear the music is the same way as if the composer had indeed had that conscious intention.'[13]
    As shall become apparent later on, my intuition, in entertaining Peacocke's thought experiment, differs radically from his. But before I get to that some clarification is necessary with regard to the concept of authorial intention itself; and to that clarification I now briefly turn.

4. Where's the Intention?

Having proposed as a thought experiment, or an intuition-pump, if you will, an intentionless hearing of the thematic and emotive relationship between the first and last movements of Op. 131, Peacocke then gives just the merest suggestion of a *volte-face*, where he writes: 'Even if the composer did not have the intention to write a theme that uses the elements of the fugue theme, it may be that the unconscious psychological explanation of why that particular theme struck him as a good way of continuing the movement is that it is in fact related to the theme of the sad fugue as described.'[14] Is *intention*, then, being sneaked up the back stairs under the guise of *unconscious* intention? Is unconscious intention to blunt the thought experiment by doing the same work that conscious intention is supposed to do, but that the thought experiment is supposed to suggest is unnecessary? I will leave these questions unaddressed. To do otherwise would lead us astray of the main point.

---

[13]   Peacocke, 'What Is the Role of Authorial Intention in Determining the Correct Way to Hear a Piece of Music?', 305.
[14]   Ibid.

Suffice it to say, whatever pre-conscious or unconscious mechanisms give birth to the themes, motives, and other compositional ideas in the musical genius's conscious mind I consider a mystery forever sealed to human scrutiny, as I have argued at length elsewhere.[15] Nor is it the stage in the compositional process where authorial intention enters the picture. One does not – one cannot – *intend* to get a good idea for a theme, although one can, of course, intend to do other things that might, in the event, end up producing a good idea for a theme.[16] But how the inversion of the fugue subject popped into Beethoven's extraordinary head is irrelevant to the question of authorial intent. It was Beethoven's conscious decision to *use* that theme, the inversion of the fugue subject, rather than some other, for the main theme of the finale, that is the authorial intention at issue.

Peacocke's thought experiment, then, I will take to be this. Imagine that Beethoven decided to use the theme that enters at bar 21 of the finale, never mind how it occurred to him, without being consciously aware, without intending it to be a virtual inversion of the fugue subject in the first movement, and without being consciously aware, without intending to have the emotive contrast to the fugue subject in the first movement Peacocke takes it to have. Imagine further that you know for certain, never mind how, of the lack of authorial intent. Would you *still* be correct in hearing the theme as an inversion and having the emotive contrast as described? Peacocke's intuition is that it would still be correct. That intuition we must now critically examine.

5. Two Relationships: Two Intentions

As I pointed out earlier, Peacocke's example embodies two very different musical features: one an expressive property of the finale theme, the other a purely musical one, which is to say, the 'property' of its being a virtual inversion of the fugue subject in the first movement. The former is a feature that, as Peacocke has it, we hear 'metaphorically-as', in Peacocke's words, 'defeating the sadness and

---

[15]   See Peter Kivy, *The Possessor and the Possessed: Handel, Mozart, Beethoven, and the Idea of Musical Genius* (New Haven: Yale University Press, 2001), *passim*.
[16]   Ibid.

passivity expressed in the first movement'.[17] But there is no reason whatever to invoke hearing metaphorically-as for the latter feature. It just is an 'objective fact' that the finale theme is the near perfect inversion of the fugue subject. It is not an inversion metaphorically of the fugue subject (whatever that would mean).

And recognizing this leads to the following conjecture. If the two features of the finale theme differ as stated, perhaps they differ in another way as well. Perhaps one of them is intention-free and the other intention-bound.

In what follows I am going first to suggest that there may be some reason for thinking that whereas the expressive quality of the finale theme *is* intention-bound, the thematic relation of inversion is not: or, in other words, it would *not* be correct to hear the finale theme metaphorically-as 'defeating the sadness and passivity expressed in the first movement' if it could be shown conclusively that Beethoven did not intend it to be heard so, but it *would* be correct to hear the finale theme as an inversion of the fugue subject in the first movement whether or not Beethoven intended it to be so heard. In the end, however, I will argue that, appearances to the contrary notwithstanding, *both* features of the finale theme are hostage to authorial intent. Furthermore, the claim is that both extra-musical features in general, for which the expressive quality of the finale theme is a token instance, and the pure musical parameters in general, for which the inversion of the fugue subject is a token instance, are intention-bound, their other differences notwithstanding.

6. Intention, Meaning, and Representation

To begin with, it should be noted that the whole flap over the relevance of authorial intention to interpretation began with, and continues to focus largely upon *meaning*: in particular, the meaning of literary works. That being the case, it is easy to see why there should be a strong intuitive pull towards intention-bound interpretation. For where the *meaning* of an utterance, whether spoken or written, is in doubt, what we want to ask the speaker or writer is: What did *you* mean by that? It is what the speaker or writer *intended* to convey that answers our question; that resolves our doubt.

I take it I am arguing here, albeit informally, in a Gricean vein. And in the great man's own words: first, 'my account of the cluster of

---

[17]   Peacocke, 'What Is the Role of Authorial Intention in Determining the Correct Way to Hear a Piece of Music', 305.

42

notions connected with the term "meaning" has been studded with expressions for such intensional concepts as those of intending and believing….';[18] second, 'An utterer is held to convey what is normally conveyed (or normally intended to be conveyed), and we require a good reason for accepting that a particular use diverges from the general usage…';[19] and third, 'in cases where there is doubt, say, about which of two or more things an utterer intends to convey, we tend to refer to the context (linguistic or otherwise) of the utterance and ask which of the alternatives would be relevant to other things he is saying or doing….'[20]

Now I am perfectly well aware that when one moves from conversational meaning, and ordinary written communication, to literary works of art, the issue of intention becomes far from crystal clear, and intuitions are conflicting rather than unanimous. Nonetheless, that a literary work of art cannot mean what is conclusively shown its author could not have intended it to mean, remains, I think, the firmer, more plausible intuition: the intuition to beat; the pre-systematic intuition.

Furthermore, this intuition passes easily from semantic meaning to representational content. In other words, a work of art can no more represent what its creator could not have intended it to represent than it can mean what its creator could not have intended it to mean. No one has articulated this more forthrightly than Richard Wollheim, where he compares seeing things in natural objects with seeing things in representational paintings. 'With clouds, rocks, sand', he points out, 'it is no more correct to see one thing in them than another'. But when it comes to paintings (say) things are quite otherwise. 'With Titian it is correct to see Venus in a particular stretch of canvas, and incorrect to see anyone or anything else there.' And the criterion of correctness in the latter case Wollheim has no hesitation placing squarely in *intention*. 'The criterion comes from the intentions, the fulfilled intentions of the artist…in so far as those guided the artist's hand and are retrievable from the work.'[21]

At the end of my slippery intention slope I am going to suggest that a strong intuition – certainly *my* intuition – pulls in the direction of authorial intention for all those musical features that require for

[18]   Paul Grice, *Studies in the Way of Words* (Cambridge, Mass. and London: Harvard University Press, 1989), 137.
[19]   Ibid., 222.
[20]   Ibid.
[21]   Richard Wollheim, *The Mind and its Depths* (Cambridge, Mass.: Harvard University Press, 1993), 188–189.

their perception what Peacocke calls hearing 'metaphorically-as'. There is a very strong intuition abroad, I suggest, that if Bach could not possibly have intended the cembalo cadenza in Brandenburg 5 to be heard as a call to liberty, it is incorrect to hear it so. And ditto for expressive properties as well. Of course the presence of intention is not a sufficient condition for hearing metaphorically-as, any more than, on the Gricean account, is it sufficient for meaning. Intentions can, needless to say, fail of their goals. There is a strong intuition, though, I am urging, that it is a necessary condition, though not a sufficient one.

What, however, of the pure musical parameters? What about Beethoven's inversion of the fugue subject? Here we may have found a sticking place on our slippery slope of intentions. This, I conjecture, is why.

It appears to me that all of the *obvious* cases we have looked at, where intuition pulls towards authorial intention as a criterion of correct interpretation, are cases which we want to describe as involving conceptual *content*, broadly conceived, of some kind: either semantic or representational or expressive. Furthermore, I think that in all of the musical cases in which it seems appropriate to say, with Peacocke, that we are hearing music 'metaphorically-as' one thing or another, we also want to describe what we are concerned with as *content*, broadly conceived.

But when we come to the pure musical parameters – when we come to Beethoven's inversion of the fugue subject in the finale, and the like – we are not dealing with content, even broadly conceived, nor with Peacocke's hearing metaphorically-as. Furthermore, someone might well claim that in such cases she feels no pull at all of intuition towards authorial intention as a corrective to listening. After all, *whatever* Beethoven's intention, or lack thereof, it is just a plain objective 'fact' of the matter that the finale theme is a virtual inversion of the fugue subject, as 'inversion' is defined. So even if one lit upon incontrovertible evidence that Beethoven had no intention of making the finale theme an inversion of the fugue subject, an inversion it remains; and that's that.

Thus a plausible position seems to be emerging where authorial intention is a necessary condition for 'content' broadly conceived, in absolute music, for what Peacocke calls hearing metaphorically-as, but *not* for the pure musical parameters. But in what follows I want to question the plausibility of this dualism. In particular, I want to argue that authorial intent is as necessary a condition for the pure musical parameters as for musical 'content', broadly conceived. In short, it's intention all the way down.

7. Thought Experiments

To motivate my argument I want to return to what I referred to earlier as Peacocke's 'thought experiment', to wit, that Beethoven was not aware of the musical relationship between the finale theme and the fugue subject: which is to say, the finale's theme being an almost perfect inversion of the fugue subject was *unintentional*. And I want to begin by considering what I will call the 'improbability quotient'. For I think that the probability, or, more to the point, the *improbability* of the thought experiment in question has a lot to do with which direction our intuitions should take. I think that it is implicit, although not stated outright, in the thought experiment, that Peacocke views it, needless to say, as counterfactual, but not, for all of that, as *wildly* implausible. And I believe this underestimation, as I see it, of the thought experiment's implausibility quotient is of some import in regard to where our intuitions go.

How impossible *is* it that Beethoven did not intend the finale theme to be and to be heard as an inversion of the fugue subject? I do not know how to measure such probabilities. Let us say it is not *as* improbable as Rembrandt's not intending the daubs of paint on the canvas known as *The Polish Rider* to be and to be seen as a representation of a man on horseback. But I want to insist that the improbability quotient of the inversion's being unintentional is, never the less, in the same ballpark as *The Polish Rider*'s being an unintentional representation-like pattern of paint looking for all the world like a representation of a man on horseback. For this reason alone we should be very suspicious of the easy conviction that the Beethoven example is as obvious as Peacocke makes it out to be. To discover that the inversion was unintentional would be stunning indeed, as would be the discovery of the unintentional resemblance of the paint daubs to the representation of a man on horseback: perhaps not *as* stunning, but stunning enough. What is your intuition about the painting? Would the unintentional 'representation' be a representation? And if not, why would your intuition be any different in the case of the unintentional 'inversion'?

In the conclusion of my paper I want now to expatiate on this point, with the purpose of showing that the dualism outlined above, in which content, broadly conceived, is intention-bound, but the pure musical parameters not, is an untenable dualism, for all of its initial plausibility. The pure musical parameters, I shall argue, are on all fours with content, broadly conceived, in being, as well, strictly intention-bound.

8. Craft without Skill?

In using the inversion of the fugue subject for the main theme of the final, in Op. 131, Beethoven was of course doing something that was to become increasingly prevalent in nineteenth-century instrumental music: imparting what came to be called 'organic unity' to a work through thematic unification. That aside though, theme-inversion is part of the bag of tricks that comes under the head of, to appropriate Paul Hindemith's famous book title, *The Craft of Musical Composition*.

Western art music, at least from the advent of polyphony, has been deeply imbued with the concept of craft. The composer learns his trade at any given time in music history by laborious industry in order to master all of the particular techniques of counterpoint, harmony, theme construction, variation, and manipulation that have defined the various musical styles from the twelfth century to ours.

Any student with moderate musical abilities can master many of these techniques and in the event, for example, write a 'correct', if uninspired fugue in Baroque style, or strict but boring polyphony in the style of Palestrina. The craft of musical composition, however, is not to be confused with the craft of making shoes or re-pairing automobiles. For the musical craft, like any other artistic craft, when mastered by genius, is craft at the genius level, and is as 'inspired', if you will, as any other aspect of the musical art. No amount of assiduous application to the technique of canon can produce the *Goldberg Variations* without the genius to go with it.

The conclusion I am pushing towards here is that the craft of musical composition, for which Beethoven's inversion of the fugue subject has been the poster boy, is a species of *skill*, namely, skill at the genius level. Furthermore, the perception and appreciation of this genius-level skill is an absolutely essential feature of our aesthetic experience of Western art music.

You can perhaps see, now, where the argument is carrying us. If, *per impossibile*, I were to discover that Beethoven did not intentionally make the main theme of the finale of Op. 131 the virtual inversion of the fugue subject, but that it just 'happened', I would perforce cease to appreciate it as an instance of the composer's skill, *qua* genius, in the craft of musical composition. This, *pace* Peacocke, must be a non-trivial, indeed a profound change in my attitude towards and appreciation of the finale theme and its relation to the fugue subject. It cannot be business as usual to stop hearing the finale theme as an intended inversion of the fugue subject and start hearing it instead as a 'happy accident'. But to drive this point home, imagine now some additional thought experiments.[22]

(1) A kind of child prodigy begins composing music, having heard it a good deal in his home. Without any instruction at all, he produces, after a while, a musical composition that displays all of the artifices of strict counterpoint: inversion, diminution, augmentation, stretto, imitation, canon, invertible counterpoint – the lot.

(2) There is a possible world in which everyone, quite naturally, comes to be able to compose music much in the natural way they come to speak their native tongue, which displays all of the artifices of strict counterpoint: inversion, diminution, augmentation stretto, imitation, canon, invertible counterpoint – the lot.

Surely, one might argue, these are cases in which the 'craft', as I call it, is unintentional. Yet surely, so the argument continues, we would still admire, enjoy, appreciate the craft so displayed, as we would displayed in a fugue by Bach with conscious intent. Why *shouldn't* we? After all, it is just plainly *there* to be admired, enjoyed, appreciated.

The second thought experiment is, I think, more easily dealt with than the first. So I will get to it straightaway.

A possible world in which the craft of musical composition were acquired by all in the same way as their native tongue, or where walking a tight-rope were acquired by all in the same way as ordinary walking on level ground, would, of course, be a world without any such thing as the 'craft' of musical composition, properly so-called, or the 'skill', properly so-called, of tight-rope walking. And in such a possible world the 'craft' of musical composition and the 'skill' of walking the tight-rope would no more be admired, enjoyed, appreciated, in the way they are in our world any more than we admire, enjoy, appreciate speaking in our native tongue or walking on level ground in our world.

The first thought experiment presents difficulties, mainly, because it is open to a variety of interpretations. I shall offer four, and following each, my response.

(1a) The child prodigy in question composed his works in the eighteenth century (say), being now, of course, deceased. And we are apprised of the supposed circumstances under which he composed from contemporary documents: letters, diaries, and so forth.

---

[22]   These thought experiments were set in train by a question posed to me by Hong Yu Wong during the discussion period following the presentation of this chapter as a lecture to the Royal Institute of Philosophy, London, 12 November, 2010.

But none of these documents reveals specifically that he knew what all these artifices were, or what they were called. We infer from their presence in his works, quite rightly, that, with regard to these artifices, he was an autodidact, taught himself strict counterpoint, and intentionally employed said artifices in his music for the usual reasons. We admire, enjoy, appreciate these displays of skill as we would in the works of a composer who acquired them in the usual way, from instruction.

(1b) The child prodigy in question is the same as the one in (1a) except that he is quoted in a document as saying, when asked, that when he wrote these juvenilia, so full of contrapuntal artifice, he had no idea what they were, what they were called, or what he was doing when he wrote them into his music. It was like 'automatic writing' or 'speaking in tongues'. Should we still regard them as the artifices they appear, admire, enjoy, appreciate them as instances of skill and craft?

The answer is affirmative, and here is why. We should take a leaf in this regard from Hume's book, which is to say, the essay 'Of Miracles', and argue thus. Which is more probable, the incredibly unlikely, indeed near 'miraculous' occurrence of contrapuntal artifices as above described completely unintended, by 'accident', as it were, in a musical work, or the falsity of the document that affirms such an improbably, 'miraculous' occurrence?[23] I say the latter is more probable. The work trumps the document. So we are fully justified in admiring, enjoying, appreciating the skill displayed in the prodigy's work as we would in the work of any other, more 'normal' composer.

(1c) The child prodigy is a living composer and at some point in his life imparts to someone in conversation the very same 'information' contained in the historical documents in (1b). The response should be as in the previous case.

(1d) The case is the same as in (1b) and (1c) – whether the composer is past or present being immaterial – but we *know*, with absolute certainty, and *know* that we know, never mind how, that the historical documentation, or oral communication, is imparting absolute truth: that the contrapuntal artifice is in the composition through no

---

[23]   I am thinking particularly of the passage which reads, in part: '...I desire anyone to lay his hand upon his heart, and after a serious consideration, whether he thinks that the falsehood of such a book, supported by such a testimony, would be more extraordinary and miraculous than all the miracles it relates...' See. David Hume, *An Enquiry Concerning Human Understanding*, ed. Eric Steinberg (2nd ed.; Indianapolis and Cambridge: Hackett, 1993), 90 (Section X).

knowledge or intent of the prodigy, who composes without any concept of the contrapuntal artifice that, through some 'miraculous' workings of nature, creeps, without his conscious agency, into his work.

What is our intuition here? By hypothesis work does *not* trump documentation or oral communication of lack of intent. And if our intuition is that in this (truly extraordinary) case the work should be treated in no way differently from a work by Bach, that we should hear the work as exhibiting contrapuntal artifice in the same we do in the fugues from the *Well-Tempered Clavier* adduced above, then the claim that intention is a necessary condition on the pure musical parameters – which is, of course, the thesis of this exercise – seems not to stand up.

But is it really so obvious where our intuition goes in this highly implausible thought experiment?

Assuming that it is not a regular occurrence but a singular one, my own intuition is that I would treat the prodigy's work much in the same way I would treat a complex stain on a wall that closely resembled the drawing of a human face or figure. I would, in other words, treat it as a 'natural object', a 'natural wonder', so to say. As such, clearly, it would *not* be admired, enjoyed, appreciated as a work of skill and genius, any more than would the stain on the wall. We might perhaps say that we treat the stain 'as if' it were a drawing, the contrapuntal artifices 'as if' they were inversion, diminution, and the rest. In both cases, however, we are appreciating extraordinary natural objects that bear an *appearance* of human art. And that is a very different kind of appreciation from that which characterizes our encounters with real drawings and fugues. So, in conclusion, let me bite this bullet and say, baldly, that the musical work in (1d) does *not* exhibit inversion, diminution, stretto, canon, imitation, augmentation, no matter how much they resemble the 'real thing'. And there's an end on it.

In fact, nevertheless, it is a nice question whether an accidental or fortuitous sequence of notes can rightly be called an 'inversion' of a theme in the first place, anymore than an accidental or fortuitous design in the sand can be called an English 'sentence' or a stain on a wall a 'representation' of a face. But putting aside the question of whether or not it makes sense to *call* the finale theme an 'inversion' of the fugue subject, if unintended as such, the gnawing question remains: Is it 'correct' to hear the finale theme as an inversion of the fugue subject, if the inversion was unintentional?

Let us confine ourselves, as we pretty much have throughout, to the absolute music repertory in the Western art-music canon. The 'objects', if I may so call them, of this repertory are craft-objects:

factum non genitum. Furthermore, they are generally described by those whose business it is in *functional* terms, which is to say, the parts are to be understood, wherever possible, as performing some sort of perceivable function in the overall plan and structure of the musical work. That being the case, the passage from the pure musical parameters to authorial intention is direct and unproblematic. There is no function, I think it will readily be granted, without intention: without there being a rational agent or designer that is the originator of the functional part. There are no 'accidental' functions.[24]

My conclusion, then, is that as musical content, broadly conceived, pulls us intuitively towards authorial intention, through the concept of meaning, so the pure musical parameters pull us intuitively towards authorial intention, through the concept of function. A dualism, in this regard, although plausible on first reflection, will not withstand critical scrutiny. It is intention all the way down. For without authorial intention as criterial for the correct interpretation of the pure musical parameters, there is neither compositional skill to admire, nor function to be heard. And that, I think is an intolerable result.

Rutgers University
New Brunswick
peterkivy@aol.com

---

[24] I am leaving out of consideration here biological functions, such as the 'function' of the heart to pump blood, the 'function' of the kidneys to do whatever it is they do, and so on. The analysis of biological function is, of course, tied to the theory of evolution and natural selection, and is irrelevant to present concerns, which are, of course, about 'crafted', man-made objects, for which the generalization 'no function without a giver of the function' still holds, intentionless biological function notwithstanding.

Popular Song as Moral Microcosm: Life Lessons from Jazz Standards

JERROLD LEVINSON

I

In a recent paper devoted to my topic, music and morality, my fellow philosopher of music Peter Kivy makes a helpful tripartite distinction among ways in which music could be said to have moral force.[1] The first is by embodying and conveying moral insight; Kivy labels that *epistemic* moral force. The second is by having a positive moral effect on behavior; Kivy labels that *behavioral* moral force. And the third is by impacting positively on character so as to make someone a better human being; Kivy labels that *character-building* moral force.

Kivy is decidedly skeptical about the prospects of pure instrumental music, or what he calls 'music alone', to possess the first or second sort of moral force, and only slightly less so for its prospects to possess the third sort. But he rightly points out that that third sort of moral force – what might alternatively be described as music's power to shape for the better, albeit in subtle ways, what kind of person one is – is largely, if not wholly, independent of the first two sorts, the epistemic and the behavioral, and might be manifest where they are absent.

Before returning to Kivy's three sorts of moral force, however, I want to underline a fourth way in which music can be moral. This fourth way is through music's having moral *quality*, whether or not it possesses, in consequence, moral *force*. What I mean by moral quality is a matter of the mind or spirit reflected in the music, and most particularly, in the nature of its expression, both *what* it expresses and *how* it expresses that. Moral quality in music is not a function simply of what emotions, attitudes, or states of mind are expressed, but of how they are expressed – with what fineness, subtlety, depth, honesty, originality and so on. Music can surely display moral quality whether it is optimistic – as for instance, the first movement of Dvořak's 'American' Quartet – or pessimistic – as

[1] Peter Kivy, 'Musical Morality', *Revue Internationale de Philosophie*, Vol. **62**, No. 246 (2008): 397–412.

doi:10.1017/S1358246112000264 © The Royal Institute of Philosophy and the contributors 2013
Royal Institute of Philosophy Supplement **71** 2013

for instance, the first movement of Mahler's 'Resurrection' Symphony. What matters is the nature of the mind or spirit that shows itself through such expression, and more generally, through its management of all aspects of the musical medium, expressive, formal, and aesthetic.

The fundamental criterion of musical moral quality, perhaps too crudely framed, is whether the mind or spirit displayed in the music is such as to elicit admiration and to induce emulation, or instead such as to elicit distaste and to induce avoidance. If the former, the music has positive moral quality; if the latter, the music has negative moral quality; if neither, then the music is simply morally neutral.

But why, one may ask, does such a property of music deserve the label of *moral* quality, and not simply *aesthetic* quality? Before answering let me re-label the property in question as *ethical*, rather than *moral*, quality, appealing to a broad sense of 'ethical' that is familiar to us from Aristotle and the Stoics, comprising all aspects of character relevant to living a good life, and not only those corresponding to the moral virtues narrowly understood. With that relabeling in place, I see no way to avoid replying, to the question of why the display of an admirable mind or spirit makes for ethical quality in music, that it is simply because some minds or spirits are ethically *superior* to others, in the sense that they are such as to conduce to living a good life or to living as one should. Music can thus have ethical value in the sense of presenting exemplars of admirable states of mind that are conducive to, perhaps even partly constitutive of, living well, even if no demonstrable effect on character is forthcoming. And ethical value of this sort, one may add, in general makes music that possesses it *artistically* more valuable as well, artistic value being a broader notion than aesthetic value, plausibly covering rewards afforded by a work that are not directly manifested in experience of it.

So music might, in principle, have ethical quality without that resulting in moral force of either the behavioral or the charactering-building sort. But in fact it is difficult to believe that repeated exposure to music that is ethically superior, in the sense I have indicated, should have as a rule *no* effect on character at all. And that is because of the plausibility of a contagion-cum-modeling picture of what is likely to result from such exposure. Just as spending time with certain sorts of friends invariably impacts on character, if perhaps in a transitory manner – this is what parents have in mind in classifying their children's pals as on the whole either 'good influences' or 'bad influences' – so does keeping company with certain music rather than other music.[2] It seems manifestly better, for one's psychological and spiritual well-being, to spend time with music of sincerity, subtlety, honesty, depth, and the like, than with music of pretension, shallowness or vulgarity.[3]

As noted earlier, Kivy does not entirely discount the notion that purely instrumental music might have moral force, at least of the character-building sort, but the possibility that he is willing to grant is slender indeed. Here is what he says:

> One might argue that, at least in some sense or other, great music uplifts us; makes us, for the period of the listening experience, feel a kind of exaltation... And even though this experience has no lasting beneficial effect on our characters...it would not be wrong to say that during the experience, at least, we are better people...Thus absolute music shares with many other human activities the propensity to produce in human beings a kind of ecstasy that might seem appropriate to describe as character-enhancing, consciousness-raising, and, therefore, in some vague, attenuated sense, morally improving, *while it lasts*.[4]

I have a few comments on this. First, as regards the feeling of uplift or exaltation that Kivy acknowledges can be the result of listening absorbedly to certain music, music in which one seems to be in the presence of a great mind or spirit – surely this effect normally endures for some time *after* the listening experience, and does not cease as soon as listening ends. Second, it is necessary to insist, *pace* Kivy, that any ethical benefit of music, if it is to be deserving of that name, must involve an effect on character that *endures* to some extent – that is, which outlives the occasion itself. Music that is only 'morally improving' while one is listening to it is not, to my mind, really morally improving, but rather only music that provides a temporary if pleasant *illusion* of moral improvement. But third, the mechanism of music's possible character-building force strikes me as both less obscure and more robust than it does Kivy. I have already touched on this, in mentioning the likelihood of contagion and modeling effects, but I now elaborate further.

---

[2]   I here echo the claim made by Wayne Booth on behalf of great literature in his well-known book *The Company We Keep* (University of California Press, 1988).
[3]   For further reflections in this vein, see my 'Evaluating Music', in *Contemplating Art* (Oxford University Press, 2006).
[4]   Ibid., 411–2.

Jerrold Levinson

Though they are not sentient, musical works are somewhat like *persons*. They possess a character, exhibit something like behavior, unfold or develop over time, and display emotional and attitudinal qualities which we can access through being induced to imagine, as we listen to them, personae that embody those qualities.[5] In short, musical works are person-like in psychological ways. If so, then it hardly seems implausible that music regularly frequented will have moral effects on one, just as will being in the company of, and spending time with, real persons. This may transpire through the mere contagion or rubbing off of mental dispositions; or through a conscious desire to model oneself, in thought and action, on impressive individuals in one's environment; or through a less conscious identification with and internalization of attractive personalities with which one has contact. Why should something similar not generally occur through exposure to a given range of minds and spirits in music?

Let me be more concrete. Judging from the mind or spirit that comes across from their respective musics, Haydn would, I think, be a good choice of companion on a desert island, Tchaikovsky rather less so. It would perhaps here be fair to specify a *particular* Tchaikovsky, say that of the Piano Trio or the Fourth Symphony; these do not correspond to individuals I would care to be marooned with. On the other hand, I would willingly share my desert island with the Tchaikovsky of the 'Souvenir de Florence' or the Third Symphony. And what goes for Haydn and Tchaikovsky as imagined desert island companions holds as well for the proportion of time one would be well advised, on ethical grounds, to allow Tchaikovsky's music, or at least certain stretches of it, to occupy one's ears as opposed to Haydn's music.

Mention of Haydn naturally raises the issue of the ethical value of *humorous* music, especially skillfully and wittily humorous music of the sort Haydn produced in abundance, and of the intimate connection between *humor* and *good humor*. It is surely significant that most *humorous* music is also *good-humored* music: that it is, on the one hand, funny or amusing, and on the other hand, mood-improving and spirits-lifting. This observation provides a basis, perhaps, for affirming the inherently positive ethical worth of humorous music, but its development will have to wait for another occasion.

---

[5]   See my 'Sound, Gesture, Space, and the Expression of Emotion in Music' and 'Musical Expressiveness as Hearability-as-Expression', in *Contemplating Art*, op. cit.

Leaving music aside for the moment, let us remind ourselves briefly of ways in which the other arts, most notably those of literature, theatre, and cinema, can contribute to moral education. Novels, plays, and films can offer imaginative acquaintance with concrete moral situations, represented in specific ways and from particular perspectives, and embodying concrete moral perceptions of them, engagement with which can aid us to better understand ourselves and others, and so to better conduct our lives. Such artworks, it should be stressed, need not *prescribe* moral stances in order to facilitate our efforts to define ourselves and to appreciate the selves of others; they need only *present* morally relevant situations sensitively and believably, allowing us a valuable exercise of our moral faculties. Such artworks generally serve to enlarge our moral imaginations, making us more capable of adopting the points of view of others and of empathizing with them. Even if an increased awareness of the subjectivity of others does not itself constitute moral improvement, it is clearly a prerequisite to it, in that without such awareness we are less able to take the interests of others into account and so to treat them as ends rather than means.

The foregoing should all be roughly familiar as a defense of the moral relevance of arts such as literature, theatre, and film. But as the ancient Greeks were keen to emphasize, music arguably also has a place in moral education, the production and reception of some music serving to make us more fully human, despite representing no concrete individuals, scenarios, or situations. And that is largely because of the person-like character of music, remarked on before, whereby music can embody personal qualities, and thus affect one in somewhat the same way that persons do. Music, through its form and expression, audibly manifests attitudes, emotions, and other states of mind, and these states of mind, to which we are exposed when attending to music, can clearly be of greater or lesser moral worth. Thus on the one hand there is music that exudes maturity, strength, courage, resignation, vitality, and determination; on the other hand there is music that exudes immaturity, cowardice, fecklessness, megalomania, hypocrisy, and superficiality. Some music reflects a process of thought that compels admiration and uplifts us; other music reflects a process of thought that inspires dismay and depresses us. Can it make no difference in what sort of musical atmosphere, ethically speaking, one chooses regularly to bask?

So much for the ethical dimension of instrumental music. I turn now to the main subject of this paper, the ethical import of song, and the role in such import of both the articulate component (the words) and the purely musical component (the notes).

Jerrold Levinson

II

As regards song, or texted music generally, claims of moral insight, which correspond to the first sort of moral force recognized by Kivy, and claims of character-building potential, which correspond to the third sort of moral force recognized by Kivy, are generally held to be less extravagant, and to have a more solid basis, than comparable claims for textless music. And the same goes for claims of what I characterized above as ethical *quality*, as distinct from moral force in any of Kivy's senses.

Still, the contribution of the musical element *per se* to whatever moral force or ethical quality a song ends up possessing surely remains crucial, and presents an enduring puzzle. Put bluntly, how is it that music can reinforce, amplify, or almost create single-handedly, the moral force or ethical quality of a text that would otherwise not seem particularly notable in that respect? I address that question towards the end of this essay, after having looked at an array of specific examples.

One of my purposes in examining a number of songs from the jazz standard repertoire – which to a large extent overlaps with what is called the Great American Songbook – is to underline that the ethical dimension of art is not something that is only of issue in regard to unconventional performance art, transgressive theatre, propaganda films in the mode of Leni Riefenstahl, homoerotic photographs in the mode of Robert Mapplethorpe, or intentionally provocative novels in the mode of Michel Houellebecq. That is to say, of art that, whether self-consciously or not, is in forthright opposition to prevailing mores. The ethical is, I suggest, a dimension in one way or another present in virtually all art, even the declaredly amoral literary art of an Oscar Wilde or Vladimir Nabokov, the purely abstract visual art of a Piet Mondrian or Mark Rothko, and the abstruse musical art of a Pierre Boulez or Milton Babbitt.[6]

I begin by contrasting the Rube Bloom song 'Day In, Day Out' with two somewhat similar songs, 'You Go to My Head' and

---

[6] Nor do I mean to suggest that ethical quality is the exclusive prerogative of songs in the repertoire from which I draw my examples. Many songs from the rock, folk, and blues genres also exhibit such quality. Consider Leonard Cohen's 'Everybody Knows', whose poetic cynicism, smooth transitions from global to personal concerns, jewel-like mandolin accompaniment, and rich background vocals all contribute to its ethical impact.

'Night and Day'. These three songs all have more or less the same theme, namely, the unparalleled effect of the beloved on the one who loves, and how the sway of the beloved over the lover amounts to a kind of possession, calling possibly for eventual exorcism. And all three songs exhibit, of course, a measure of ethical quality in virtue of their musical excellence and taste and the mind that such excellence and taste manifests. 'Night and Day' and 'You Go to My Head' are as fine, or perhaps even finer, from the musical and lyrical point of view, as 'Day In, Day Out'.[7] But I suggest that they embody less, if anything, in the way of moral insight, and that their ethical quality is thus less than that of 'Day In, Day Out'.

'Day In, Day Out' offers, first of all, a picture of amorous absorption even more revealing than that offered by the other two, turning on the figure of the beloved as a recurring tattoo, coursing through one's blood and permeating one's being, and the idea that the presence, the sight, the touch of the loved one utterly transforms the world, whatever the weather may happen to be.[8] But what probably most distinguishes 'Day In, Day Out' from the other two songs is its quasi-narrative aspect, which makes the phenomenology of love it conveys even more vivid and affecting. This is most noticeable in the bridge, which sketches a paradigm scenario in the lover's daily existence: 'Day out, day in, I needn't tell you how my days begin. When I awake I awaken with a tingle, one possibility in view, that possibility of maybe seeing you.' And the narrative momentum of the bridge is continued in the chorus that follows, 'Come rain, come shine, I meet you and to me the day is fine, then I kiss your lips, and the pounding becomes, the ocean's roar, a thousand drums', leading sweepingly to the emotional climax and vocal high point of the song, 'Can't you see it's love, can there be any doubt'.

With 'Day In, Day Out' one doesn't just *grasp* the nature of the lover's possession by the beloved through a series of original and poetically arresting images of intoxication, as in 'You Got to My Head', or through a sequence of alternatingly besotted and bemoaning apostrophes to the beloved, as in 'Night and Day'. One rather *lives* that possession itself, albeit vicariously, in virtue of the narrative, albeit fragmentary, that the song contains. And it is most of all in that

[7] To note just one respect in which the music of 'You Go to My Head' is not only beguiling on its own terms, but incredibly well-fitted to the sentiment of its lyric, the octave leaps at the beginning of the vocal line at each of three stanzas of the chorus are a perfect sonic emblem of the intoxicating effect of which the lyric so eloquently speaks.

[8] Another song that foregrounds that idea is Gershwin's 'A Foggy Day'.

illuminating vicarious experience that the surplus ethical quality of 'Day In, Day Out' resides.[9]

It should not, of course, be surprising that a narrative dimension, even if it is not essential to a song's having ethical import, can nevertheless contribute to its having such import. For a song is then able to draw, although to a limited degree, on the same resources possessed by novels and plays for evoking complex emotional responses to concrete situations and facilitating ethical insight into them.

Consider next the song 'As Long As I Live'. One thing that makes this song special is its uncommonly bluesy feel, of which Harold Arlen was, among the great American song composers, the past master. But another thing, and one more germane to our theme, is the genius of the lyricist, Ted Koehler, in following the line 'Maybe I can't live to love you as long as I want to' with the seemingly throwaway explanatory remark 'life isn't long enough'. For that is an unexpected and beautifully colloquial way of telegraphing how love, in effect, always aspires to forever, knowing all along that it is bound to finitude and must necessarily come to an end. The repeated amorous pledges of the speaker to love for all time are all the more poignant because they invariably raise in our minds the question of whether loving someone is something that one can reasonably *promise* to do. More likely, it is only something that one can promise to *try* to do, or that one can earnestly *hope* to do, for only as long as one lives.

III

Let us now look at the other side of the coin, turning our attention to songs that deal not with the thrill and exhilaration of love, but with the ache and desperation of its loss or absence. Pride of place here must go to Don Raye and Gene De Paul's 'You Don't Know What Love Is'. Probably no song conveys better the pain of loving

---

[9]   Alec Wilder, an authority on American popular song, offered this encomium of 'Day In, Day Out', one that responds to its special quality from a somewhat different, yet entirely compatible, angle: 'I was astounded by both the melody and the lyric...It was unlike any song in the pop field I'd ever seen...fifty-six measures long. The melodic line soared and moved across the page like a lovely brush stroke. It never knotted itself up in cleverness or pretentiousness. And it had, remarkable for any pop song, passion.' (Quoted in Philip Furia, *The Poets of Tin Pan Alley* (Oxford University Press, 1992), 122.)

hopelessly, long after love has flown.[10] First, the despairing and soul-sick lyric is perfectly matched by, and fitted to, music of precisely the same character. But second, the idea that fully appreciating the value of love requires losing it or going without it for some time is one that rings completely true, at least to this listener. Naturally one might easily *understand* that truth in the abstract – say, in the manner in which Tolstoy's Ivan Ilych, before his fatal accident, had always grasped the syllogism 'All men are mortal; Caius is a man; Hence Caius is mortal', not seeing that it had any particular relevance to him – but a song like 'You Don't Know What Love Is' makes you *feel* its truth, in the most concrete fashion. And therein lies its not inconsiderable ethical value.

In a less wrenching, though perhaps no less moving, vein is the Rodgers and Hart standard 'It Never Entered My Mind'. This song, imbued with wistful regret and rueful musing, brings home as few others do how fragile love is, how often underappreciated, how often taken for granted, its inevitable departure from some oppressive notion of perfection being allowed to get in the way of estimating it at its proper value. The sublime rightness of the bittersweet images of life after love – such as ordering orange juice for one, being uneasy in one's easy chair, wishing that the other might get into one's hair again – have rarely, if ever, been equaled in the annals of song. The song's jilted lover seems, as one commentator puts it, 'almost bemused by her own heartache and understatedly characterizes it as mild discomfort.' But we see and hear through that, and have no trouble suffering along with her empathically.

Consider now another love song – it hardly needs mentioning that love is the overriding subject of the songs in this repertoire, accounting for perhaps ninety percent of them – but one that stresses neither the joy nor the sorrow of love, but instead the mystery that so often triggers and sustains it, namely, the perception of the other as beautiful. 'You Are Too Beautiful', another gem we owe to the team of Rodgers and Hart, straightforwardly conveys in its text the irrational power of human beauty, its dominion over the will, and its capacity to short-circuit, or even wholly disarm, moral assessment. The text is perfectly seconded, and its truth effectively illustrated, by the song's utterly beautiful, wholly unfussy, melody, one that is almost entirely diatonic, not needing any chromaticism for chromaticism's

---

[10] A strong second-place showing, however, must be accorded at least three other songs from this repertoire, 'Angel Eyes', 'Estate', and 'When Your Lover Has Gone'.

sake in order to lend it interest. There is ethical quality here as well, and not all of it resides in the luminous beauty and simplicity of the music itself; some of it resides in the wisdom of the sentiment conveyed by the words.

A more complex song, 'Sophisticated Lady', is full of sympathy for the woman of the title, though a sympathy qualified by criticism of the choices she has made, which the song regards as reflecting a basically evasive adaptation to the reality of disappointed love. The music of this standard is as sophisticated as the lady it helps to portray, and perhaps in a way that is similarly a bit forced, the bridge being almost unsingable in its unbridled chromaticism and unusual harmonic relation to the chorus that precedes it.[11]

Its ethical dimension aside, 'Sophisticated Lady' is a particularly interesting song from one point of view: it is an example of a strikingly successful joint creation[12], the conjunction of an original instrumental by Duke Ellington and lyrics added subsequently by Mitchell Parish, where the composer and lyricist harbored rather different conceptions of the subject, that is, the sophisticated lady, in fashioning their respective contributions. Parish's sophisticated lady, as is evident from the song, is a blasé and jaded creature of the night, vainly attempting to escape the emptiness in her soul; but the sophisticated ladies that Ellington had in mind were the proper, well-dressed, middle-class, cultivated African-American schoolteachers of his Washington youth.

IV

For the sake of contrast I now draw attention to a standard that seems to me not just of *lesser* ethical value than those I have been discussing, but possibly of slight ethical *disvalue*. For if songs can have positive ethical value on the grounds I have been sketching, then presumably they can have negative ethical value, or ethical disvalue, as well. At the

---

[11]   The main key of the song is Ab major, while the bridge is in G major, only a half-tone down but harmonically quite remote from Ab. What is especially hard to negotiate for a singer is the transition from the last note of the main section to the first note of the bridge, separated by the bedeviling interval of a tritone.

[12]   I note here the rather unsympathetic, and in my opinion obtuse, view of this song taken by Philip Furia. (See *The Poets of Tin Pan Alley*, op. cit., 257–8.)

least the song is of dubious ethical quality, even though it is, as regards both its lyrics and its music, of a high order.

The standard in question is called 'Everything Happens to Me', and represents, in a vein of apparent endorsement, an attitude of mind that is arguably not worthy of admiration, emulation, or sympathy, an attitude one might describe as one of self-indulgence and self-pity. The attitude represented comes through clearly in the opening stanza: 'I make a date for golf, and you can bet your life it rains. I try to give a party, and the guy upstairs complains. I guess I'll go thru life, just catching colds and missing trains. Everything happens to me'. The second stanza of the song delivers more of the same.

Plainly, one would do well not to dwell in the company of a persona as self-absorbed as that which such sentiments reflect, someone who feels that the ordinary small annoyances and inconveniences of life have somehow singled him out for special and unfair treatment. One wants to take this whiner by his lapels and ask, what will you do if you ever confront a real problem or experience a serious setback? To be fair, the closing stanza of 'Everything Happens to Me', which reflects bemoaning more worthy of sympathetic response, turning as it does on misfortune in love, somewhat offsets the initial impression of outsized self-pity.[13] And both the song's harmonically surprising bridge and some nice chromatic touches in the song's main melody add an undeniable poignancy to the protagonist's complaint. Nonetheless, in the final analysis the song leaves something to be desired, ethically speaking.

This prompts me to a more general reflection concerning songs of equivocal ethical quality, such as 'Everything Happens to Me'. The crucial issue is whether a song not only *expresses* or *portrays* undesirable character traits, but in addition, does so in a way that amounts to *endorsing* or *condoning* them. Only if the latter is true will they clearly count as bad company for a listener on ethical grounds. And a song might conceivably also be ethically bad company if the implied author, while not endorsing or condoning the undesirable traits

---

[13] 'I've telegraphed and phoned, and sent an air mail special too. Your answer was goodbye, and there was even postage due. I fell in love just once, and then it had to be with you. Everything happens to me.' Furthermore, when sung a certain way 'Everything Happens to Me' can be redeemed in performance, if the singer manages to neutralize what's unappealing about its persona by inhabiting it in a wistful yet knowing manner. The performance by Chet Baker comes closest, of those I have heard, to achieving that.

Jerrold Levinson

displayed, fails to clearly *reject* or *distance* himself from the undesirable traits or obnoxious attitudes expressed or portrayed.

Still, mightn't the displayed character of the imagined speaker of the song be bad company *even if* the implied author is critical of the song's imagined speaker? Perhaps. That is to say, the mind of the song's persona might be a bad thing to spend too much time exposing oneself to, even if the implied author is blameless because implicitly criticizing or distancing himself from the persona depicted. Yet clearly, it is worse if the implied author appears to view the persona in a sympathetic or even just neutral light.

V

If any of the songs I have chosen for examination manages to achieve the ethical quality I am claiming for them, then surely the song 'What's New?' does so. Like 'Sophisticated Lady', 'What's New?' is one of those vocal standards that began life as an instrumental and then achieved a new identity once words had been attached to it by someone other than the composer. With the text in place, 'What's New?' emerges as a musical dramatic monologue, one half of a conversation between ex-lovers, the other half of which is only implied, yet readily imagined.

Note first that 'What's New?' achieves a satisfying unity between its opening and its closing couplet: the phrase 'you haven't changed' in the former becomes 'I haven't changed' in the latter. This is a small change, grammatically speaking, but one that adds to the song's very special poignancy: the first phrase is a remark directed to outer appearance in a vein of polite compliment; the second phrase is a naked confession of inner sorrow. And the falsely cheery 'adieu' – preferably pronounced a l'americaine as 'adyoo' – at the end of the bridge serves as a perfect hinge to the heartbreak of the final chorus, with its almost unuttered 'I still love you so'.

'What's New?' achieves a truly impressive depth of characterization in such a short space. We are led to both admire and empathize with the protagonist's quiet suffering, with the brave face he assumes in the situation. A song like this fosters understanding of the risks and rewards of romantic engagement, and helps one to feel from the inside what it is like to harbor love for someone who has long ago ceased to care. Sensitive audition of 'What's New?', it may not be too much to claim, plausibly puts one in a better position to understand situations of this sort, to assess them morally if called for, perhaps even to deal with them better if one finds oneself in them.

VI

I here offer a few illustrations of how these exceptional songs, when treated in a jazz context, can make, ethically speaking, a greater or a lesser impact. I am thinking of ways in which specific interpretive choices made in performance by the singer of a song can serve to enhance, whereas others can serve to blunt, its inherent ethical quality.

Regarding 'What's New?', suppose that instead of a smooth descent on the words that follow the repeated refrains of 'what's new?' the singer offers instead a halting one, almost stopping on each word, something like this, 'how'..'did'..'that'..'romance'.. 'come'..'through'. If not overdone this can underline the vulnerability of the song's protagonist and his or her effort of keeping pain in check – trying, though not really managing, to affect an insouciance not felt – making that persona all the easier to empathize with, and making the song all the more effective on the ethical plane.

Regarding 'It Never Entered My Mind', both the song's tone of melancholy regret and its poignant portrait of one who wised up too late are arguably best served by a slow tempo and a legato vocal delivery, one that helps to conjure up an atmosphere of wistful reminiscence. A too lively tempo, a too blithe or jaunty vocal delivery, can undermine the effectiveness of this song, and its ethical value in particular.

Regarding 'Day In, Day Out', by contrast, adopting a slow, hardly swinging, tempo can make for an outing that is musically interesting, and can succeed in conveying a nice sense of relaxation. But such an approach also makes it difficult to convey the feeling of amorous exhilaration that is, to my mind, at the heart of the song and an important source of its ethical quality. Thus such an approach is probably not an optimal choice for bringing out what is best and most distinctive in that song.

VII

It is high time to venture some general reflections, difficult as they are to arrive at, on the ethical power of popular song. The crucial question, it seems, is this: How can setting to music fairly ordinary sentiments and observations – such as the ones we have encountered in this repertoire – make those sentiments and observations so much more affecting or compelling, and hence manage to invest them with what I have called ethical, or life-enhancing, quality? Is it a mere additive effect? Is it a kind of delusion? Are we being duped?

Jerrold Levinson

We can formulate a couple of rather difficult conundrums here. The first is this: Is it simply that due to our pleasure in the music as such we end up attributing more validity to the sentiments or observations conveyed by the words than we would otherwise do? Or is it rather that setting the words to music in a particular fashion somehow provides a kind of corroboration of the sentiments or observations conveyed by the words? And the second is this: When a song moves us or touches us, and also conveys a substantial thought or distinctive perspective, does the thought or perspective seem more true or apt in part because the song has moved or touched us, or does the song move or touch us in part because the thought or perspective, musically enrobed, seems more true or apt? These are conundrums I am not sure how to resolve, but I push on in the hope of shedding some light on them.

Recall that of the four sorts of moral relevance that music might have that were canvassed at the beginning of my talk, three seem to remain live possibilities for the songs we have surveyed, namely *epistemic moral force*, *character-building moral force*, and *ethical quality*. To take the first of these, if a song manages to have epistemic moral force – that is, a capacity to embody and communicate moral insight – it seems that that will depend almost entirely on the words, words capable of conveying an articulate content. Since I want to focus on the specifically musical contribution to a song's moral import, I will accordingly here leave the issue of epistemic moral force to the side.

As regards ethical *quality*, however, and the *character-building* moral force that may be consequent on that, at least two things are clear. The first thing is that the ethical quality of the *purely musical component* of the song will contribute, all things being equal, to the ethical quality of the song as a whole, something it is thus better, for the good of one's soul, to spend time with. For instance, that the music of 'Sophisticated Lady' reflects a finer, nobler, more searching mind than the music of, say, 'Cherokee' – a sturdy old standard that yet served as a basis of improvisation for many great jazzmen – is at least part of why 'Sophisticated Lady' has a higher ethical, and not only aesthetic, value than 'Cherokee', and hence a higher artistic value as well. And the second, and most patent, thing is surely that the *particular manner of joining words to music* in these songs also accounts in part for whatever ethical quality the songs end up having, though in ways it is exceedingly hard to generalize about.

One clue to the special ethical quality that songs in this repertoire can have may be the element of exceptional *condensation, concision* or *compression* they exhibit. In experiencing a great jazz standard well delivered, one has a sense of getting to the heart of a subject, of being presented with its essence, because of the brevity of the medium and the consequent intensity of focus, where all must be said and sounded in no more than three or four minutes, as opposed to the hours involved in the unfolding of, say, a novel, film or opera. In a great jazz standard every note, every word seems to count, and the economy of means seems somehow to underline the justness or rightness of what is being expressed.

Of course, as has often been noted, condensation, concision and compression are also part of the power of *poetry*, a good poem often capturing in a small span of words a whole world of thought or feeling. Still, in song there is something additional: not just condensation, concision and compression, but the conjunction of two *quite different* vehicles of significance or orders of meaning-making – articulate words and inarticulate sounds – which in their interpenetration often manage to convey a single content, and to do so more powerfully than either is able to do on its own.[14]

A great song, one that is not only beguiling in its music and worldly wise in its words, but compelling in its precise marriage of the two, has ethical quality, one might suggest, partly in virtue of serving as an emblem of harmonious and mutually enriching cooperation, a prime goal of interpersonal relations and of social life more generally. And when one responds positively to such a song – acknowledging on an emotional level its utter rightness and fineness of tone – one participates imaginatively in the ideal of sublime interaction that the song represents.

There is also, finally, an undeniable aspect of *liberation* involved in the joining of articulate thoughts or sentiments to music. For it is a curious fact that one allows oneself to sing, or to hear sung, or to compose as a song, what one would be too inhibited or too embarrassed to simply speak, or hear spoken, or offer as a poem. Why? Well, it seems as if music inaugurates a sort of charmed unreality, licensing the expression of feelings too direct or too unguarded to survive without musical protection. And such emotional license, if not overindulged in, may count as an ethical benefit of engaging with songs such as the ones I have examined.

[14] Perhaps the special satisfaction derived from song is partly rooted in some systemic awareness of the two halves of one's brain being singularly united in the comprehension of what is hearing, on the assumption of the right hemisphere as the main locus of musical processing and the left hemisphere as the main locus of verbal processing.

Jerrold Levinson

One last remark. I know that my own life, at any rate, would be considerably poorer without the benefits that exposure to and involvement with the best songs in the jazz standard repertoire can afford, and poorer as much ethically as aesthetically. And I am sure, as well, that that is not just the case while I am actually listening to them.

University of Maryland
august@umd.edu

Is there still life in Still Life?

ANTHONY SAVILE

> Auch kleine Dinge können uns entzücken
> Auch kleine Dinge können teuer sein
> (Paul Heyse)

In his literary autobiography, *Le vent Paraclet*, Michel Tournier records how during his time at the Lycée Pasteur in Neuilly he and his fellow classmates found a source of great hilarity in their favourite *bêtisier*, a volume called *Pensées de Pascal*, in which one learns that painting is a frivolous exercise that consists in imperfectly reproducing objects that are themselves quite worthless. Fairness to Pascal – far from Tournier's mind in those early days – demands that that offending *pensée*, which belongs in the sheaf of *Vanités*, be seen more as a summary of Saint Augustine's views than as a record of Pascal's own, and one that was rooted in a tradition stemming from Plato that deprecated all varieties of mimesis. Setting historical adjustment aside and reining back on the boys' sophisticated amusement, one may well wonder whether the view Pascal records does not contain a grain of truth. Are there not indeed kinds of painting that we prize, yet which are well chosen butts of this criticism? In particular, still life painting concerned to record the trivia of domestic life, pots and pans, fruits and meats, glasses and all sorts of everyday tableware looks to be sharply exposed to Pascalian scorn. If this Platonic or in Augustine's case, neo-Platonic, attack on painting is to be warded off in general then it had best be done here where it appears at its most pressing. And if it cannot be warded off here, then still life painting at least is moribund, probably lifeless, *nature morte* mort indeed.

Here I propose to explore a line of thought that stems from Schopenhauer's reflections about the nature and value of our experience of painting and ask whether there may not be something in his ideas fit to draw the sting of the contempt. What makes Schopenhauer a nice choice as still life's champion is that what he aims to do is not just to confute Platonic or neo-Platonic doctrine, but to show that in the finest painting we are given irreplaceable access to what the true Platonist esteems above all else, to Forms or Ideas. If some version of that thought can be made plausible in regard of still life painting, the neo-Platonist of Augustinian stamp

doi:10.1017/S1358246112000161   ©The Royal Institute of Philosophy and the contributors 2013

will be shown to have closed his eyes there to the very thing that should keep them firmly open. As deft a rebuttal as one might wish for – if only it can be made out.

First a little crude exposition. Our world is the world as we represent it, and the perceived character it takes on is fundamentally a reflection of our needs, interests and desires. The urgencies of the moment, together with our long term goals and strivings, give our world its colour and its tone, but they distort our grasp of it as it is independently of those concerns. By contrast, in our more contemplative aesthetic engagement with the arts we are relieved from the treadmill of everyday life and its subservience to the imperious will, and there we can enjoy a far less distorted view of things. There, Schopenhauer thinks, we can be shown by the artist of genius the inner core and substrate of the world – Will – as it takes on perceptible shape and acquires immediate and adequate objectification unclouded by the clamouring of desire. In the arts we are offered a view of the world not as it usually apprehended, that is for us, *für uns*, but as it is in itself, *an sich*. The beautiful is just what manifests the *Ding an sich* (scilicet, *Wille*) as an object of knowledge and as such qualifies as Platonic Idea, something that is fully real, entirely generic in nature and immune to the vicissitudes of passing time.

In the aesthetic contemplation of things – be that in nature or in art (though primarily in art) – Schopenhauer holds that we find two things going on: first, we experience relief as we free ourselves, even if only briefly, from the pressures of will, the endless cycle of desire, its satisfaction and then the renewed onset of desire. Secondly, through our enjoyment of its beauty, art supplies us with pure knowledge. This cognitive satisfaction has its effect beyond the aesthetic moment in that it acts as what Schopenhauer called a Quietive, encouraging us to resign ourselves to our condition rather than pointlessly battling against it. Such is the lesson he took to lie at the heart of the Christian ethic and that of Eastern religions too. While this sense of relief is primarily what we gain from the beauties of nature and the minor arts, in the arts that concern themselves with human matters (especially history painting and poetry) the cognitive aspect of the story is to the fore and it is there that we are moved more surely beyond the momentary freedom that is provided by any restful quietive gain.

So much by way of bare summary. Clearly there is much here that is not particularly encouraging. But let me pick out the central matter to pursue. At the heart of the story – and what has to be preserved if anything worthwhile is to be made of it – is the idea that the best art provides a desirable correction or adjustment to our customary every-day way of seeing and thinking about things, in Schopenhauer's eyes the theoretical replacing the practical, pure knowledge standing over against end-directed representation. More specific is the idea that the crucial adjustment Schopenhauer had in mind was the exchange of the *für uns* representations of specific matters by *an sich* generic ones. So we should be able to ask whether in still life painting there are plaus-ible cases that might serve to illustrate the point. Examples of a sort that look broadly supportive of the view come readily enough to mind.

The first I offer is the sort of *trompe l'oeil* painting that detaches the things that collect around us or which we collect around ourselves and displays them in settings that set them off against ourselves. Such, for example, are Wallerant Vaillant's *Letter-rack* in Dresden (Figure 1)

Figure 1. Wallerant Vaillant, *Letter-rack* (1658) © Gemäldegalerie Alte Meister, Staatliche Kunstsammlungen Dresden.

Anthony Savile

Figure 2. Samuel van Hoogstraten, Still Life (1666–68), oil on canvas (63×79cm). © Vereingung der Freunde der Staatlichen Kunsthalle, Karlsruhe.

and Samuel van Hoogstraten's *Steckbrett* in Karlsruhe (Fig. 2). The *trompe l'oeil* aspect of these seventeenth century works has the effect of showing these objects – to put it tendentiously – as they really are, as opposed to the way in which they are usually seen, bound by the framework of our practical concerns – letters being read, written, sanded and sealed or, in the case of the *Steckbrett*, articles that serve the everyday practical activities of their owner. Here though, the person is quite absent and these objects take on an insignificance that displays them for what they are in themselves, not so much trinkets as junk (junk, just because they have no existence beyond the concerns of the persons they serve). These witty pictures do not strip those objects of their significance; they reveal them for what they are, insignificant.

Given that, for Schopenhauer, these generic items must be counted as specimens of a low grade objectification of the *Ding an Sich* they would have been welcomed by him more for their provision of relief or detachment from the pressures of practical life – tiresome communication with others, say, in the case of the notes and letters, or the labours of toilette for social effect or work in the writer's studio in that of the *Steckbrett* – than for any far reaching insight into they might provide about the world. For that we need to turn elsewhere where more is at stake than pretty conceit.

An example that looks better able to bear the burden is provided by Juan Sanchez Cotán's *Quince, Cabbage, Melon with Cucumber* in San Diego (Fig. 3). It is no longer a *trompe l'oeil* but a painting that offers to view items of the natural world displayed in a space from which onlookers feel themselves firmly excluded. It is a world in which those fruit and vegetables have almost only spatial relations to one another, and even there they are arranged in a carefully crafted but entirely mysterious way. It is as if their order emphasizes their ultimate independence of one another and, of course, of us, and so epitomizes the artist's prime concern for the *an sich* rather than the mere *für uns*.

Without any reference to Schopenhauer the art historian Norman Bryson has commented on Cotán's work in terms that would have struck a chord. He writes: 'Cotán's paintings aim to persuade vision to shed its worldly education, – its sloth, the blurs and entropies of vision that screen out everything in creation except what the

Figure 3. Juan Sánchez Cotán, *Still Life with Quince, Cabbage, Melon and Cucumber* (c1602) © San Diego Museum of Art (http://www.TheSanDiegoMuseumofArt.org).

Anthony Savile

world presents as spectacular. Against these vices of fallen vision, Cotán administers his antidote: hyper-reality.'[1]

But hyper-reality or *Ding an sich* with a purpose, one should say: in its period and place, in deeply Catholic Spain of the late sixteenth century, Cotán's work was an invitation to spiritual exercise – meditation from a distance on the wonder of God's creation in its smaller parts and a reminder of our duty to adore Him through appreciation of that wonder. Even the geometrical disposition of those fruits intimates a divine order and in its mystery further emphasises our subservience to a higher power which we are called to worship. So at least in that case, unlike the two *trompe l'oeil* ones, the reward of the picture is in part an ethical one that extends well beyond the kind of pure cognition that Schopenhauer would have encouraged us to find there.

Indeed, for him the religious-cum-ethical teaching of Cotán's work could not sit at all well with the Platonic Idea he favoured, for the God that is posited there had no reality and was, as far as Schopenhauer could see, just a fable, whereas Platonic Ideas can only be of what is truly real. And it won't do for him to say that the true subject of the picture is the Will as objectified in fruit and vegetables (as he does in relation to the work of his favourite painters, Raphael and Correggio) for that then makes those works' ethical aspect incomprehensible, substituting resignation to our alienated situation for their more positive redirection of practical thought.

To make progress and to preserve a healthy sense of reality in our dealing with still life painting two adjustments recommend themselves. First, as even the hyper-reality of the Cotán makes clear, at the heart of such pictures is a thought about the relation between what is depicted and ourselves. Even though we feel ourselves to be excluded from the strange world of those familiar fruit, the idea to which we are led is nonetheless about our relation to the order they would reveal. Schopenhauer's idea that relief from pressures of the will demands that we abstract from all thought about the relation of depicted subjects either to each other or to ourselves cuts us off from what enables them to make most sense. Then, secondly, if we are to account for what lies at the heart of a picture like Cotán's, the idea of pure knowledge that comes with the reintroduction of Platonic Ideas must be enlarged to embrace such normative elements as come with making the first adjustment.

---

[1] Norman Bryson, *Looking at the Overlooked*, (Reaktion Books, London, 1990), 64. My illustrative examples are all to be found in Bryson's book, and I have made free use of some of his incisive commentary.

Figure 4. Francisco de Zurbarán, *Metalware and Pottery* (1658–64) ©
Museo Nacional del Prado – Madrid (Spain).

It may be that it would be less misleading to speak more modestly
of reflective knowledge of how things are for us rather than of pure
knowledge of Ideas while still preserving much of what is most interesting in Schopenhauer's thought. For instance, he insists that we are
concerned with types or species rather than individuals – and about
the Cotán it is right enough to say that at least there is no answer to
the question: Which quince is there on display? Which melon? Just
a melon; just a quince. (Interestingly, Schopenhauer pursues that
theme even when it comes to portraits, insisting that each individual
typifies a generic aspect of humanity – and maybe the appeal of portraiture itself lies less in capturing likenesses of individuals we care
about than in its exploration of the extraordinary ways in which
spirit takes on bodily form.) Then, secondly, and for Schopenhauer
quite centrally, the vision that the artist offers us may well act as a corrective to or adjustment of the way our view of the world comes to be
deformed and distorted under the pressures of practical exigency,
egotistical velleity and the like.

These points can be illustrated in the work of another Spanish still
life painter of the early seventeenth century, Francisco de Zurbarán.
His study of *Metalware and Pottery* in the Prado (Fig. 4) situates its
objects in strict geometrical formation, somewhat like the fruit and
vegetables of Cotán, but here the space is one that invites us in
rather than excludes us, and the objects visibly bear on them the
marks of the human hand in their making as well as the way they
are adapted to the movement of the body in the ways they are
fashioned to be lifted and moved about.[2] This picture too, like

---

[2]   See Bryson, op. cit. note 1, 72.

Cotán's, invites us to meditation, but, unlike it, exploits the thought that in human artefacts we also find scope for adoring God's work, for, a seventeenth century spectator might reflect, not only did He create the world for man, man too is His creation and in properly admiring human artefacts we give thanks for that generosity of God's in our regard.[3]

In both these cases I think we are struck by the way in which the apparently trivial material – the humble objects of the *bodega* or the *cantanero* – is revealed as having a significance that we might not have expected. They work on us by removing those objects from their immersion in everyday activity that directs attention away from them and focuses it on the immediately given instead. Fruit and vegetables encountered in everyday life are on their way to the table and consumption; pots, glasses and other vessels, mere containers of future nourishment and thirst-quenching pleasure, but in the picture those aspects of their common presence recede. It would be misleading – as well as pretentious – to think of these objects as being invested with some metaphysical or transcendent significance, for what is actually going on is that they are being shown really to have that retrieved significance for us, one to which the picture teaches us to be alert in the life we lead beyond the picture's frame. That is, the view the picture offers us of its subject has its value not just in its purely aesthetic character but far more in the way in which it contributes to the rich and complex way in which such everyday things are incorporated in the conception of the world that we unconsciously build up through our interaction with its humbler contents and their surroundings. The connection between Schopenhauer's formulation in terms of pure knowledge of Ideas and what we have here is found at the point of what I call a reflective incorporation of such things in our internalized conception of the world.

Nevertheless, the examples I have mentioned could well be seen not so much as illustrative of Schopenhauerian theory as a warning against trying to carry it through. After all, the first of them seems to come closest to the *an sich* of their subjects, yet more as a conceit than as revelatory of their essence. And as we try to preserve something of that essence in the Cotán and the Zurbarán, what emerges quite plainly is that that is only achieved as we focus on the

---

[3]   That we properly see those pots metaphorically as people, in the way Christopher Peacocke has recently suggested (*British Journal of Aesthetics,* 2009). strikes me as fanciful and out of keeping with the picture's seventeenth century spirit. That is not to say that they cannot be so seen.

significance the depicted objects have in relation to ourselves and not as they stand quite independent of all humane considerations.

The ground is made muddier than it need be by Schopenhauer's insistence on the Platonic image, and his Augustinian adversary may think that to protect his own position it suffices to throw cold water over that aspect of his thought. So while Plato's Ideas are *auto kath' auto*, and must putatively surface in art as such if they are to do so at all, the recognition that we should be looking in the direction of the sense things are shown to have for us indicates that something is already giving way. Then too it could be observed that Plato's Ideas were of themselves necessarily inaccessible to sensible experience, yet what Schopenhauer offers us in their name is apparently sensibly recorded in the finest painting. Thirdly, and this is something that demands more than passing comment, the timeless validity and stability of Ideas does not look likely to be replicated in the shifting patterns exhibited by the arts in all their various guises, the painting of still life included.

So should we allow that the adversarial case is made and turn our backs on Schopenhauer in the supposition that there is nothing to take away here from his teaching in the aesthetic chapters of his volume? Certainly not for the reasons just mentioned. Maybe the appeal to Plato is florid and overdone, but the central message is that one leading value of painting – not the only one of course, but certainly a leading one – is to be found in its cognitive deliverances; and a message of subsequent but striking importance is that the arts supply a route to that goal, or good, which is otherwise often unavailable or available only with difficulty. It is only if these claims should fail that the verdict will finally turn out to be negative and it is primarily with them in mind that we should square up to his deflection of the attack recorded in Pascal's *Pensées*.

At the very outset, though, it might seem that the fundamentally cognitivist position that we are being offered is not one that can be safely occupied. Knowledge of how things are supposits truth in all its cases, yet are there not pictures to which the Schopenhauerian idea ought to extend but whose would-be cognitive claims involve opposites that cannot be plausibly combined. An instance of the sort I have in mind is provided by the so-called 'inverted' still life morality of Joachim Beuckelaer's *Well-stocked Kitchen* in the Amsterdam Rijksmuseum (Fig. 5), where the foreground images display tables of enjoyable plenty and abundance, while almost indiscernible in the background scenes from the gospel story play out. There in view, but easily overlooked, are the Flight into Egypt and Christ in the house of Mary and Martha, and their being visibly

Anthony Savile

Figure 5. Joachim Beukelaer, *Well-Stocked Kitchen* (1566) Oil on panel, 171×250cm © Rijks Museum, Amsterdam.

overlooked serves as a reminder of what we have forgotten or neglected, the repulsive side of that foregrounded surfeit. And if those two examples are contested as lying beyond the still life genre that concerns me or are just too far-fetched to illustrate the point convincingly, the Cotán supplies another case. The melon and the quince we see there come across at once as humble and majestic, both modest and grandiose, something that is central to any full appreciation of that marvellous work.

At its heart the market stalls cannot be at once gloriously and repulsively abundant; majesty and humility cannot both properly characterize the same fruit at the same time. And the peculiar image of reality that Schopenhauer wanted to exploit would get lost if one sought to respond to the difficulty by saying that such pictures display knowledge both of what is the case (hedonic abundance or majesty) and also of what ought to be sovereign, ascetic restraint or humility as preached by the Reformed Church, i.e., of what ideally is the case. For as Schopenhauer uses his image, what the artist achieves is always grasp of the real as opposed to the ideal and the challenge posed by such conflicts as these pictures face us with cannot be resolved by reifying the ideal alongside yet opposed to

76

the actually real. And of course the challenge is not limited to a few pictures that show up both conflicting features. That is just a vivid illustration of the more general point that the supposed cognitive reward looks under threat as soon as we acknowledge that distinct pictures can claim our approval yet offer to our view what are dubiously combinable features of the same things.

What this hesitation about the cognitivist project should do is not make us abandon it, but be clear about the way the knowledge it has in view is identified. Talk of the essence of things, of Ideas, of *Dinge an sich* naturally encourages the thought that we have in mind knowledge and truth about the world as it is independently of us, where all truths can coexist and where there are no conflict-generating contraries. But once the move is made from the natural world to the Schopenhauerian 'world as representation' and which we have got used to speaking of as the *Lebenswelt*, or as what Kant had once called 'second nature',[4] that constraint no longer applies with any bite. The artist of talent can make it compelling that the world for us is structured one way and also in a way that is at odds with that first, as is achieved in the 'inverted' cases. Again, different artists, sensitive to potentially opposed features of things that engage us, can display their being thusly disposed in one case and in another to an equally powerful but opposed conception of those same things without there being any incoherence in our supposing that they both achieve cognitive insight.

Something that Schopenhauer could well draw on to outflank the criticism and to make his own point is his insistence that the artist is less concerned with the individual than with the generic, a point we have already met in noting that Cotán is not painting any particular melon and quince, but just a melon, just a quince. And while no melon or quince in the world of nature can possess incompatible properties, the way in which we respond to melons and quinces and their like in our *Lebenswelt* can and often does encompass strains to which individuals of the natural world are hardly subject. So the best response to the critically offered reflection is not to dismiss it, but to redirect it so that its base is given the proper weight, encouraging us to see that the phenomenon it highlights sits well within the cognitivist's field without being at odds with it.

In sum then, as long as we remember that we have to do with second nature, with 'the world as representation' in the best way of taking that famed phrase, the cognitivist need not be daunted. He

---

[4]   The idea surfaces in §49 of the *Critique of Judgment* and is prefigured there in §23.

will abjure any attempt to treat the world as we represent it as, at its best, the world as it is in itself and so free of inconsistency, but instead more modestly express an interest in capturing aspects of it that reflect our very mixed internalized attitudes towards that world – attitudes that may themselves be incommensurable and evidently at odds with one another. Within Schopenhauer's world as representation, taken as our *Lebenswelt* as we have it and as not a boring version of Berkeleyian or Kantian idealism there is ample room for conflicting opposites, and no bar to the painter seeking to exploit that fact. Witness the Cotán and the Beuckelaer.[5]

A corollary – though one without any specific application to our thought about still life – is this. As long as the represented world is thought of as an approximation to the world of first nature then it is natural to think of artistic success, when the cognitivist programme is running, as adding knowledge to knowledge already acquired, and constrained by the usual logical demands of consistency and coherence. Then it will be found quite natural to think of the historical succession of great artists somewhat in the way we sometimes think, ideally and naively maybe, of the succession of great scientists – at their best cumulatively contributing to our progressive understanding of the world, one that approaches closer and closer to an ideal limit (realistically conceived). As we look back over the past in the grip of that picture, it hard for us not to think that the arts of the past are bound to be inferior to those of the present even as we foresee that what we achieve in the present is due to be surpassed and rendered obsolete by what the future will bring in its place.

Perhaps we can even see that the dismissive attitude that I have presented Schopenhauer as aiming to explode is itself a natural expression of that would-be 'progressive' conception of art. For in the end the cognitivist goal could only be perfectly achieved when there was a complete match between what the real world is like and the way it is mirrored in art – an idea of perfection that seemed to early thinkers to be already pointlessly achieved in the painting of Zeuxis and Apelles. The point would still stand even if later eyes, trained to detect mismatches between represented and representation even in the most convincing *trompe l'oeil*, will have had to wait for Luciano Ventrone or some other hyper-realist to attain that goal. As long as things are seen like that, the familiar jibe about the frivolity of making copies of what we already have is quite understandable and not easy to resist.

---

[5]   Maybe this is a point at which to sympathize with Walt Whitman's 'Do I contradict myself? Very well, then, I contradict myself. I am large. I contain multitudes'.

However, refocus the cognitivist's target as 'the world as representation', richer in its way than the world of nature, and neither of those points gains purchase. We can of course allow that there is progress in art: but only in the sense of movement from one rewarding point to another and not as movement towards some antecedently fixed end state. Once that is accepted, any judgment of superiority we are inclined to feel about the figurative work of our own day or its more or less recent past over that of earlier periods cannot be supported by an Augustinian or Pascalian conception of perfect reproduction. That is true even though we may think that what we prize in the still life painters' art is the way in which it can capture so accurately the way things are for us. Now the old jibe falls flat: the cognition that the artist arrives at and offers to the viewer is precisely of something that we do *not* already have, where we think of that 'already' as what is supplied by the world of nature. What is given to us beyond that is a display of how the world of nature enters into our lives in relation to our own place in it, where that place embraces the 'what it is for us' in as broad a sense as we like to give that phrase.

Trying to maintain his position, the Augustinian may think that he can concede the point, but that his criticism still holds good. After all, the *Lebenswelt* that the artist makes manifest is a world that is *ours* through and through and so is surely *already* in our possession. And in that case isn't it idle to attach ourselves to facsimiles of it?

At this point we do well to remind ourselves here of the demand made by Schiller and Hegel that the artist be primarily concerned to find externalizations of what is internal, where the leading thought there is that we do not grasp what is actually internal until it is given adequate external expression. Of course our lived lives have the character they do, yet very often, they have that character without our being more than dimly aware of it. It takes distance to see what we are about, and in the practical urgency of getting things done that distance all too easily eludes us. Engagement with painting can provide the distance – so in the case of the 'inverted' pictures they can get us to see gluttonous surfeit *as* gluttonous or, to take another famous example of the genre, that of Chardin (Fig. 6), to find in our everyday domestic surroundings a delicacy and tenderness that we would otherwise quite miss.[6] The externalization of these

---

[6] The *locus classicus* of this thought is Proust's early essay 'Chardin et Rembrandt', one to which writers on Chardin regularly recur (*Proust, Essais et Articles*, ed. T. Laguet, Gallimard, Paris, 1994, 68–78). The contrast between forgetting and overlooking is important. We can only forget what has already occupied the mind, whereas what we overlook does not

Anthony Savile

Figure 6. Jean-Simeon Chardin, *La Table d'Office* (1757) courtesy of Le Musée de Beaux Arts, Carcassonne (who, generously, did not charge for their reproduction permission).

attitudes and their like in still life makes us aware of the internal, the inner life that is ours in our immediate environment and to which in our day to day business we are are insensitive or even incapable of grasping before we find its expression in the artist's work. This, I suggest, is what we should make of Schopenhauer's thought that in our aesthetic life we find the intellect resisting the deforming pressures of unremitting will, yielding rare access to the elusive *an sich* of things. (When the world as representation is identified as the *Lebenswelt* his expression '*an sich*' naturally rings alarm bells, but we should not suppose it stands for nothing; rather, it must pick

---

touch it. In a brief comment on Proust Richard Wollheim has suggested that the pleasure we come to find in domesticity and which we derive from Chardin is not something that we had previously overlooked but something that had not been consciously within our grasp. It is a quality which can be retrieved from unconscious awareness (which is where Prost locates it) only by our having looked at Chardin, by having looked at representation (*Painting as an Art,* Thames and Hudson, 1987, 99).

out a rich and reflective '*für uns*' that stands over against the depleted '*für uns*' of habit and jaded familiarity and also of what we are no more than unconsciously aware.

May there not be another intellectual mistake that in his *a priori* mode the Augustinian is trading on at this point beyond the misidentification already discussed? Perhaps. A view of mentality that comes with Descartes and which is explicitly endorsed by Spinoza is of what is transparent to the subject. Consciousness is necessarily *for* the subject and that transparency brings with it willy nilly consciousness of the subject's mental life (for Spinoza, iteratively so). So it could appear that the inner world of which the artist makes us aware is indeed already ours and hence its reproduction in art quite superfluous. But, of course, consciousness is indeed for a subject, yet only in the sense that consciousness belongs just to minded subjects. It is an entirely different matter to suggest that a subject is necessarily consciously aware of all his mental states. Of some he is, of others not. And the universal generalisation of that modest truth cannot be used to buttress the 'already' that is at the heart of the critic's complaint.

Maybe he will accept this too, and as a last *a priori* gasp hold out for the painter's externalized knowledge being frivolous and scarcely of value and, staking his colours to that mast, saying that along with much other knowledge about ourselves that we could acquire (How many hairs are there on my head? How long does my genome reveal I am likely to live?) what the still life painter shows us about the near to hand is hardly worth the effort of creating or the expense of acquiring. Nobody would be drawn to the crudest version of that reflection – one that comes in the version that the examined life is not worth living *either* – but one can again observe that there is a misleading philosophical assumption from which that thought may well spring: to wit, that the test of the less than frivolous can only be mounted on a base that is other than self-centred, in this case a base that is unbiased in our own peculiarly human direction. By contrast, once we recognize that any test for frivolity and its opposite can not but be geared to our own standards and preoccupations generated from within the sort of lives that are ours and what sort of persons we are and can decently aspire to be, that last plank of the negative and denigratory case also gives way.

All this does of course still leave open the question of my title - whether there is still life in Still Life. For even if still life at its best gives expression to the attitudes we have unconsciously or unself-consciously to our domesticity, its surroundings and decoration and so on, is there any reason to think that the art of the past has not already exhausted the field? (If not, and if the field is as it were constantly renewed, must we say that in the present we lose what the past once gave its own contemporaries?). Only the initial running together of the *Lebenswelt* with the world of first nature would give the rhetorically implied answer to that question any plausibility. True, the world of nature is basically stable and discoveries we make about its structure do tend to accumulate over time, while what in the main gets jettisoned are the mistaken beliefs that what had made up our conception of the world were in fact truths about it – believed in their day to have been discoveries, though not in fact being so. But the world of our imagination and understanding, 'second nature' is not like that. The character it has is constantly shifting in response to social, political, economic, philosophical and religious changes, and we must expect those changes to make themselves felt in the way in which we can best internalize our nearest surroundings (including our clothing, food, domestic furniture and so on) as they respond to those pressures on it. Seeing still life painting as of value for us on account of its ability to provide an externalization of the changing place these items have in our inner lives, recognizing the changing nature of that inner life, is at once to see that the insights acquired through the artistry of the past do not exhaust the field. So, as far as the cognitivist defence of the genre goes, there is indeed and indeed there will always still be room for still life – room that, once we acknowledge our need for it, we might reasonably expect to be fulfilled.

A word about the past. Is there an asymmetry here between real accumulating discoveries about the world of nature and replacement in the world of imagination (or representation) of established ways of thinking by the new, the cognitive gains delivered by paintings of the past being displaced by those of the present? If that were so to any marked degree then what spoke most clearly to its near contemporaries may strike us moderns as curiosities, and if the work of the past does still hold appeal for us it will do so for different reasons: as an antiquity; as an example of dazzling technique; as historical document and so on. What would be lost is the power that that art once had to anchor in the minds of its beholders the inner world it once displayed, just because and to the degree that that inner world is not any longer the world that once it was. For us nostalgia would have taken over from the vivid immediacy that our predecessors once enjoyed.

That is not how things stand. What seems more nearly true is that changing times make for adjustment of the inner life, make for changes of emphasis, so that the emergence of new ways of thinking and feeling that are added to the older ones alter the potency of the old without entirely reducing it to nothing. We are unlike the Catholic Spaniards of the sixteenth and seventeenth centuries, but their inner world still plays positively in our own, not just nostalgically so. Otherwise the Cotáns, the Zurbaráns and the Chardins could only move us under interpretations that do not really fit them. So in this respect we are all Whitmanesque; we are all large; we all contain multitudes.

So much for the past. What is still lacking is any sense that the bare painted externalization of the inner world I have spoken of plays back into any re-forming of that world, as it surely must. Clearly, just to be shown a flash photo or image of the inner can rightly be thought of as of little import if we do no more than simply acknowledge it and pass on to the next temporary focus of interest. It will only make its due effect through being easily available to be held before the eye. Now that might be supposed to be assured by the simple fact that the achieved still life image is fixed – the painter has captured what he is after, and once sealed by the varnish it does not move. But that is not all – it's not just that the image has to be stable, but *access* to it needs to be stable and undisturbed too if it is to have any truly forming and reforming effect. And this brings me to a further reason for thinking that still life still has a life.

As the power of particular fine work comes to be recognized, so pressure mounts for it to be made publicly available, and today that means to be conserved and presented in the museum, where it is the fate of most significant painting sooner or later to end up. Yet there, as Paul Valéry once remarked, it is that we become superficial.[7] Venus is transformed into document – and the last place where it is now possible to renew ourselves is in the confused and confusing assemblage of riches that the gallery prides itself on putting on show. What we need for intimate still lifes to make their effect is presence in the home where they can still be taken in at leisure and without distraction, and where what they rewardingly show becomes part of the fabric of life from day to day, and so can form and refresh that daily life. As it happens that is now something that can better be achieved by new work before the moment comes for it to serve out its days amid what Ruskin once called 'the general lumber of the great pillage-reservoir galleries'.[8]

---

[7] 'Le Problème des musées' in *Pièces sur l' Art, Paul Valéry, Oeuvres*, La Pléaide, Vol 2, 1290–94. Valéry was not the first to view museums askance. Sixty years or so before Ruskin had spoken of them as 'places of execution of pictures' (*'A Joy Forever'*, §93).

[8] In *Praeterita* Vol. II, §197. See too §94 of *A Joy Forever* : 'But great good is also to be done by encouraging the private possession of pictures; partly as a means of study (much more being always discovered in any

Anthony Savile

Finally, among other things that the future life of still life depends on is the existence of intelligent patronage, the patronage of clear sighted individuals of fine taste, sensitive to the value that this genre of painting can offer. In the mid-1930s Valéry observed that 'there is never any shortage of talented men of imagination born to artistic creation; but often what they need and is in short supply – indeed it is singularly lacking today – are those indispensable amateurs and connoisseurs whose pursuit of their very personal pleasure and the exercise of their very special intelligence is corrupted neither by the prospect of good business deals, nor by the success of their writing, nor by any ambition to be ahead, or on the crest, of fashion's wave'.[9] Perhaps the existence of such figures is even more precarious today than it was when Valéry wrote those lines, making still life's future less assured than it might otherwise be. One thing that could make both them and it rather less precarious is clarity about what is at stake.[10]

Kings College, London
anthony.savile@kcl.ac.uk

---

work of art by a person who has it perpetually near him than by one who only sees it from time to time) and also as a means of refining the habits and touching the hearts of the masses of the nation in their domestic life'.

[9] In his own words, 'Je crois bien que les hommes doués pour concevoir, et nés pour créer ne manquent jamais; mais il leur manque souvent – il leur manque singulièrement aujourd'hui, ... ces amateurs et connaisseurs incorruptibles, chez lesquels ni l'espoir de faire une bonne affaire, ni la prestige de la plume, ni l'ambition de précéder ou de suivre la mode ne troublaient la poursuite de leur volupté personelle et l'exercise de leur intelligence originale' (from the *Préambule* to the catalogue of the 1935 Paris *Exposition de l'Art Italien*, ibid., 1346).

[10] I am grateful to Mr.David Woods for pointing out how little sympathetic Plotinus, the arch neo-Platonist, was to the style of criticism from which I started out and in consequence how the view that Pascal records should not be called neo-Platonist in an unqualified way. In particular he drew my attention to *Enead V*, Tractate 5, Section 1. "Still the arts are not to be slighted on the ground that they create by imitation of natural objects; for, to begin with, these natural objects are themselves imitations; then, we must recognise that they give no bare reproduction of the thing seen but go back to the ideas from which Nature itself derives, and, furthermore, that much of their work is all their own: they are the holders of beauty and add where nature is lacking. Thus Pheidias wrought the Zeus upon no model among things of sense but by apprehending what form Zeus must take if he chose to become manifest to sight."

On Cinematic Genius: Ontology and Appreciation

PAISLEY LIVINGSTON

The word 'genius' is often associated with the idea that artistic creativity is entirely a matter of an involuntary sort of inspiration visited upon the individual artist.[1] My aim in referring to cinematic genius is not, however, to defend that dubious thesis, but to direct attention to the remarkable artistic achievements that some film-makers, working individually or in collaborative teams, have managed to bring about in their intentional and often painstaking creation of cinematic works. Genius, as I understand it, is the exceptional ability to do something difficult, such as the intentional making of an innovative and valuable work of art. My central claim in what follows is that our longstanding and legitimate interest in manifestations of this kind of skill has important implications for a number of interrelated issues in the philosophy of art, and in particular, for some of the questions taken up in the ever-expanding literature on the ontology of works of art.

I begin by evoking some of the central questions in the ontology of art and recommend one approach to their solution. In the second section of the paper I discuss aspects of a particular case in some detail, namely, Mira Nair's (2004) cinematic adaptation of William Makepeace Thackeray's (1848) *Vanity Fair*. One upshot of this discussion is that when we take into account what it means to appreciate a cinematic adaptation as such, we discover additional support for the recommended approach to the ontological questions. In the final section of the paper, I examine some implications for our understanding of the nature of cinematic works and conclude with remarks on the distinction between multiple and singular art forms.

---

[1]   For background, see my 'Poincare's "Delicate Sieve": On Creativity in the Arts', in Krausz, Michael, Dutton, Denis and Bardsley, Karen (eds.), *The Idea of Creativity* (Leiden: Brill, 2009), 129–146; 'Creativity', in Borchert, Donald (ed.), *The Encyclopedia of Philosophy*, 2nd edition (Detroit: Macmilland, 2006), Vol. **2**, 688–691, and *Art and Intention: A Philosophical Study* (Oxford: Clarendon, 2005), chapter 2.

doi:10.1017/S1358246112000215   ©The Royal Institute of Philosophy and the contributors 2013
Royal Institute of Philosophy Supplement **71** 2013   85

Paisley Livingston

I

The most basic and central question to which contributions in the ontology of art address themselves concerns what kinds of things works of art are.[2] It is asked, then, whether all sorts of works are plausibly thought to belong to a single overarching category of entities, and if so, what category that is. Related questions include how particular works are to be individuated, and under what conditions they may be created and destroyed.

With regard to the first question, a central dispute concerns the distinction between multiple and singular works, the thought being that if both of these categories are applicable to the arts, monism about the ontology of art is false. And indeed many philosophers have argued that while some works are 'multiple' in the sense of having, at least in principle, more than one instance, another very basic category of works is made up of those that are in some sense singular or non-iterable.[3]

The latter assumption has been contested. For example, in his fairly brief, enigmatic yet highly influential essay of 1936, Walter Benjamin contrasted the cinematic work's mechanical reproducibility to what he called the 'auratic' status and function of works such as Leonardo's *Mona Lisa*.[4] According to Benjamin, the essential genius of the cinema as a medium and art form is its disruption of the traditional, quasi-religious ideology of the uniqueness or individuality of the work of art. Other philosophers, such as C. I. Lewis

---

[2]   For instructive surveys, see Currie, Gregory, 'Art works, ontology of', in Craig Edward (ed.), *The Routledge Encyclopedia of Philosophy* (London: Routledge, 1998, 2010); retrieved April 08, 2011 from http://www.rep.rout ledge.com/article/M012; Davies, Stephen 'Ontology of Art', in Levinson Jerrold (ed.), *The Oxford Handbook of Aesthetics* (Oxford: Oxford University Press, 2003), 155–180; Gracyk, Theodore, 'Ontological Contextualism', in Davies, Stephen, et al. (eds), *A Companion to Aesthetics*, 2nd edition (Malden, MA: Wiley-Blackwell, 2009), 449–453, and Thomasson Amie, 'The Ontology of Art', in Kivy Peter (ed.), *The Blackwell Guide to Aesthetics* (Oxford: Blackwell, 2004), 78–92.

[3]   Davies, Stephen, 'Ontology of Art', in Levinson, Jerrold (ed.), *The Oxford Handbook of Aesthetics* (Oxford: Oxford University Press, 2003), 155–180.

[4]   See Benjamin, Walter, 'L'œuvre d'art à l'époque de sa reproduction mécanisée', *Zeitschrift für Sozialforschung* **5** (1936), 40–66; 'Das Kunstwerk im Zeitalter seiner technischen Reproduzierbarkeit', in Tiedemann, Rolf and Schweppenhäuser, Hermann (eds.), *Gesammelte Schriften*, Vol. I:2 (Frankfurt am Main, Suhrkamp, 1980), 431–469.

in 1946, Andrew Paul Ushenko in 1953, and Peter Strawson in 1958, have reasoned that as a matter of metaphysical if not technological possibility, *all* of the artefacts associated with works of art, and perhaps the works themselves, could have multiple instantiations.[5] If they are right, then the 'auratic' belief in a work's individuality would be illusory in all art forms, and not just the cinema. The thesis that at least some works are particulars as opposed to types or universals still has its adherents, however. For example, in a paper on the relations between art and technology, Anthony O'Hear defends what he calls the 'singularity thesis', which is the idea that works of art, or at least those 'of distinction', are necessarily individual and unique.[6]

The debate between the advocates of contrasting 'monist' and other views on the work of art continues in the contemporary literature. I return to this topic below, but shall first recommend a very general approach to the more general question of the nature of works of art.[7]

Various philosophers who have commented on the problematic nature of topics in the ontology of art have suggested that at least part of the problem resides in a 'process/product' ambiguity inherent in the term 'work' (and related terms in other languages, such as *Werk*, *œuvre*, *opus*, etc.).[8] If this is right, then a first attempt at explicating a concept of works can adopt any one of three basic strategies: eliminate the product and retain the process; eliminate the process and retain the product; and finally, retain both process and

---

[5]   Lewis, C. I., *An Analysis of Knowledge and Valuation* (La Salle, IL: Open Court, 1946), Ushenko, Andrew Paul, *Dynamics of Art* (Bloomington, IN: University of Indiana Press, 1953), 21–25, Strawson Peter F., *Individuals* (London: Methuen, University Paperbacks, 1959), 231, n.1; see also his 'Aesthetic Appraisal and Works of Art', in *Freedom and Resentment and Other Essays* (London: Metheun, 1974), 178–88, at p. 183: 'There is no reason for regarding the members of some classes of works of art as essentially particulars, rather than types. All works of art, certainly, are individuals; but all are equally types and not particulars'.

[6]   O'Hear, Anthony, 'Art and Technology: An Old Tension', in Fellows, Roger (ed.), *Philosophy and Technology* (Cambridge: Cambridge University Press, 1995), 143–158; reprinted in *The Landscapes of Humanity: Art, Culture and Society* (Exeter: Imprint, 2008), 126–142.

[7]   For a survey, see my 'History of the Ontology of Art', *Stanford Encyclopedia of Philosophy* (2011); http://plato.stanford.edu/entries/art-ontology-history/

[8]   A fairly early, and generally overlooked example is Boas, George, *A Primer for Critics* (Baltimore: The Johns Hopkins University Press, 1937).

product, for example, by understanding the concept of the work as somehow covering their relation.

The first of these options has been attempted by various philosophers. Robin Collingwood is an early example, at least if we take literally those formulations in which he clearly states that the work is the artist's 'activity'.[9] This line of thought has the disadvantage of neglecting the evidence that artistic creation is not always a process undertaken with no product in view. In many cases, the artist's activity is clearly intended to eventuate in some finished, perceptible item that can be put on display and attended to, and this sort of practice is central to the worlds of art. To say that the work is the activity alone and in no wise the product of this activity is implausible because it simply denies this fact.

The second option amounts to thinking of works as finished products only. St Thomas Aquinas can be interpreted as espousing this option when he contends that art 'does not require the artist to proceed well, but to make a good work' because 'the good of art is considered not in the artist himself, but in the product [opus]'.[10] This position is sometimes promoted as the ordinary or common sense view. Proposals that diverge from it are labeled 'revisionist' and attacked as inconsistent with ordinary usage. And indeed we are apt to say that the *Mona Lisa* is to be glimpsed inside the thick glass case in which it is housed at the Louvre. Do not such utterances refer to the work of art as a discrete material object having a determinate spatio-temporal location, which is certainly not the case with the process of Da Vinci's making of the picture, which apparently took place over twelve years? The second type of explication of 'work', then, has the apparent advantage of setting aside the intangible and fleeting thoughts and actions of the artist so as to seize upon the final product, which remains to be identified as the work of art itself.

A first problem with this position, however, is that if some works are happenings or performances (which arguably belong to the category of events), then not all works of art are reducible to, or are even partly constituted by a product, if by this is meant a particular physical or abstract artifact. It would indeed be a stretch to classify the action undertaken by a performance artist, such as Chris

---

[9] Collingwood, Robin George, *The Principles of Art* (Oxford: Clarendon, 1938), 281–282.
[10] Aquinas, St. Thomas, *Summa Theologica*, Ia IIae q. 57 a. 5. Cited by Tatarkiewicz, Władysław in *History of Aesthetics, II: Medieval Aesthetics* (The Hague: Mouton, 1970), 261. The context is an argument for the necessity of prudence to virtue and a good life, but not to goodness in art.

On Cinematic Genius: Ontology and Appreciation

Burden's having himself shot in the arm, as a 'product'. A second problem with this general approach to the ontology of works is that it is hard to square with our demonstrable and justifiable interest in the artistic artefact, taken not as a detachable product, but as the manifestation and upshot of the artist's purposeful activities and abilities, reference to which is necessary to the correct classification of the item. The latter point is made by Kant in the *Kritik der Urteilskraft* when he distinguishes between works and natural items such as honeycombs. Kant claims that the former, unlike the latter, involve the exercise of freedom, and he adds immediately that by this he means that a work, unlike the honeycomb, arises 'durch eine Willkür': 'through a capacity for choice that grounds its actions in reason'.[11] It should be noted, however, that Kant did not explicitly square off against the above-cited thesis advanced by Aquinas, and in the same paragraph §43 he contrasts *Werk* (*opus*) to *Wirkung* (*effectus*), aligning the artist's *Produkt* with the former terms, and the honeycomb with the latter.

Against the thesis that the work is simply the artist's product or effect, it can be argued that some of the identifying or essential features of the work involve the artist's activities, and more specifically, aspects of the process whereby the artefact or event was generated. It will not do to try to explain this by saying that reference to the artefact's relations to the agent's actions is purely epistemic, or in other words, merely our (optional) way of experiencing or thinking about the product. A work, we say, is skillful or inept to some degree, and a judgement of this sort does not refer uniquely to the intrinsic properties of a physical object or artefact, but instead bears upon a relation obtaining between the content and quality of the artist's intention and the actual results of the actions the artist undertakes in an effort to realize those intentions. A skill is a capacity to succeed in attempts at doing something difficult; to say that a product is skillful is to imply that the action whereby it was made was the activation of such an ability. An inept yet lucky attempt is contrasted, then, to a skillful action in which the agent realizes the aim as intended.

---

[11] Kant, Immanuel, *Kritik der Urteilskraft. Kants gesammelte Schriften*, Vol. **5**. (Berlin: Walter De Gruyter, 1902 [1790]), paragraph 43; Guyer, Paul and Matthews, Eric (trans.), Guyer, Paul (ed.), *Critique of the Power of Judgment* (Cambridge: Cambridge University Press, 2000),182. For a discussion of Kant's definition of art and its relation to some more recent views, see Guyer, Paul, 'From Jupiter's Eagle to Warhol's Boxes: The Concept of Art from Kant to Danto', *Philosophical Studies* **25**:1 (1997), 83–116.

Paisley Livingston

What, then, is the link between skill and artistic value? Here we must be very careful, since the bold and straightforward theses on this topic are false. The successful realization of some artistic intention cannot alone *suffice* to endow a work with a corresponding artistic merit, since the intended feature can be artistically worthless. And if there can be valuable, but unintended artistic properties, as I think we should recognize, intention is not *necessary* to artistic value either. So we have to look for more subtle correlations.

One possibility is that the *intentional* realization of an intended goal could contribute to artistic value in a context where other conditions (including conditions on the quality of the intention) are satisfied. As I have already implied, we should acknowledge the existence of artistic serendipity, which is what happens when the artist goes looking for one sort of good thing, does not find it, but luckily comes up with some other kind of good thing. Even if we grant the existence of artistic serendipity, perhaps the successful realization of at least some artistic intentions is *necessary* to the creation of any work of art having significant artistic value. This weaker necessity thesis can be tested by asking whether there is or could be a highly valuable work of art, *all* of the significant artistic merits of which were the unintended consequences of the artist's inept attempts to endow the work with artistic qualities vastly different from those it actually possesses. I do not know of any such cases and think that such a thing is highly unlikely, but perhaps this is merely the product of my inability to imagine the glories of a totally serendipitous work, that is, one in which all of the mediocre features conceived of and attempted by the inept artist were luckily supplanted by marvelous artistic qualities.

There is another way to support a thesis to the effect that whether an artistically valenced property has been intentionally realized can make a difference to some of the work's artistic values, and hence ought to be recognized as potentially contributing, in more or less direct ways, to the overall artistic merit (or demerit) of the work. Such a thesis can be supported by reference to a sub-category of valuable artistic properties which can only be realized when the artist's intentions match the subsequent output. An example of properties falling into such a category is a stylistic feature the value of which necessarily pertains to the manner in which the artist designs and executes that feature in the making of the work.[12] An artistic feature

---

[12]   'Style' and 'stylistic' are, of course, amongst the most contested and ambiguous terms in aesthetic discourse. On one usage, these terms are employed to refer to the manner or mode involved in some feature or collection

referred to as 'semi-archaic' is an example of an artistic property belonging to that category, as it is a property that is only valuable when intentionally realized (as when an artist, such as Sassetta, chooses to combine rival or seemingly incompatible options or features in a particular historical situation). If features of a work are semi-archaic by design, then these features carry one artistic valence, but if they are merely the result of ineptitude or happenstance, they carry another, negative valence.

Such considerations concerning one aspect of artistic value and its appreciation support the idea that the process/product ambiguity at the heart of the concept of a work should be maintained. A work, then, should be conceived of as comprised of a result as well as an intentional activity converging on that result. With this in mind, the work of art as a whole should be distinguished from the product alone, or what can be called the artistic vehicle, such as a painted surface, a string of linguistic symbols, a sequence of sounds, bodily movements, or whatever other perceptible or cognizable arrangement may be put on display for some audience to contemplate.

In employing the term artistic 'vehicle' here, I follow a usage adopted, for example, by H. S. Goodhart-Rendel in 1934, as well as by such philosophers as Stephen C. Pepper and C. I. Lewis, and a few contemporary figures, including David Davies.[13] In old-fashioned medicinal parlance, the vehicle is the sugar that makes the medicine go down; those who dislike the medical and other connotations of the word may prefer to follow Jerrold Levinson, Gregory Currie and others in speaking of artistic 'structures'.[14] With regard to the cinema, it is appropriate to use the term 'audio-visual display' to refer to the vehicle or structure of a cinematic work, though it may be worth noting that many film scholars think there are cinematic 'texts', probably because they have in mind the Barthesian idea of *un texte* (or even *du texte*) as anything it can be amusing to interpret. Or perhaps

---

of features of a work or works; cf. Prown, Jules David, 'Style as Evidence', *Winterthur Portfolio* **15**:3 (1980), 197–210.

[13] Goodhart-Rendel, H. S., *Fine Art* (Oxford: Clarendon, 1934), 3–4, Pepper, Stephen C., 'The Individuality of a Work of Art', *University of California Publications in Philosophy* **20** (1937), 81–97, *The Basis of Criticism in the Arts* (Cambridge, MA: Harvard University Press, 1945), *The Work of Art* (Bloomington: Indiana University Press, 1955), Davies, David, *Art as Performance* (Malden, MA: Blackwell, 2004).

[14] Levinson, Jerrold , *Music, Art, and Metaphysics* (Ithaca, NY: Cornell University Press, 1990), Currie, Gregory, *An Ontology of Art* (London: Macmillan, 1989).

Paisley Livingston

what leads film scholars to refer to moving images as texts is some
more general (and in my view dubious) 'semiotic' notion that anything that is meaningful or has content is a text.

One key reason for insisting on a work/vehicle distinction (which is
different from the distinction between a work and its multiple instances) is this: a work of art is more than the perceptible item (or
type of item) an artist may intentionally put on display, since the
work includes relations between that item and relevant aspects of
the artist's activity and attitudes, including intentions, decisions,
and a way of devising, making, classifying, and displaying the
vehicle or structure. In those happy cases where the intended properties of a work have been realized as intended, this is not an intrinsic
feature *of the vehicle*, but it is a feature of the work. The overall explication of the concept named 'work of art' that best accommodates
these points is our third, 'skill-inclusive' option, which identifies
the work as a process/product relation.

Is this a revisionary proposal? If 'revisionary' means anything that
deviates from a literal acceptance of all ordinary usage, the answer is
'yes', since one of the proposal's entailments is that what is located in
the box at the Louvre is the artistic vehicle (the poplar board), not the
work of art. But is revisionism necessarily a bad thing? It is common
sense, and not at all revisionist, to observe that revisionism would
only be a mistake if we knew that the *status quo* could not be improved.
That is usually quite hard to establish, however, especially when it
comes to the vagaries of ordinary usage. Philosophers of art would
do well, I think, to look beyond the revisionary/non-revisionary di-
chotomy (and what may or may not be a Strawson-inspired appeal
to a 'descriptive' metaphysics).

In any case, the broad approach to the conception of works that I
have just sketched does not lack distinguished historical antecedents
as well as the sophisticated 20th-century proponents mentioned
above. For example, when Leon Battista Alberti attempted to generalize about excellence in architecture, or what he called 'concinnitas',
one of his concerns was to characterize 'lineamentis', which can be
translated, at least if we follow Bastoli, who was responsible for bringing Alberti's Latin into the vernacular, as 'disegno' or 'design'.[15]

[15] Alberti, Leon Batista, *De Re Aedificatoria* (1486), I, 4-4v. http://
echo.mpiwg-berlin.mpg.de/ECHOg.de/ECHOdocuView?url=%2Fmpiwg
%2Fonline%2Fpermanent%2Farchimedes%2Falber_reaed_004_la_1485&toc
Mode=thumbs&viewMode=text_dict&pn=1; (accessed 28.9.2011);
*L'architettura (De re aedificatoria) di Leon Battista Alberti trodotta in
lingua fiorentina da Cosimo Bartoli. . . con l'aggiunta de disegni* (Florence:

Design in turn is understood as 'a product of human ingenuity' (ingenio), but also as a project [une preordinazione] 'executed with learned ingenuity, intelligence, and talent ['animo ingenio et erudito' for which Bastoli wrote 'condotto da anima e da ingegnio buono']. Such was Alberti's general characterization of one of the privileged objects of appreciation. More generally, skill and intention-related properties, such as design, figure amongst the objects of artistic appreciation, and we should only accept an account of works that is consistent with this assumption.

In order to make this point and some of its implications more tangible, in the next section of this paper I discuss a particular example. This discussion will set the stage for a return to the theoretical issues in the final section of the paper.

II

My example belongs to an important category of cinematic works in which the relation to a literary or other anterior work invites and guides specific comparisons that are meant to inform both the experience and appreciation of the work. I have in mind the category of cinematic adaptations, for to appreciate an adaptation *as such* is to weigh the qualitative differences and similarities between the adaptation and the work that served as its source or model.[16] Cinematic adaptations belong, I propose, to the larger category of overtly imitative works, that is, works explicitly or conspicuously modelled on anterior works, and where the target audience is meant to be aware of this modeling relation. In some cases, such as in a pastiche or a

---

Lorenzo Torrentino, 1550); Alberti, Leon Batista, *On the Art of Building in Ten Books*, Rykwert, Joseph, Leach, Neil, and Tavernor, Robert (trans.) (Cambridge, MA: MIT Press, 1988), 7. I am aware that there is a tendency in the literature on Alberti to stress the neo-Platonic assumptions in his aesthetics, and there is a good basis for this in his remarks on beauty. See, for example, Gadol, Joan, *Leon Battista Alberti: Universal Man of the Early Renaissance* (Chicago: University of Chicago Press, 1969). Yet the rather non-Platonic, positive emphasis on the artist's ingenuity is an element in the text to which many of Alberti's translators and commentators have also been attuned.

[16] For background to this remark, see my 'On the Appreciation of Cinematic Adaptations', *Projections* 4:2 (2010), 104–127. I am grateful to Trevor Ponech for valuable collaboration on the topic of cinematic adaptations.

Paisley Livingston

parody, the source is not a particular, identifiable work, but a category or style of works, such as westerns or science fiction or the distinctive life-work of a famous author. In other cases, an overtly imitative work is conspicuously based on a particular model, and the audience of the adaptation is expected to entertain comparisons between the adaptation and its model so as to grasp various aspects of the adaptation's intentional design. Whereas some imitative works of this sort are designed to remain highly faithful to the model, others are not, and instead exhibit creative differences from that model while also remaining overtly imitative in other respects. In some cases it is a matter of a transgressive manifestation of the distance from the anterior model, but in other cases there is a more or less harmonious combination of imitative and innovative traits.

Consider now the 2004 cinematic adaptation of Thackeray's *Vanity Fair*. This is a very fine instance of the hybrid category referred to above. For those who know something about the filmmakers and the novel, it is easy to observe that this is not an adaptation the makers of which slavishly sought a high degree of fidelity to the source, yet as it is an adaptation, the work was of course meant to carry over a number of key features (or more accurately, types of features) of that source. In both the film and the novel, the central character is a *parvenue* or social climber named 'Rebecca Sharp'. In the novel Becky is a deeply villainous figure, a mother who intentionally and systematically mistreats her child. Yet in the film, the homonymous character is a rather more sympathetic figure, not simply one portrait figuring alongside the others in a very long gallery of *vaniteux*.

Plenty of evidence supports this broad contrast. In interviews in which she discusses the approach adopted in the making of the film, the director and co-author of the script, Mira Nair, admits that her Becky is a 'rascal', but repeatedly praises the character's intelligence, artistic talent, and selfless acts of friendship. One finds little or no evidence of any such selfless acts in the novel. The subtitle of Thackery's work is 'a novel without a hero', but Nair and her multiple collaborators have not made a film without a heroine. Money, and those who have it, such as Lord Steyne, are the real problem in the film's story, not the efforts and schemes of those who, like Rebecca and her artist father, are born with talent but without money.

To develop these points in a bit more detail, let us consider how the movie-makers have rather cleverly adapted the episode in which Becky has managed to get herself invited to the home of the lecherous Lord Steyne. This is already something of an achievement for the social climber, but Rebecca still faces the problem of getting the

94

On Cinematic Genius: Ontology and Appreciation

aristocratic women to stop 'cutting' her. Taking pity on her, and perhaps in an effort to placate her husband, Lady Steyne finally asks Rebecca whether she will sing. Here is what Thackeray's narrator tells us about what happens next:

> 'I will do anything that may give pleasure to my Lord Steyne or to you', said Rebecca, sincerely grateful, and seating herself at the piano, began to sing.

> She sang religious songs of Mozart, which had been early favourites of Lady Steyne, and with such sweetness and tenderness that the lady lingering round the piano, sate down by its side, and listened until the tears rolled down her eyes.[17]

The treatment given to this material in the film is quite novel and nothing short of marvelous. Film-making is often a richly collaborative endeavor, and the scene in question is a good case where cinematic genius is a matter of the harmonious contributions made by a group of creative people. Nair deserves authorial credit for having skillfully solicited and orchestrated contributions from a variety of talented people, including Julian Fellowes, who co-authored the script with Nair; Beatrix Aruna Pasztor, who was responsible for the costume design; Allyson Johnson, the editor, and Declan Quinn, cinematographer.

With regard to the artistic brilliance of the scene in question, special mention should be made of the Canadian composer Mychael Danna, who provided an inventive and lovely musical setting to Tennyson's poem, gorgeously sung by Custer Larue. In this regard, the adaptation explicitly diverges not only from the novelistic source but from the historical record. When Lady Steyne asks Becky what song to play, she names Tennyson's poem, as though the music that follows were some well-known composition. This is clearly a deliberate anachronism, yet in my view it has a cogent artistic motivation in the context of a hybrid adaptation aimed at a deliberate refashioning of the *parvenue*. Nair and her collaborators did well in deliberately swerving away from having the movie's Rebecca hypocritically lend her voice to a rendition of 'O Gottes Lamm', or one of the

---

[17] Thackeray, William Makepeace Thackeray, *Vanity Fair: A Novel without a Hero*, Tillotson, Geoffrey and Kathleen (eds.) (Boston: Houghton Mifflin & Co., Riverside Edition, 1963), 474. For those using other editions, the passage is to be found at the end of chapter 49. In the novel, Becky's singing does not win over the other ladies, who keep up a 'loud and ceaseless buzzing and talking'. Here there can be no reasonable doubt that the filmmakers intentionally diverged from the novelistic source.

other relatively obscure religious songs by Mozart. Instead, Nair's Rebecca honestly wins her audience, just as Nair courts hers, with the beauty and power of a song of erotic mystery and intimacy. In Thackeray, Becky manages to charm Lady Steyne largely because she stirs up the Lady's childhood associations; Becky fails, however, to charm the other women. In the film, Becky seduces everyone who witnesses her performance. In Thackeray, Rebecca's oft-mentioned musical talent is adduced as another illustration of a moralist's contrast between an all-too-scarce moral virtue, on the one hand, and beauty, talent, and the other worldly vanities on the other. In the film there is instead a harmonious celebration of artistic virtuosity exemplified by Becky's adept performance of a fascinating song.

While the cinematic medium has its own specific artistic techniques, films can also nest or embed the expressive devices of many other art forms, such as, most obviously, music, dance, and costume, but also, interior design and the statues and pictures that are depicted within a set. A film can also nest within itself another work of art. Very briefly, a work nests another work when at least part of the vehicle of that work is observable in the vehicle of the nesting or matrix work.[18] For example, the words of Tennyson's poem are audible in Becky's song. In a sense, the specifically cinematic genius of this scene is its very combination of an array of nested artistic vehicles.

A systematic analysis of the scene, and of its relation to the work as a whole, would take quite some time, and in what follows I single out only a few aspects. At the beginning of the scene, Becky enters a roomful of enemies. Her social exclusion is visually highlighted by the contrast between her black dress and the white and red gowns worn by the others. An overhead crane shot shows how Becky quite literally attempts to break into the closed circle of the women gathered about a round table, looking at drawings. When Becky approaches, the others flee in a kind of choreography of social exclusion. As Becky begins to sing, Nair and her team draw masterfully upon two of the most powerful cinematic devices: close-ups and reaction shots. The fictional performance of Becky is a composite of the actresses' expressive mimicry and the singer's dubbed-in voice. Shots of the actress pretending to sing are intercut with shots that depict

---

[18]   For background and a more detailed explication, see my 'Nested Art', *The Journal of Aesthetics and Art Criticism* **61**:3 (2003), 233–245, and 'Artistic Nesting in *The Five Obstructions*', in Hjort, Mette (ed.), *On The Five Obstructions* (London: Wallflower Press, 2008), 57–75.

the responses of the onlookers, whose faces progressively shift from cool disdain to a reluctant acknowledgement of talent, and finally to complicity and genuine aesthetic delight. Whatever else they make think of her, the audience must acknowledge and admire Becky's talent.

A few comments on the use of lip-synching in this scene may be in order. In a purely musical context, the use of this device is hardly an artistic virtue, yet the valence somehow shifts in the context of Nair's film, where no deception is involved. We can admire Reece Witherspoon's skill, not at singing, but at pretending to sing, just as we can admire the director's selection of a superior voice for the part; Witherspoon is a performer in the work as opposed to one of the work's authors, so there is no reason to conclude that she ought to have sung the part herself, or that her failure to sing is a flaw in her performance. Finally, we may note that in her commentary on the film, the director has generously identified a cinematic source that provided some inspiration for the scene, Bollywood director Guru Dutt's 1957 film, *Pyaasa*. It is true that both films include lip-synched song sequences in which a singing figure interacts dynamically with a crowd of onlookers, but the one in Dutt's film lacks the restraint, precision, and elegance of Nair's scene.[19]

Some readers may wonder what my points about adaptations have to do with the distinction between the work and its vehicle and with the considerations introduced above about works as product and process. An answer to that question can be formulated by turning our backs on the messiness of actual artistic examples and referring to a schematic, imaginary example devised in the manner of Jorge Luis Borges' oft-mined 1939 story of Pierre Menard.[20]

Imagine, then, that two film-makers (or teams thereof), A1 and A2, work independently. Rather surprisingly, they somehow end up making cinematic displays (or 'texts' if you insist) that are indistinguishable.[21] Call these Vehicle 1 and Vehicle 2 of Work 1 and Work 2,

[19]   Readers are invited to compare the song sequences, which are available at http://www.youtube.com/ watch?v=GeqU0maaQL0 and http://www.youtube.com/ watch?v=wFQc6PyAf5I (accessed 28.9.2011).
[20]   To my knowledge, the first argumentative use of this source in English in the context of aesthetics was Anthony Savile's, 'Nelson Goodman's "Languages of Art": A Study', *The British Journal of Aesthetics* **11**:1 (1971), 3–27. For other references, see 'History of the Ontology of Art', *Stanford Encyclopedia of Philosophy* (2011); http:// plato.stanford. edu/entries/art-ontology-history/.
[21]   By 'indistinguishable' I mean competent or normal observers cannot perceive any intrinsic differences between the two items and so would

made by A1 and A2, respectively. Both vehicles bear a number of striking resemblances to a particular novel, N, published prior to their making. The author of Work 1 intentionally based his film on N, conceiving of the film rather standardly as a cinematic adaptation of this particular, anterior work. Yet the author of Work 2 was blithely unaware of N, and so in creating his film was in no way intent upon making an adaptation of it. Nor was A2 basing his work on other works that were modeled on, or direct sources for N. One might conclude, on the basis of the resemblances between N and Work 2, that the latter lacks historical if not psychological creativity: even though A2 was innocent of copying N, 'somebody else got there first', and the film therefore lacks one kind of novelty. In such a context, it would, however, be a blunder to classify Work 2 as an adaptation. So as we scrutinize the qualities of Vehicle 2, it would be an error to think in terms of the ways in which the maker(s) intentionally copied or diverged from N, whereas the tracking of these very same sorts of qualities would be wholly appropriate in an assessment of Work 1, which cries out to be understood in relation to its source as well as to its maker's particular manner of understanding (or misunderstanding) that source. It follows, then, that while the vehicles are type-identical, the works are not, and from this fact, given some relatively uncontroversial assumptions about identity, it follows that the works are not identical to their vehicles. Instead, the work is the relation between a vehicle and the episode of its making, or the product as well as the process. To appreciate a work, as opposed to the vehicle alone, one must know certain things about the artist's intentions and decisions, as well as about the features of the historical context within which the artist was acting.[22]

---

classify them accurately as tokens of the same type of audio-visual display. If these observers had no independent knowledge whether they were experiencing a screening of Vehicle 1 or Vehicle 2, they would, after a particular screening, have a 50% chance of correctly identifying which one they had just seen. For the sake of the argument, I stipulate that the credits in Vehicle 1 make no reference to the novelistic source, perhaps because it was deemed too obvious to require mention. This makes A2's ignorance of N a glaring weakness, but that only reinforces the point about the artistic differences between Work 1 and Work 2.

[22] This more general thesis was, of course, argued for in a more eloquent and less roundabout way by Erwin Panofsky in his essay, 'The History of Art as a Humanistic Discipline', in Greene, T. M. (ed.), *The Meaning of the Humanities* (Princeton: Princeton University Press, 1940), 89–118. The

It follows from these remarks that the successful appreciation of an adaptation requires a lot of knowledge, not only about the features of the source, but about how that source has been understood by the makers of the adaptation. The appreciator also needs to know which of the source's features the adaptors do and do not intend to carry over into the adaptation. Appreciation is a fallible enterprise: of course the appreciator may lack some of this knowledge, and the available evidence may require careful sifting.

Here, for example, is a tangle related to the Thackeray example. One of my central claims above about the relation between Nair's and Thackeray's works is that Becky in the novel is a far more villainous character than the Becky in the film. Yet Nair's co-author of the script, Julian Fellowes, has denied that in the novel Becky is really a villainess. Thackeray, he claims, 'had to pretend' that Becky was not the heroine.[23] I confess that I do not find it cogent to conjecture that when Thackeray wrote in a way that coherently invites us to imagine a character who does a lot of obviously evil things, he was only pretending to do so, and 'thus' the character does not really do these evil things *in the story*. The list of Becky's misdeeds in the story is quite long, and the only way to delete or shorten that list would be to argue that the *narrator* is lying or otherwise unreliable. The author, then, would only be pretending to endorse everything the narrator says about what happens in the story, but the discerning reader would detect the irony and suspend the make-believe. Yet I see no evidence to support the postulation in Thackeray's *Vanity Fair* of an authorial irony with regard to the descriptions of the story events that are proffered by the seemingly omniscient narrator. Thackeray very obviously uses the device of the unreliable narrator in the case of the first-person account in *Barry Lyndon* (Barry is more villainous than he presents himself as being) but there is no such first-person narration at work in *Vanity Fair*. Even if Nair et al. genuinely intended to be faithful to Thackeray's intentions by making Rebecca a positive heroine, and even were we to grant the

---

greatest (unintended) achievement of post-structuralist art theory was prodding analytic philosophers into developing increasingly elaborate justifications of traditional humanistic positions.

[23]   See his remarks as cited in Muir, John Kenneth, *Mercy in Her Eyes: The Films of Mira Nair* (New York: Applause Theater and Cinema Books, 2006), 220–223. Like all statements about artistic intentions, this is one is fallible, both as a characterization of Fellowes' effective intentions, but also as a description of the overarching intentions behind the making of the film as a whole.

accuracy of Fellowes' claim about the conjectured unreliable narration or authorial pretense in the novel, the film could not have been genuinely faithful to the novel in realizing such an intention because Thackeray's putative ironic or indirect strategy of characterization would have been left behind. It is far from apparent, in any case, that the film as a whole was actually designed with this sort of fidelity in mind, and thus I am reluctant to ascribe to its makers a failure in attempting to achieve any such thing. Instead, the more straightforward conclusion is that while Thackeray's book has no heroine, Nair's film does. Nair's Becky is a talented *parvenue* whose tough circumstances explain the liberties she takes with what is presented as a conventional and largely hypocritical set of imperial mores.

III

With the discussion of the example in mind we can identify some of the kinds of artistic properties that are the object of one important species of artistic appreciation; for shorthand, I refer to these properties as pertaining to artistry, understood, following Alberti, as talented and intelligent choice and skilful purposeful activity in the realization of an artistic design. The appreciation of artistry, I have suggested, requires attunement to the artist's actions and choices in a context.

To return to the ontological issues broached earlier, the questions to which we must address ourselves are these: what kind of item is it that can be the bearer of the properties involved in artistry? What kinds of entities are they, and are they multiple or singular?

To begin with the distinction between the work of art and the artistic vehicle, it is generally allowed that in the case of film, the artistic vehicle is not a unique object, but a *type* of text or display. Two people can experience two distinct tokens of the same type of audio-visual display at the same time but in different places. This is the case because various technologies can be used to encode a type of display that is then instantiated in particular screenings or projections effectuated by the relevant machines. As Noël Carroll has observed, such a screening is not like the performance of a musical or theatrical work, as normally no artistry is involved in such mechanical operations as using a projector to screen a film.[24]

---

[24]   Carroll, Noël, *Theorizing the Moving Image* (Cambridge: Cambridge University Press, 1996).

Or in other words, the projectionist's performance, while valuable and important, is not one of the objects of artistic appreciation. Mention should, however, be made, in passing, of hybrid traditions in which musical and other performances enhanced screenings of films. For example, in Japan, *kowairo setsumei* (translated literally as 'voice colouring') was provided by a group of performers who, seated out of sight, improvised dialogue during the screening of a 'silent' film.

Setting aside various hard questions about the nature of cinematic vehicles, I turn now to the question of the relation between the vehicle and the work. What, finally, is a work if it is not the discrete and detachable product of the artist's creative activity? The crux is to say something sufficiently accurate and informative about the nature of the complex, relational entity which is a work of art, and there remains significant disagreement amongst philosophers on this score, including those who agree that the work is a relation between a structure or vehicle and an artist's (or artists') attitudes and creative activities in a context.

A good part of this disagreement hinges on the right way to provide a highly general characterization of the action artists undertake in relation to the vehicle of a work.[25] The traditional inclination is to invoke some concept of creation or making, understood broadly as being instrumental in and responsible for intentionally bringing something into existence for the first time. Yet objections to this traditional idea have been raised. If the vehicle is an abstract type or a universal, it is reasoned, this item cannot have been literally created as a result of the activities of a spatio-temporally located agent. This assumption, which may not be well-founded, is what motivates some philosophers to say that the artist *discovers* or *indicates* an artistic structure, but does not genuinely create one. My view is that it is preferable for a variety of reasons to say that the artist intentionally creates, makes, or chooses a primary instance or token of the vehicle; the artist makes various choices regarding the primary token's features and this vehicle's possible and appropriate reproductions. As appreciators of works, we are interested in the difference made by the artist's purposeful and potentially skillful manipulation of artistic media, and talk of a rather cerebral 'discovery' of pre-existing *abstracta* does not correspond to the object of this sort of well-entrenched interest. Also, if we remember that in some art forms, such

[25] For an informative discussion of this issue, see Nussbaum, Charles, 'Kinds, Types, and Musical Ontology', *The Journal of Aesthetics and Art Criticism* **61**:3 (2003), 273–291.

as dance and mime, the vehicle is itself a matter of physical actions and gestures (as opposed, say, to the making of some artefact or arrangement of objects), it is especially awkward to have to say, as some philosophers would have us say, that the artist's role in the production of a work of art is to discover or select a type of movement or action that is the artistic structure. Instead, it is preferable to say that the artist creates a work by performing intentional actions, where some of these actions generate or constitute or otherwise give rise to a first, and in some cases, the only instance of the perceptible vehicle of the work.

With regard to cinematic works, while it may appeal to some philosophers to imagine that all possible types of audio-visual displays 'always already' exist along with all other abstract items, it seems unhelpful and irrelevant at best, and ludicrous at worst, to think that what the film-makers are doing in their painstaking labours in those 'fields of technology' that are the film set and film studio is to 'indicate' or 'discover' a pre-existent audio-visual display. Did Nair and her collaborators merely discover the audio-visual images of the heavily costumed Reece Witherspoon et al. as they prepared and then filmed the 'Crimson Petal' scene, or did they not substantially *create* this part of the multiply instantiable artistic vehicle of the work they were inventing? And is this skillful act of creation not one of the key bearers of the kind of value that is necessary to what we recognize as the artistic merit of the work?

As I have just implied and do not tire of repeating, the vehicle is not equivalent to the work. Nor is it accurate to say that the vehicle is an *instance* of the work, though the temptation to employ such a confusing locution persists. The vehicle of a work does not fully manifest or constitute that work; the vehicle conveys some of the work's features, but it does not carry all of them, as some of the work's features pertain to attitudes and actions that are not, strictly speaking, intrinsic properties of an artistic vehicle.

As has often been observed in the literature, this approach to the nature of works does some violence to ordinary language, since we regularly say we see and hear the film, by which we mean the cinematic work, whereas we cannot literally see and hear the work if it is not only an audio-visual display, but the determination of that display as the vehicle of a particular finished work by this (individual or collective) author. But I do not see why this kind of linguistic consideration should be decisive if we are doing philosophy, which should not be a matter of always speaking roughly and efficiently, but of trying, within the limits appropriate to the subject matter, of saying something reasonably precise, sometimes at the cost of elegance and discursive economy (the current sentence being a very good example). And the proposed approach to art's ontology and appreciation is, I maintain, firmly anchored in well-entrenched artistic practices that have a solid motivation in our perennial interest in certain forms of agent-related artistic value.

I shall conclude with a few remarks about the bedeviled topic of the multiple or singular nature of the work of art and/or artistic vehicle. This topic is not, I believe, reducible to a single question. One can, for example, ask, of any given artistic vehicle, whether it admits of an artistically perfect reproduction; it is another question to ask whether the work of art, of which this item is the vehicle, is a unique entity or something admitting multiple instances or occurrences. So one sort of question is about vehicles, as in: can the vehicle of the *Mona Lisa* be adequately reproduced? Or could there be two distinct yet artistically equivalent performances of the *Hammerklavier* sonata? Another sort of question, which is not a matter of questions about artistic vehicles, is about works, as in: could there be two *Hammerklavier* sonatas? Not two performances of that work, but two compositions referred to by that name? If we follow Currie in thinking that the work that bears this title is in fact an action *type*, it follows that there could be two or more tokens or instances of this type.

A good part of the disagreement on such difficult questions arises from philosophers' divergence with regard to the nature of the modality that is deemed decisive in saying whether a given artistic entity is multiple or singular. For example, since he reasons in terms of logical possibility, C. I. Lewis deems all artistic vehicles to be multiple, even if the current techniques of reproduction are highly imperfect. Similarly, Currie reasons that a work of art is an action *type* because it is metaphysically possible for more than one artistically equivalent event to take place in contexts where all artistically relevant factors are equivalent. For Currie the event is a certain type of discovering of something in a certain type of context, and since the event and its components are not numerical individuals, but schematic types, the work logically admits of multiple instances. Yet someone who is interested in the value of specific artistic accomplishments could agree with these observations as a matter of logic and metaphysics, yet argue that this is not the sort of possibility that is most relevant to our appreciation of the artistic value and status of a work. If we think in terms, not of what is logically or metaphysically possible, but in terms of what is probable given the history of the arts in our world, the singular nature of the artist's achievement in a particular context comes to the fore. It is

Paisley Livingston

logically possible, of course, that a twin Nair created a twin *Vanity Fair* based on a twin Thackeray novel on a planet that is a perfect image of our own. Perhaps such a strange event is also nomologically possible, since given what we think we know about the laws of physics, no law of nature would have to be violated for this to take place. Yet even if this much is allowed, it may be rejoined that this is an extremely unlikely event that in no way figures within the scope of our artistic appreciation. Nair's work is to be appreciated only in relation to the context and tradition in which her relation to Thackeray emerged, for it is in this context that she and her collaborators have found an interesting response to the challenge of adaptation, a response involving both the following and breaking of the rules of fidelity to a prized literary source.[26]

Lingnan University
pl@ln.edu.hk

[26] Versions of this paper were presented at the Royal Institute of Philosophy and at the University of Kent, Canterbury, and I am grateful to members of the audience for their questions and comments. Thanks are due as well to Rafael De Clercq and Kelly Trogdon for criticisms of a draft of the paper. This research has benefited from financial support from the Research and Postgraduates Studies Committee of Lingnan University, Hong Kong.

The Poetic Image

MARTIN WARNER

1. Romantic Image

> The unpurged images of day recede;
> The Emperor's drunken soldiery are abed;
> Night resonance recedes, night-walkers' song
> After great cathedral gong;
> A starlit or a moonlit dome disdains
> All that man is,
> All mere complexities,
> The fury and the mire of human veins.
> . . . . . .
> Astraddle on the dolphin's mire and blood,
> Spirit after spirit! The smithies break the flood,
> The golden smithies of the Emperor!
> Marbles of the dancing floor
> Break bitter furies of complexity,
> Those images that yet
> Fresh images beget,
> That dolphin-torn, that gong-tormented sea.

W. B. Yeats's great celebration of the human imagination, 'Byzantium',[1] of which these are the first and last verses, is concerned with the tension, reconciliation and movement between two types of sensibility, the sensual and the spiritual, that of natural life and that of transcendent symbol, in this poem imaged as 'the fury and the mire of human veins' and as 'bird or golden handiwork . . . of changeless metal'. In it, as Richard Ellmann puts it, 'the teeming images, "that dolphin-torn, that gong-tormented sea", flood up to the marbles of Byzantium itself, where they are at last brought under control by "the golden smithies of the Emperor"' – himself, *inter alia*, an image of (one sort of) poet.[2]

[1]   *The Collected Poems of W. B. Yeats* (London: Macmillan, 1950), 280–1.
[2]   *Yeats: The Man and the Masks* (London: Faber and Faber, 1961), 273–4.

doi:10.1017/S1358246112000252   © The Royal Institute of Philosophy and the contributors 2013
Royal Institute of Philosophy Supplement **71** 2013   105

Martin Warner

We are here in the world of what Sir Frank Kermode memorably designated that of the 'Romantic Image', of a vision of the creative imagination capable of begetting works of art with 'lives' of their own, each with all its parts in some organic-like relation. The Byzantine Emperor is a multifaceted and resonant image, far from a mere allegorical figure, encompassing civilizing and cultural as well as distinctively poetic control, yet also transcendence of the temporal,[3] with the context determining which facet or facets have priority. But also a problematic image; however multifaceted, the Emperor would hardly be recognizable as a kindred spirit from the perspective of Yeats's Crazy Jane with her 'unpurged images', or of Shakespeare's 'poet's eye, in a fine frenzy rolling'.

Two of the key emblems of Kermode's Romantic Image are to be found united in Yeats: the organic Tree and the movement with a kind of stillness of the Dancer. For such poetry meaning and form are united as are dancer and dance, with the resulting poetic force being indissolubly connected with and through internal reference, like blossom on a tree. Kermode notes that 'the Image, indeed, belongs to no natural order of things. It is out of organic life; but it is easier and less dangerous to talk about it in terms of the organic than in terms of the mechanical.'[4] The latter mode of discourse had led in the eighteenth century to the analysis of poetic images in terms of the 'association of ideas' understood in terms of deterministic psychology such as that of Hartley, which seemed to leave no room for the creative imagination championed by the leaders of the Romantic movement for whom the most powerful poetic thought is through images which possess organic vitality, like the tree and the dancer.

In England one thinks of Coleridge and Wordsworth, and a little earlier of Blake, while in Germany of A. W. Schlegel's distinction (developed by Coleridge) between allegory and 'the personification of an idea' on the one hand and the 'independent reality' of the symbol on the other.[5] And in France, half a century or so later, the

[3] F. A. C. Wilson, drawing on Yeats's 'heterodox mysticism', takes the Emperor to symbolize God and interprets the passage from natural life to transcendent symbol as that from this life to the next. (*W. B. Yeats and Tradition*, London: Victor Gollancz, 1958; 231–243, esp. 242; also 15). On my account this 'mystical' dimension of the poem images a form of human creativity. 'Byzantium' contains both aspects; it is the nature of the Romantic Image to be multifaceted in such ways.

[4] *Romantic Image* (London: Routledge & Kegan Paul, 1986), 92.

[5] *A Course of Lectures on Dramatic Art and Literature*, trans. John Black and A. J. W. Morrison (New York: AMS Press, 1965), Lect. VI, 88.

Symboliste poetry and theorizing of Baudelaire and Mallarmé provide influential parallels; as Kermode remarks, 'The Symbol of the French is . . . the Romantic Image writ large'.[6] This points to a delicate terminological problem, that of sorting out some of the different uses of the terms "image" and "symbol", to which I shall return, but brings out that in their opposition to the realisms and naturalisms of their day the *Symbolistes* sought to move by means of evocation from the discursive towards the autonomous Image.

Baudelaire's importance, T. S. Eliot maintained, lay 'not merely in the use of the imagery of the sordid life of a great metropolis, but in the elevation of such imagery to the *first intensity* – presenting it as it is, and yet making it represent something much more than itself', such elevation being related to the poet's use of language.[7] While for Mallarmé 'to *name* an object' is radically to reduce a poem's power; rather, 'to *suggest* it, that is the dream. It is the perfect use of this mystery that constitutes the symbol, displaying or evoking a state of soul [*état d'ame*]'.[8] Further, when the imagery which represents 'something much more than itself' symbolizes not simply the poet's emotions, ideas or states but an ideal which transcends them, the poet may juxtapose apparently incongruous images so that the mind will not rest on any single one, but see through all of them to what lies beyond; in somewhat similar fashion words may be detached from their normal referents and have their senses modified by their relationships with those which surround them. Mallarmé uses the analogy with music, which can suggest without tying the mind to irrelevant particularities, hence Arthur Symons's famous description of Mallarmé's best poetry: 'every word is a jewel, . . . every image is a symbol, and the whole poem is visible music'.[9] And out of these imagistic and symbolical traditions emerged the characteristic twentieth century (especially Modernist) conception of the poem as an autonomous complex image, or coordinated set of images, liberated from ordinary discourse, with form and meaning interdependent.

[6] *Romantic Image*, op. cit., 5.
[7] 'Baudelaire', in his *Selected Essays* (London: Faber and Faber, 1961), 426.
[8] *Oeuvres complètes*, 2 vols., ed. Bertrand Marchal (Paris, 1998–2003), II. 700. A 'principle' summarized by Arthur Symons as 'to name is to destroy, to suggest is to create'. (*The Symbolist Movement in Literature*, London: William Heinemann, 1899, 132)
[9] *The Symbolist Movement in Literature,* op.cit, 129.

Martin Warner

But caution is necessary here. Not everyone influenced by these traditions put a premium on gradual accumulation. Ezra Pound's Imagist and *haiku*-like 'In a Station of the Metro' gains its power from compression:

> The apparition of these faces in the crowd;
> Petals on a wet, black bough.[10]

Nor did they all seek delicate evocation or oppose all forms of literary realism. The classic Imagist poem by William Carlos Williams, 'The Red Wheelbarrow', which also owes something to the Japanese *haiku* model, presents a single visual image (*not* a symbol) very directly, focussing on the concrete representation of an object, and in place of the juxtaposition of multiple images we have the curious disposition of stresses and hesitations suggesting a continually failing attempt to reach for a completed pattern in the experience with which we are presented:

> so much depends
> upon
>
> a red wheel
> barrow
>
> glazed with rain
> water
>
> beside the white
> chickens.[11]

This image is relatively static, more Tree than Dancer, but when the Dancer begins to move – expressing perhaps 'the fury and the mire of human veins' – we typically find not merely movement but also multiplicity, and here our philosophical consciences should begin to stir if they have not done so already. What sort of understanding is properly involved when we seek to relate to the poetic 'movement' of images which are said to possess organic vitality which 'it is murder to dissect', with a different kind of life from that of prose propositions, since here meaning and form are united? And when the words through which we engage with the images may be detached

---

[10] *Lustra of Ezra Pound with Earlier Poems* (New York: Alfred A. Knopf, 1917), 50.
[11] *The Collected Poems of William Carlos Williams, Volume I 1909–1939*, ed. A. Walton Litz and Christopher MacGowan (Manchester: Carcanet, 1987), 224. For convenience, I on occasion refer to this poem using its conventional designation, as above, but strictly it is untitled.

from their normal referents, with their senses modified by their relationships with those which surround them, in what appears to be a more radical manner than that conceived in terms of Paul Grice's rules for conversational implicature?[12] Or, considered from a different perspective, when we engage with 'Those images that yet / Fresh images beget', how are we to understand images poetically begetting images? In France, one notes, the *Symboliste* movement found its final form through the work of Valéry with the focus shifting from the achieved poem as an end in itself to the poetic process as the proper object of poetic contemplation, while in England Pound abandoned 'Imagism' for 'Vorticism', seeking to find a term that would encompass the Image in, as it were, 'movement'.[13]

Introducing his translation of St.-John Perse's *Anabase* which he declared, despite its apparently being written in prose, to be a poem, T. S. Eliot maintained that 'the sequence of images coincides and concentrates into one intense impression of barbaric civilization', arguing that 'there is a logic of the imagination as well as a logic of concepts' and that it is in these terms, together with the pattern of 'stresses and pauses', at least as much as by reference to versification, that poetry may be distinguished from prose.[14] This appears to suggest at least one type of response to the concern I expressed about how we are to understand the poetic 'movement' of images. Kermode, writing in the mid-twentieth century, identifies Eliot's notion of a 'logic of the imagination' as characteristic of the 'modern' as distinct from the 'Metaphysical' poet,[15] so before engaging with these issues directly we might do well to widen our historical perspective, in the course of which it will prove useful to clarify some key terms.

2. Image and Symbol

'Imaging is, in itself, the very height and life of Poetry' affirms Dryden,[16] setting himself combatively against critics for whom

---

[12]   See especially 'Logic and Conversation' in his *Studies in the Way of Words* (Cambridge, Mass. and London: Harvard University Press, 1989) 22–40.
[13]   Kermode's word, *Romantic Image*, op. cit., 85.
[14]   *Anabasis: A Poem* (London: Faber and Faber, 1959), 10–11.
[15]   *Romantic Image*, 152.
[16]   'The Author's Apology for Heroic Poetry and Poetic Licence', in *Essays of John Dryden*, 2 vols. (ed.) W. P. Ker (Oxford: Clarendon Press, 1900), I. 186.

imagery, even in poetry, was mere decorative illustration, while retaining a broadly mimetic orientation. He invokes Longinus in support, who maintained that 'images' (φαντασίαι) contribute greatly to weight, grandeur and energy in both poetry and oratory; Longinus glosses "φαντασίαι" as "ειδωλοποιίαι' (mental pictures), and the word as being appropriate when 'you seem to see what you describe and bring it vividly before the eyes of your hearers'.[17] Dryden reads this as poetry making 'it seem to us that we behold those things which the poet paints'. But the poet is not confined to visual images. John Clare combines hearing with sight as he presents the 'solitary' crane: 'Cranking a jarring melancholy cry / Thro' the wild journey of the cheerless sky' ('March'), and Tennyson combines smell and hearing (with suggestions of warmth and taste) in 'And many a rose-carnation feed / With summer spice the humming air' (*In Memoriam* § CI). Further, as C. Day Lewis remarks, in the case of Shakespeare's 'Finish, good lady; the bright day is done, / And we are for the dark' (*Antony and Cleopatra* V ii), 'although it presents no picture to the eye, it speaks in the language of sight'.[18]

With this move we conveniently reach a conceptual boundary, that which separates what Sir Peter Strawson characterized as two 'areas of association': in the first imagination is 'linked with *image* and image is understood as *mental image* – a picture in the mind's eye or (perhaps) a tune running through one's head'; in the second 'imagination is associated with invention . . . or insight'.[19] The example also indicates that and how this boundary is porous; to see this it will be useful to make a philosophical detour.

Claims about the poet making 'it seem to us that we behold' something points to Strawson's 'mental imagery' in a manner that may tempt us into the snares of psychologism. Visualization is an unevenly distributed capacity and the same appears to be the case with respect to the aural, tactual and other dimensions of the imagination; this led E. J. Furlong to speculate that some of those 'ill-disposed to imagery . . . [who] write off "mental imagery" in any form' might lack such capacities.[20] Douglas Hedley identifies Gilbert Ryle as one with such an ill disposition: 'Ryle's theory of imagination as principally propositional pretending, and his

---

[17] *On the Sublime* xv. §§ 1–2.
[18] C. Day Lewis, *The Poetic Image* (London: Jonathan Cape, 1947), 18–19.
[19] 'Imagination and Perception', in his *Freedom and Resentment and Other Essays* (London and New York: Routledge, 2008), 50.
[20] *Imagination* (London: George Allen & Unwin, 1961), 70.

expulsion of mental images, is an instance of a sophisticated theory banishing rather mundane facts of common human experience.'[21] But Ryle's notorious dictum, 'Roughly, imaging occurs but images are not seen', is not 'expelling mental images' in this sense; rather, as he says, 'visualising . . . is a proper and useful concept, but . . . its use does not entail the existence of pictures which we contemplate. . . . I do have tunes running in my head, but no tunes are being heard'.[22] Images, that is, are not literally seen because the concept of "seeing" is being used in an extended or figurative sense when it is used in the context of visualization, not because mental imagery is to be somehow 'written off'. As Hidé Ishiguro put it, 'Ryle's point is that when I picture something, what I am doing does not satisfy the ordinary accepted concept of seeing'.[23] It may be that Dryden would not dissent; he claims not that in imaging 'we behold those things which the poet paints' but rather, imaging in poetry 'makes it *seem to us* that we behold those things which the poet paints'.

This is not to say that Ryle's analysis is beyond criticism. Ishiguro argues that it is distorted by the 'implicitly assumed dogma that there are no occurrences of mental acts . . . which are not in some *de facto* way connected with publicly observable phenomena', and that this arises from mistakenly supposing that recognizing that 'the meanings of words expressing mental activities are connected with certain patterns of behaviour' commits one to such a claim.[24] Wittgenstein, like Ryle, insists on the interpersonal, public, status of criteria for the use of mental words and expressions, that they cannot be given solely in terms of our having certain inner experiences, but this does not disable him from using the concept of imaging in exploration of noticing aspects. He lists a number of ways the line drawing of a triangle might be seen, as a triangular hole, as a solid and so on, and remarks 'it is as if an *image* came into contact, and for a time remained in contact, with the visual impression', later concluding that 'The concept of an aspect is akin to the concept of an image. In other words: the concept "I am now seeing it as . . . ." is akin to "I am now having *this* image".' He goes on, 'Doesn't it take imagination to hear something as a

[21] *Living Forms of the Imagination* (London & New York: T&T Clark, 2008), 46.
[22] *The Concept of Mind* (London: Hutchinson, 1949), 247–8.
[23] Imagination', in Bernard Williams and Alan Montefiore (eds) *British Analytical Philosophy* (London: Routledge & Kegan Paul, 1966), 160.
[24] Ibid., 177, 172.

Martin Warner

variation on a particular theme? And yet one is perceiving something in so hearing it.'[25]

The notion of "imagination" covers a family of meanings, only some of which imply the use of mental imagery, but these latter, together with Wittgenstein's account of "seeing as", are crucial to two of the most impressive analyses of the role of imagination by contemporary philosophers, those of Mary Warnock and of Roger Scruton.[26] Mary Warnock gives priority to approaching 'the concept of the imagination as *that which creates mental images*', declaring Wittgenstein's claim that 'seeing an aspect is akin to having an image' to be an essential 'clue' to understanding how it is that 'at least part of our perceptual experience must be described in terms of the significance which we attach to what we perceive'. She concludes: 'Imagination is our means of interpreting the world, and it is *also* our means of forming images in the mind. The images themselves are not separate from our interpretations of the world; they are our way of thinking of the objects in the world.'[27] This conclusion has a familiar ring; as Strawson puts it:

> The thought of something as an x . . . is alive in perception of it as an x . . . just as the thought of an x . . . is alive in the having of an image of an x . . . . This is what is now sometimes expressed in speaking of the *intentionality* of perception, as of imaging. But the idea is older than *this* application of that terminology, for the idea is in Kant.[28]

Roger Scruton similarly argues that while there is indeed a variety of phenomena 'grouped under the heading of imagination', there are 'links of an important kind' between them and that, 'in effect, there is only one concept expressed in the use of this term'. Wittgenstein's probings play a significant role in Scruton's account of these interrelations, for which 'imagination involves thought which is unasserted', and 'imagining is a special case of "thinking of x as y"'; later Scruton notes that the phrase 'seeing X as Y' can in certain contexts substitute for 'thinking of X as Y'.[29] With

---

[25]   *Philosophical Investigations.* trans. G.E.M. Anscombe (Oxford: Basil Blackwell, 1958), II, §xi, 200e, 207e, 213e.
[26]   Mary Warnock, *Imagination* (London: Faber and Faber, 1976), chap.IV; Roger Scruton, *Art and Imagination: A Study in the Philosophy of Mind* (London: Methuen, 1974), chaps. 7 & 8.
[27]   *Imagination*, op. cit., 192, 194.
[28]   'Imagination and Perception', op. cit., 69.
[29]   *Art and Imagination*, op. cit., 91, 97–8, 117.

respect to images, he maintains that if we wish to know what an image is, 'looking inwards' is liable to put us on the wrong track; rather, 'we must ask "What is it about another that enables us to say of him that he has images?"' In this context he notes, 'an image is always an image *of* something – imagery has the intentionality characteristic of thought'; also that imagery 'is an object of immediate knowledge' and, further, that 'the principal criteria for saying that a person is having an image, or picturing something, are verbal – they consist largely in descriptions he would be prepared to offer of an absent or non-existent thing', though he concedes that 'a man might express his image by drawing or pointing to a picture'. These criteria together 'place imagery in the category of thought'. However, 'all our ways of referring to images seem to suggest an element of experience over and above the constitutive thought'. This experiential element is conceptually important because when one refers to an image that one has, one 'describes it in terms of a genuine experience, the publicly observable form of which is familiar to us all'; one will describe one's 'visual image of X in terms that are equally appropriate to the experience of seeing X'. The 'connection between imagery and its verbal expression' helps 'explain the formal (conceptual) properties of imagery'. This implies 'an analogy between the two processes of imagery and sensory experience'. However, for Scruton, the analogy is 'irreducible': 'A man will be unable to indicate in *what* way his image is "like" a particular sensory experience, although he will feel that to describe his image in terms of a sensory experience is appropriate, and indeed inevitable.'[30]

We are back, it seems, with Longinus and Dryden. In deploying a pictorial rather than descriptional approach to images, maintaining that imaging in poetry 'makes it seem to us that we behold those things which the poet paints', Dryden is drawing on that analogy between imagery and sensory experience which grounds one's propensity to envisage one's image of a rose as the seeing (and/or smelling or even feeling the petals) of a rose, and hence to describe one's 'visual image of X in terms that are equally appropriate to the experience of seeing X'. And here we may begin to see how it might be that 'Imaging is, in itself, the very height and life of Poetry', for the verbal criteria for images can be significantly different from those for concepts.

Concepts, of course, have both a subjective (psychological) and an objective (linguistic) side; they play a role in human thinking as constituents of the propositions we entertain, but are identified, as well as

[30]   Ibid., 94, 100–101, 103, 104.

Martin Warner

being conveyed or expressed, through language – an essentially public phenomenon – thereby enabling us to determine their application to the world (though, if we follow Quine, never uniquely). Those images that are the concern of poetry are similarly Janus-faced. But here one may distinguish two stages of analysis. As Scruton notes, there is a criteriological level at which we can describe (or draw or point to a picture of) the image we are entertaining, and where description is involved standard conceptual relations may obtain, though perhaps with significant dependence on implicature and taking note of the poverty of non-technical language in describing features of 'olfactory and gustatory images'.[31] Williams does, in a sense, describe his image of a red wheelbarrow, glazed with rain water beside the white chickens.

But at what one might call the properly imaginative level, whereas concepts are identified by their inferential relations and truth conditions when embodied in propositions or sentences, with images such criteria may not be applicable; here evocation and resonance may take the place of inference, and truth conditions give place to a notion such as "appropriateness". To stay with the red wheelbarrow, the opening words ('so much depends / upon') – at once open-ended and inviting scrupulous attention at once to the image and the text –, the distinctive arrangement of stresses and pauses suggesting a continually failing attempt to reach for a completed pattern, the impression of precision, particularity and immediacy, together with the use of the curiously appropriate word "glazed" with its aesthetic undertones, all help intensify the effect of entering into a moment of perception, focussed in an image, resonating with a greater order of which it is a part.

The 'Red Wheelbarrow' resists analysis in terms of 'seeing X as Y' at any but the criteriological level, but with our other Imagist poem, Pound's 'apparition of these faces in the crowd; / Petals on a wet, black bough', it is otherwise. An image of faces in the Paris Metro is fused with the perception of beauty in the midst of bleakness, as found in the delicacy of petals on a wet, black bough, under the rubric of that ambiguously resonant word "apparition". We have here the evocation of an image coming into contact with a visual impression (it seems indeed to have been the representation of an actual experience), conveying a distinct emotion through an unexpected similarity. And through this evocation we, the readers, are invited to imagine what it would be like to have such an experience, sharing that emotion. Such 'imagining what it is like', notes

[31] Ibid., 105–6.

Scruton, has closer affinities with 'knowledge by acquaintance' than it does with 'knowledge by description',[32] hence presumably our sense that poetry is capable of conveying a distinctive form of immediacy.

The significant role of 'seeing X as Y' in certain forms of poetic imaging casts light on Aristotle's contention that for the poet 'the greatest thing by far is to be a master of metaphor. It is the one thing that cannot be learnt from others; and it is also a sign of genius ['ευφυία, a gift of nature], since a good metaphor implies an intuitive perception of the similarity in dissimilars' (*De Poetica*, 1459a5–8). Pound's image is not strictly a metaphor ('giving the thing a name that belongs to something else'; 1457b6–7), but it also gains its force from an original perception of the similarity in dissimilars. And so too, we should note, does Shakespeare's 'Finish, good lady; the bright day is done, / And we are for the dark' which, although metaphorical, is not in the strict Drydenesque sense imagistic. Both, to use C. Day Lewis's expression, 'speak in the language of sight' but, as we have seen, poetic images range across all our senses, and Lewis goes further. In Meredith's 'darker grows the valley, more and more forgetting' (*Love in the Valley*, l. 37) we have again the language of sight but, crucially,

> The poet's re-creation includes both the object and the sensations connecting him with the object, both the facts and the tone of an experience: it is when object and sensation, happily married by him, breed an image in which *both* their likenesses appear, that something "comes to us with an effect of revelation".[33]

Adequate expression in words of what one sees, hears or otherwise senses often requires precision not only with respect to the object perceived but also to the associated feelings, tone and attitude, and it is this concern 'for expressing the relationship between things and the relationship between things and feelings, which compels the poet to metaphor';[34] Lewis adds that it also 'demands that within the poem

[32] Ibid., 105.
[33] *The Poetic Image*, op. cit., 23; the quotation is from John Middleton Murry's essay 'Metaphor' in his *Countries of the Mind: Essays in Literary Criticism* (London: Oxford University Press, 1937), II. 4.
[34] Ibid, 25. Compare Anthony O'Hear, *The Element of Fire: Science, Art and the Human World* (London and New York: Routledge, 1988), 104–5: 'A literal description of a feeling or attitude I have will not precisely delineate it, nor will it bring out the way in which it is not an object for me, but

Martin Warner

the images should be linked by some internal necessity stronger than the mere tendency of words to congregate in patterns'. In Thomas Nashe's 'Brightness falls from the air; / Queens have died young and fair' ('In Time of Pestilence') the two lines are tied together, he suggests, by 'emotional logic'; 'the sadness of evening and the sadness of untimely death illuminate each other reciprocally', leading him to designate the whole complex a single 'image'.[35]

It should be clear that in being driven to metaphor in such a way, or to 'breed an image' that unites 'both the facts and the tone of an experience', the poet needs insight and even creativity; the freshness of an image can be an integral part of its capacity to convey vivid conviction to the reader – hence Aristotle's belief that mastery of metaphor is not something that can be gained at second hand. The need for such insight, of course, is at the very least not diminished when the experience presented is invented rather than 'recreated'. In poetry, therefore, the boundaries between Strawson's two 'areas of association' for the imagination, that of mental imagery and that of inventiveness or insight, are porous.

Further, because poetic images are apt for presenting objects in the context of an experience, and hence as part of a relationship, the boundary between image and symbol is in poetry also porous. For Mallarmé, it will be recalled, displaying or evoking a 'state of soul' is 'the dream' of poetry, and 'it is the perfect use of this mystery that constitutes the symbol', for an image may represent much more than itself, whether an emotion, state, idea, or ideal, particularly when juxtaposed with other – perhaps at first sight incongruous – images. And when such incongruous images are thus united so that they reciprocally point beyond themselves, as through Nashe's 'emotional logic' to symbolize a distinctive form of sadness, the whole complex is often not unreasonably called an "image", in an extended use of the term. It is a development of this line of thought that lies behind Kermode's identification of both Tree and Dancer, each

---

something I feel, something constitutive of what I am. It is at this point that one can have recourse to metaphor or symbol, transferring certain terms from the public realm to indicate the nature of one's inner state. . . . [T]he metaphor, precisely because it is not literal, awakens intimations and a free flow of associations, where the literal closes and confines one's thought. . . . [T]he criterion of success will be to produce a metaphor which evokes the right sort of experience in one's audience.'

[35]   *The Poetic Image,* op. cit., 25, 35. If, as some suppose, Nashe's "air" is an error for "hair" this does not weaken the point; the received line has stood the test of time in a manner the proposed alternative could hardly have done.

of course a Drydenesque image in itself, as emblematic of what he designates 'the Romantic Image'.

"Symbol" is a term no less problematic than "image". Glossing with some freedom a distinction drawn by Nelson Goodman,[36] David Novitz discriminated between 'purely referential symbols', and 'literary symbols'; while the former simply represent or refer, to say of a word or phrase that it is a literary symbol 'is to say that it is being (or has been) used in a highly suggestive way to inform or even arouse an audience by conveying a certain insight, a certain mood, a certain feeling'; he notes that many literary works contain symbols of both sorts. On this account, any literary symbol can be regarded as a 'juxtapository metaphor', defined as 'the stark and incongruous verbal juxtaposition of two or more subjects and their associated ideas without any explicit predicative relationship between them' (one notes that on this account, unlike Aristotle's, Pound's two lines count as a metaphor), and 'any juxtapository metaphor can be regarded as a literary symbol' when it involves 'the transference of ideas and feelings from one subject to another'. Where analogous literary devices work 'iconically – with the help of similarities or resemblances', depending for their effect 'on their congruity rather than their incongruity', we should regard them 'as juxtapository similes, not metaphors; hence as literary images rather than literary symbols'.[37]

Novitz's idiosyncratic distinction between literary image and symbol has not caught on, but it is worth considering his contrast between two types of symbol in relation to the opposition of symbol to allegory to be found in those influenced by Blake, Schlegel and Coleridge. Schlegel, for example, contrasts the symbolical, which has a reality independent of the conceptual, and the allegorical which is 'invented' with an 'idea' in mind.[38] While for Coleridge 'a Symbol . . . always partakes of the Reality which it renders intelligible; and while it enunciates the whole, abides itself as a living part of that Unity, of which it is the representative' (the symbol, that is, is a form of synecdoche), whereas 'an Allegory is but a translation of abstract notions into a picture-language'.[39]

[36] *Ways of Worldmaking* (Hassocks, Sussex: Harvester, 1978), 58.
[37] *Knowledge, Fiction & Imagination* (Philadelphia: Temple University Press, 1987), 198–203, 192.
[38] *A Course of Lectures on Dramatic Art and Literature,* op. cit., 88.
[39] *The Statesman's Manual: or The Bible the Best Guide to Political Skill and Foresight*, in his *Lay Sermons*. Ed. R. J. White, *Collected Works*, Vol.6, Bollingen Series LXXV (Cambridge and Princeton: Routledge & Kegan

Martin Warner

There is, that is, a well-established tradition for which allegory is seen as primarily ornamental, with its elements standing referentially for what could be said otherwise (on the pattern of Novitz's 'referential symbol'), whereas the symbol functions in the manner of Novitz's 'literary symbol' (or 'image') by means of (to use his terminology) 'suggestion' to 'convey a certain insight, mood or feeling'. On the Coleridgean synecdochal model the symbol participates in the reality it renders intelligible so that one directly apprehends that which is symbolized in the act of perceiving the symbol; in this very specific sense, insight or vision gained through symbol is 'unmediated' whereas ideas conveyed through allegory are 'mediated'. One notes that Kant draws what is verbally almost the opposite moral; it is schematic representation that is said to 'directly' exhibit the concept, whereas symbolic representation does so 'indirectly', being mediated by analogy.[40] In this context it should also be noted that the terminology has been complicated by Charles Williams's influential preference, in the context of a Coleridgean reading of Dante's *Commedia*, for 'the word image to the word symbol, because it seems to me doubtful if the word symbol nowadays sufficiently expresses the vivid individual existence of the lesser thing'.[41]

That the images of good verse ought ideally to operate symbolically, in some quasi-Coleridgean sense, is of course a contested claim, and not one that would be accepted by, for example, Alexander Pope for whom 'True wit is nature to advantage dress'd, / What oft was thought, but ne'er so well expressed' (*An Essay on Criticism*, l. 297); one is reminded of Coleridge on allegory, translating 'abstract notions into a picture-language'. To bring the issue into focus it may be useful to return to Aristotle on metaphor, for metaphor is a flower of wit and also, as we have seen, deeply implicated in poetic imagery. Pope is echoing Aristotle's suggestion that metaphor can 'save the language from seeming mean and prosaic' (*De*

Paul and Princeton UP, 1972), 30. Compare: 'The allegorist leaves the given . . . to talk of that which is confessedly less real, which is a fiction. The symbolist leaves the given to find that which is more real.' C. S. Lewis, *The Allegory of Love: A Study in Medieval Tradition* (New York: Oxford University Press, 1958), 45.

[40]   'On Beauty as the Symbol of Morality', in his *Critique of Judgment*, trans. Werner S. Pluhar (Indianapolis/Cambridge: Hackett, 1987), §59, ¶¶ 351–2, 226–7.

[41]   *The Figure of Beatrice: A Study in Dante* (London: Faber and Faber, 1943), 7. Williams's use of "image" appears to have significant affinities with that later proposed by Novitz.

Poetica, 1458a33–5), giving metaphor and imagery a primarily ornamental role. But elsewhere Aristotle remarks that 'it is from metaphor
that we can best get hold of something fresh' (*Rhetorica*,
1410b13–14), and here we are closer to the Romantic Image. Of
course these two conceptions of the role of metaphor can be held together, as they were by Aristotle, for elegantly exemplary expression
can enlighten the mind and move the heart, but the (English)
Augustan poets were typically much more at home with 'inventing'
an image with an idea in mind than were the Romantics.

The so-called 'Metaphysical Poets' provide an instructive inter-
mediate case, for with them the, often startling, image (such as
John Donne's lovers as 'stiff twin compasses') is typically concept
driven (one remembers Samuel Johnson's 'the most heterogeneous
ideas are yoked by violence together')[42], but in such a way as to be
open to imagistic development which is itself conceptually rewarding; their images 'often create the argument of the poem or at least
direct its course'.[43] There is a remarkable finessing of this technique
with the initial image of 'The Love Song of J. Alfred Prufrock' (Eliot
of course being a champion of the Metaphysicals). 'Let us go then you
and I, / When the evening is spread out against the sky / Like a
patient etherised upon a table'.[44] Here we have indeed 'the stark
and incongruous verbal juxtaposition of two or more subjects and
their associated ideas' but there is no visual resemblance between
the subjects, save perhaps through a distant echo of the luminiferous
aether; the connection is, rather, 'emotional, one of mood'[45], a mood
of extreme passivity and disconnection from reality, to which the very
word 'patient' contributes. It is not so much that the resistance to
imagistic 'likeness' forces recourse from image to concept as that
the reader is forced into passively awaiting illumination from what
follows as when, for example, the passivity and disconnection of
the 'you and I' of the first line ('Oh, do not ask, "What is it?"')
seems fittingly matched by the personification of the image of the
evening's 'yellow fog' which 'Curled once about the house, and fell
asleep'. The poem is initially read sequentially but, once familiarity
is achieved, in subsequent readings the later images inform one's
readings of the earlier; the significance of each image is modified

---

[42] *The Lives of the Poets*, 3 vols. (ed.) John H. Middendorf (New Haven
and London: Yale University Press, 2010), I, 26.
[43] C. Day Lewis, *The Poetic Image*, op. cit., 57.
[44] T. S. Eliot, *Collected Poems: 1909–1962* (London: Faber and Faber,
1974), 13–17.
[45] C. Day Lewis, *The Poetic Image*, op. cit. 93.

through its relationships with those which surround it. Mallarmé's analogy with music is in place here. As with so much poetry touched by *Symboliste* poetics, 'Prufrock' can only be adequately comprehended in retrospect.

3. Imagery and 'Movement'

Let us look a little more closely at what I termed the "movement" of poetic images, though from Eliot's post-*Symboliste* perspective for which the poet may aspire through words to 'The stillness as a Chinese jar still / Moves perpetually in its stillness' ('Burnt Norton' V)[46] a better word might be their "interrelationships". A particular poetic image may be said to 'move' in a number of inter-connected senses: by being presented as changing location or context, through transformation, and since many images can, as it were, reverberate, with new dimensions and possibilities becoming apparent in different readings, a single instance of an image may also be said to 'move'; the distinction between this sort of movement and that from one image to another can be a fine one. There are, nevertheless, clear cases of the latter and, as should already be apparent, with these there are a variety of possibilities, while in any given case more than one of them may be operative. I shall be primarily concerned with change of context and the way in which a poem may 'move' from one image to another, but it would be artificial to make sharp separations here. It is worth recalling F. R. Leavis's warning that the relation of images to a poem is not at all, like that of 'plums to cake': 'they are foci of a complex life, and sometimes the context from which they cannot be even provisionally separated . . . is a wide one.'[47]

As a preliminary, it is worth distinguishing between intra- and inter-textual transitions, between the movement of images within a poem and movement from one work to another (bearing in mind that the identity conditions for a work may sometimes be problematic). Here the main difference seems to be that whereas understanding a work of art as having all its elements, including its

---

[46] T. S. Eliot, *Collected Poems: 1909–1962*, op. cit., 189–95.
[47] 'Imagery and Movement: Notes in the Analysis of Poetry (ii)', in his *A Selection From Scrutiny*, Vol. 1 (Cambridge: Cambridge University Press, 1968), 231. He adds that in considering certain types of poetic effect 'we find "imagery" giving place to "movement" as the appropriate term for calling attention to what has to be analysed'. (237)

images, in some organic relation is often normative for poetry, when one poet echoes or otherwise evokes an image from the work of another, a law of diminishing returns can soon set in if one seeks to bring the whole pattern of the earlier poem into relation with the later. For example, in the third of Eliot's *Four Quartets* Tennyson, whose famous 'haven under the hill' has already been evoked in the second poem[48] and thereby established as a 'presence' in the sequence, appears to return in a more subtle form. We are introduced to 'a voice descanting (though not to the ear / The murmuring shell of time, and not in any language)' ('The Dry Salvages' III);[49] the image, part auditory part visual, of the ear as a shell within which one still appears to hear the past rhythms of a distant sea, is powerful in itself, but is given further temporal resonance if one's own ear is also attuned, through the striking word "murmuring", to Tennyson's 'moan of doves in immemorial elms, / And murmuring of innumerable bees' ('The Princess' VII). 'Immemorial elms' may well be within the ambit of 'The murmuring shell of time', but the rest of Tennyson's 'Sweet Idyl' does not bear pressing.

Given this preliminary distinction, if we use as our primary model the movement of images within a single poem, a further set of discriminations may be made. First, there are those forms of poetry whose images seem to be governed by the development of emotion, whether or not 'recollected in tranquillity', and here one can well understand how Hartley's associationist psychology could seem so appropriate. Second, we have those images, often associated with the Augustan satiric poets, which are invented 'with an idea in mind' the development and movement of which are often concept or even argument driven; as Lewis puts it, the images 'are strung together. . . on a thread of logical argument spun out of the centre of the subject'.[50] Third, at least as far back as Homer and Aeschylus we find poetry that, with its images, is shaped by narrative; such narrative need not be understood primarily either conceptually or in terms of emotion but rather in terms of Aristotelian μῦθωος; Schlegel characterizes the *Oresteia* as symbolical rather than allegorical, to be understood in 'emblematic' terms,[51] but its development,

---

[48]   From Tennyson's 'Break, break, break'; compare Eliot's 'The dancers are all gone under the hill' ('East Coker' II).
[49]   T. S. Eliot, *Collected Poems: 1909–1962*, op. cit., 210.
[50]   *The Poetic Image*, op. cit., 65.
[51]   *A Course of Lectures on Dramatic Art and Literature*, op. cit., Lect. VI, 87–8.

indeed transformation, of images such as the Eumenides is neverthe-less more governed by narrative than by imagistic logic.

So what of that imagistic logic? This might be thought to provide us with a fourth category, that of 'Those images that yet / Fresh images beget', apparently out of their own substance, but here care is necessary. If the teeming images are but the expression of 'the fury and the mire of human veins', undisciplined by any cultural smithies, then their movement or even development is best under-stood in psychological terms and it is the business of poetry to trans-mute their restless energies linguistically into 'golden handiwork . . . of changeless metal'. We are back with a variant of our first category. The underlying fact to be reckoned with here is that 'those things which the poet paints' are necessarily painted with words, and hence poetic images cannot escape the linguistic dimension, even if only at the criteriological level. This is why any aspirations, whether Mallarméan or Pateresque, poetry may have towards the condition of music must always be that of the moth for the star; poetry is essentially conceptually contaminated in a way that music is not.

Jonathan Kertzer's critique of Eliot's proposed 'logic of the imagination', seen as distinct from the 'logic of concepts', is relevant in this context. "Logic" Kertzer understands in terms of Wittgenstein's *Tractatus* such that it is 'impossible to represent in language anything that "contradicts logic"'[52], and 'since logic is the law of all thought, whether rigorous or wayward, valid or invalid, there can be no escape from it'.[53] Any form of intelligible language can be logically analysed, and such analysis is conceptual. Interpreting Eliot's claims for a 'logic of the imagination' to be about argument, he maintains that 'As dramatic displays of thought and speech, the arguments of poetry must "second" reason'.[54] 'Reason', so understood, has a primary status to which the 'arguments of poetry' are at once subordinate and, indeed, rhetorical, capable of influencing reason's 'persuasiveness'. Poetic wit, in other words, is 'nature to advantage dress'd'. The issue is whether, given that poetic imagery must always be conceptually contaminated, there can be an imagistic logic that does not collapse poetry into rhetoric, subordinating it to Tractarian 'reason'.

---

[52]   *Tractatus Logico-Philosophicus*, trans. D. F. Pears and B. F. McGuinness (London: Routledge & Kegan Paul, 1961), §3.032.
[53]   *Poetic Argument: Studies in Modern Poetry* (Montreal: McGill-Queen's University Press, 1988), 42.
[54]   Ibid., 51.

I shall mention just two possibilities. The first, very traditional, move takes us back to the poetic image understood as symbol. We find in human experience, it is suggested, certain primordial or archetypal patterns of imagery, these being either intimations of a Divine order or else – or as well as being – derived from universal or widespread human, biological or, more generally, natural phenomena, from a supposed 'collective unconscious', or otherwise. In different ways human culture has developed what have been somewhat loosely termed "languages" of symbolic analogy, grounded in these images, the symbols typically exemplifying their archetypes synecdochally. Poetry that draws on them – from Blake to Yeats to Kathleen Raine – is shaped by those traditional relationships.[55] Those ignorant of the relevant traditions may well have had their imaginations shaped by literature that has been so informed. One's imagination is not a *tabula rasa*, and the field of archetypal or inherited images provides controls on their patterning which an individual poet's vision may transmute or, indeed, challenge. Such a move is in some ways reminiscent of our third category, with the development of images shaped by μῦθος, though here the term is not primarily to be understood in terms of narrative but rather of symbolic structure.

Birth, love, nature and death[56] do indeed look remarkably like cultural universals – they are, one notes, perennial preoccupations of poets – and no doubt cultural tradition profoundly affects how poet and reader engage with the movement of poetic imagery. Nevertheless, construal in terms of a symbolic 'language' of the primordial is far from universally accepted. One of the most influential, if perhaps not wholly convincing, critiques is that of Paul de Man who argued more than forty years ago that such a prioritizing of the symbol in a Coleridgean manner seeks to place human experience *sub specie aeternitatis* in a manner that is no longer credible, a 'defensive strategy that tries to hide from . . . the truths that come to light in the last quarter of the eighteenth century', most importantly the self's 'authentically temporal predicament'. It is not that there are no such

---

[55]   See, for example, Kathleen Raine, 'On the Symbol', in her *Defending Ancient Springs* (London: Oxford University Press, 1967), 105–22, and 'The Vertical Dimension', *Temenos* **13**, 1992, 195–212. Also Maud Bodkin, *Archetypal Patterns in Poetry: Psychological Studies of Imagination* (London: Oxford University Press, 1934). Symons advocated 'that confidence in the eternal correspondences between the visible and the invisible universe, which Mallarmé taught' (*The Symbolist Movement in Literature,* op.cit, 138).

[56]   C. Day Lewis's list, *The Poetic Image*, op. cit., 141.

Martin Warner

traditions of symbolic analogy on which poetry has drawn, but that they are no longer in good conscience open to us.[57] This takes us into areas of metaphysics and theology beyond the scope of this paper.[58]

For an alternative possibility let us return to Eliot's proposed 'logic of the imagination'. This logic he characterizes in terms of 'arrangement', 'order' and, by implication, 'movement'.[59] Yvor Winters objected early on that 'the word *logic* is used figuratively' here, indicating nothing but 'qualitative progression', 'graduated progression of feeling',[60] but the objection is widely thought to have missed the point; as Frank Kermode pointed out, 'It indicates no *progression* of any sort. Time and space are exorcised; the emblem of this

---

[57] 'The Rhetoric of Temporality', in his *Blindness and Insight: Essays in the Rhetoric of Contemporary Criticism*, 2nd edn, (Minneapolis: University of Minnesota Press, 1983), §I. 'Allegory and Symbol', 208.

[58] A vigorous response to de Man's essay has been mounted by Douglas Hedley (*Living Forms of the Imagination*, op. cit., 136–40). For de Man 'the prevalence of allegory always corresponds to the unveiling of an authentically temporal destiny', where 'self' and 'non-self' can never 'coincide' ('The Rhetoric of Temporality', 206–7), and he downplays the contrast between allegory and symbol as being of 'secondary importance', arguing that Coleridge implicitly allows figural language as such to be understood in terms of 'translucence' (192–3). Hedley replies, with some plausibility, that this in effect collapses a crucial distinction, pointing out that for Coleridge there is an '*ontological* link between symbols and the reality symbolized [which] becomes transparent in the image', but that with allegory there is 'a different relationship between the means of expression and the objects of that expression' (*Living Forms*, 138–9). De Man's rejection of any such ontological link, and hence resistance to claims for a symbolic, synecdochal, 'translucence' of the eternal through and in the temporal, appears to be in part a consequence of his accepting the self's 'authentically temporal destiny' as being crucial to the 'truths' supposed to have 'come to light in the last quarter of the eighteenth century', and coming close to implying that the associated 'secularized thought . . . no longer allows a transcendence of the antinomies between the created world and the act of creation' ('The Rhetoric of Temporality', 206–7). Such a position is, of course, incompatible with Coleridgean panentheism. De Man's assault on 'this symbolical style' as lacking 'an entirely good poetic conscience' (208) looks suspiciously like a form of *petitio* in the guise of analysis.

[59] St.-John Perse, *Anabasis*, trans. and ed. T. S. Eliot, op.cit., 10–11. These coordinates suggest an affinity with Ezra Pound's 'ideogrammic method', with concepts built up from combining concrete images; see his *ABC of Reading* (London: Routledge, 1934).

[60] *In Defense of Reason* (Chicago, Swallow Press, 1947), 62–63.

"logic" is the Dancer', that image which is 'all movement, yet with a kind of stillness', the coalescence of 'meaning and form'.[61] Eliot, it will be recalled, introduced his notion in relation to his translation of Perse's *Anabase*. In a note on the poem by Lucien Fabre to which he draws our attention it is remarked how 'symbol [may lead] to symbol, linked allusively, throughout an entire stanza',[62] and Eliot himself maintains that

> any obscurity of the poem, on first readings, is due to the suppression of 'links in the chain', of explanatory and connecting matter, and not to incoherence, or to the love of cryptogram. The justification of such abbreviation of method is that the sequence of images coincides and concentrates into one intense impression of barbaric civilization. The reader has to allow the images to fall into his memory successively without questioning the reasonableness of each at the moment; so that, at the end, a total effect is produced. Such selection of a sequence of images and ideas has nothing chaotic about it.[63]

Three features of Eliot's account are worth noting. First, though this 'logic of the imagination' is distinguished from the 'logic of concepts' they are not set in opposition, as Kertzer supposes; Eliot, after all, implies that 'incoherence' here would be a fault, and putting the supposed fault alongside 'love of the cryptogram' suggests we may read "incoherence", at least in part, conceptually. The sequence is, we are told, one of 'images and ideas'. As we have seen, poetic images necessarily have a conceptual element, and this needs to be taken into account in considering their 'movement'. Second, the criterion of 'coherence' goes beyond the purely conceptual to the imaginative; this is the force of the emphasis on producing a 'total effect' which is glossed as 'one intense impression'. We are back with that double meaning of "image" such that it can designate both a particularized scene (as in the opening line of *Anabasis*, 'Under the bronze leaves a colt was foaled') and that complex ordered arrangement of such items, here by 'allusive' linkage of 'symbols', we call a poem. Finally, as mentioned earlier, Eliot suggests that it is in these terms, together with the pattern of 'stresses and pauses', at least as much as by reference to versification, that poetry may be distinguished from prose.

61   *Romantic Image*, op. cit., 152, 85.
62   In *Anabasis*, op. cit., 94.
63   *Ibid.*, 9–10.

Martin Warner

In *Anabase*, claims Eliot, Perse, by using such 'exclusively poetic methods' has been able 'to write poetry in what is called prose' for, 'although it would be convenient if poetry were always verse, . . . that is not true'; he goes on to remark that the term "poetry", when it is applied to works in verse, 'introduces a distinction between good verse and bad verse'.[64] Putting these claims together we have the suggestion that, as well as competence in versification, where appropriate, and analogues where not, poetry worth the name displays a form of ordering in its images productive of 'one intense impression' as an aspect of its 'total effect'. Elsewhere Eliot offers a note of caution on such claims, remarking that a poet, in his critical writing, 'at the back of his mind . . . is always trying to defend the kind of poetry he is writing, or to formulate the kind that he wants to write'.[65] One suspects this may apply here. But we may nevertheless treat as worth consideration the claim that this is true of poetry as conceived in terms of the traditions Kermode associates with the 'Romantic Image', providing a rationale, at once imagistic and conceptual, for the 'movement' of its images.

4. 'The Poetic Image'

So what may we conclude concerning 'The Poetic Image'? Ultimately, I think, that the designation only makes sense in the context of a certain tradition, or set of related traditions, of poetry and of understanding poetry, but that teasing out why this is so can be illuminating. Dryden's designation of imaging as 'the very height and life of Poetry' invokes Longinus, but the latter was considering poetry and rhetoric together, and bringing what you seem to see 'vividly before the eyes of your hearers' is characteristic of both, though for different purposes. Dryden's gloss, making 'it seem to us that we behold those things which the poet paints', could similarly be applied to the orator. We do not here have an account of imaging that is distinctively poetic. The same applies when we move, on this model, to non-visual images and even, via a network of analogies, to non-sensory ones, where a mental image appears to be little more than the accusative in what we might call 'direct' imagining (or remembering, or so on), as distinct from 'imagining that'. The analogy between imagery and sensory experience gives point to

64 Ibid., 10.
65 'The Music of Poetry', in his *On Poetry and Poets* (London: Faber and Faber, 1957), 26.

126

modelling the mental images evoked by the poet in terms of pictures (and their analogues) though, as we have seen, there are pitfalls to be avoided, and also to modelling at least some of such images in terms of 'seeing X as Y' – hence the association of these images with metaphor. But such considerations apply, once again, well beyond poetry. In all these cases we conceive of images independently of poetry, the latter being identified primarily in prosodic terms, as items which the poet can use to suit his or her own purposes, 'to point a moral or adorn a tale' or perhaps, as Longinus suggests, to enthral or amaze ('ἔκπληξις).[66] On such an account poetic images are simply those images we encounter in poetry; some no doubt are more suitable than others for the various and contested ends that have been proposed for poetry, but this does not warrant the designation of a coherent class such as seems to be implied by the definite article of '*the* poetic image'.

It is when we turn to those traditions associated with what Kermode termed the 'Romantic Image', and specifically to those forms of poetry and discourse about poetry associated with it, that such a classification comes into focus, and may be seen even as having application to poetry outside such confines as far back as Homer and as far afield as the *haiku*. Poetry is most fully itself, according to this tradition, where concept, emotion and image are internally related, in the sense that they are not fully identifiable apart from each other, the prosody informs and is informed by this complex, and in those cases where narrative or other forms of μῦθος drive the movement of the whole the images are to be conceived symbolically, seen as in some way integrally related to that wider range of experience or reality they in this way render partially intelligible or otherwise available to us. Moments of poetic intensity, from whatever period or tradition, gain their effect by their approximation to this ideal, and since prosody is only one factor in the identification of poetry in this full sense, poetry can in principle be written, as Eliot puts it, 'in what is called prose', so long as there are quasi-prosodic analogues of verse.[67] Where this is not the case we find non-poetic works, novels and short stories for example, which through their own specific uses of imagery enact or otherwise engage with analogous ideals, as in Thomas Hardy, James Joyce or Virginia Woolf. When a complex of such images are united so that they reciprocally point beyond themselves, gaining imaginative and emotional force through their interrelationship, the senses of those words through

[66] *On the Sublime* xv. §2.
[67] In terms of genre, *Anabase* is plainly epic.

Martin Warner

which we engage with them being thereby modified by their relationships with the words which surround them, then the whole complex
may be termed an "image", and the designation "The Poetic Image"
comes into its own as picking out images and image complexes in
poetry, so understood, possessing the sort of vitality the Romantics
termed 'organic', prompting such questions as those of Yeats:

> O chestnut-tree, great-rooted blossomer,
> Are you the leaf, the blossom or the bole?
> O body swayed to music, O brightening glance,
> How can we know the dancer from the dance?
> ('Among School Children', final lines)[68,69]

University of Warwick
martin.warner@warwick.ac.uk

[68] *The Collected Poems of W. B. Yeats, op. cit.*, 245.
[69] My thanks to my brother, the poet Francis Warner, for comments
and reminders.

Depiction

JOHN HYMAN

§1 Analytic philosophers interested in depiction have focused for the most part on two problems: first, explaining how pictures represent; second, describing the distinctive kinds of artistic value pictures can possess, or the distinctive ways in which they can embody artistic values that extend more broadly across the arts. I shall discuss the first problem here. The main concepts I shall be concerned with are depiction, resemblance, sense and reference.

§2 My main aim is to reassess the traditional idea that representation in painting and sculpture depends on resemblances in form and colour between works of art and the objects they represent. The philosophical literature about representation has been dominated for fifty years – to its detriment, I shall argue – by the view that the traditional idea is wrong. I reject the so-called resemblance theory of representation, the theory that representational works of art are iconic signs, which Nelson Goodman attacked with devastating effect in *Languages of Art*.[1] But there are other ways of making the traditional idea precise.

The question I shall consider first is whether resemblance is a relation. This may seem remote from the interests of philosophers of art, especially since we cannot expect to be able to answer it without first clarifying the idea of a relation itself. But it is where I believe we must begin.

According to logicians, if two or more names in a true sentence are replaced by variables, the term that results will normally express a relation, which obtains between the bearers of the names. For example, if we start with the sentence 'Reggie and Ronnie are twins', and replace the names with variables we get the predicate 'x and y are twins', which expresses a relation that can obtain between two siblings. Here are a couple more examples: 'Paris is west of Moscow' yields the predicate 'x is west of y', which expresses a spatial relation; 'Scott is the author of Waverley' yields 'x is the author of y', which expresses a causal relation.

However, the logical conception of a relation has two important limitations. First, it is too broad. For there are cases where – as

---

[1]   Nelson, Goodman, *Languages of Art* (Indianapolis: Hackett, 1968), ch.1.

doi:10.1017/S1358246112000276   © The Royal Institute of Philosophy and the contributors 2013

logicians generally agree – following this procedure will not yield a predicate that expresses a relation. For example, 'Brutus killed Caesar' reports an action, but actions should not be assimilated to relations.[2] And there are other cases that are controversial. For example, it is controversial whether identity-statements, such as 'the morning star is the evening star' and 'Bronstein is Trotsky', are about an especially intimate relation in which everything stands, and can only stand, to itself.

Second, the logical conception of a relation tells us where we can normally find a term expressing a relation in a sentence – it is the part we are left with when we delete the names – but it does not tell us anything more about what a relation is. This is rather like explaining that a father is the kind of thing Russians refer to with their middle names. If we want to know more than this, we need to refer to the traditional conception of a relation, which preceded the development of formal logic.

According to *this* conception, which modern formal logic complements, but does not supercede, a relation is *a way in which one thing can stand to another thing, or several things can stand to one another*. As a matter of fact, the last clause is untraditional, since the idea of a many-termed relation was only introduced in the second half of the nineteenth century.[3] But the definition in italics captures a conception of a relation which stems originally from Aristotle's *Categories* and on which the logical conception I have described is based. Here, for example, is Locke's definition, which confines relations to two terms, and also precludes things from standing in a relation to themselves:

The Nature of Relation consists in the referring or comparing two things one to another.[4]

And here is the definition in the current edition of the OED:

An attribute denoting or concept expressing a connection, correspondence, or contrast between different things; a particular way in which one thing or idea is connected or associated with another or others.[5]

[2]   A.J.P. Kenny, *Action, Emotion and Will* (London: Routledge & Kegan Paul, 1963), ch.7.
[3]   A.N. Prior, *The Doctrine of Propositions and Terms* (London: Duckworth, 1976), 29.
[4]   Locke, *Essay Concerning Human Understanding*, 2.25.5.
[5]   *Oxford English Dictionary*, relation, 2.a.

Like the definition in italics, the definition in the OED includes many-termed relations, and it allows a man to stand in a relation to himself, for example, *being the one who shaves*, or *being the one who kills*. For these are both ways in which one thing can stand to another thing. But *being the same man as* is not a way in which one thing can stand to another thing. Nor is it a way in which one thing is connected or associated with another thing. So it is not a relation, according to these definitions, whereas it looks like a relation according to the logical conception we began with, as I pointed out earlier. I shall not attempt to adjudicate between these views.

In the relation-stating sentences I mentioned earlier, the verb phrase that expresses the relation is flanked by proper names referring to the objects it relates: 'Paris is west of Moscow', 'Scott is the author of Waverley'. These names can be replaced by descriptive terms such as 'the capital of France' or 'the Laird of Abbotsford'. But, like proper names, these terms refer to particular places, people or things. Even the sentence 'John knows a fireman', which does not purport to identify John's acquaintance, implies that there is a particular fireman John knows, since one cannot know a fireman, but not any fireman in particular.

What about statements of resemblance? Do the verb 'resembles' and the verb-phrases 'is like', 'looks like', 'sounds like', etc., express relations? The answer, I suggest, is that sometimes they do and sometimes they do not. For example, in the sentence 'Darwin looks like Socrates' the verb-phrase expresses a relation, whereas in the sentence 'Socrates looks like a satyr' it does not.

Compare the verb 'to be'. It is an elementary fact about English grammar that 'to be' is used both to express identity, as in 'Bronstein is Trotsky' and 'Cicero is Tully', and as a copular verb, as in 'Cicero is a statesman'. As I mentioned earlier, it is controversial whether identity is a relation: Wittgenstein says that it isn't in the *Tractatus*, whereas Kripke says that it is. But if we assume that Kripke is right, that identity *is* a relation, the verb 'is' expresses a relation in the sentence 'Cicero is Tully' and the sentence 'The morning star is the evening star', whereas in the sentences 'Cicero is a statesman' and 'The morning star is a planet' it does not.

The verbs 'resembles', 'is like' and 'looks like' evidently have a similar dual use, that is, they are used both to express relations and as copular verbs. 'x is like y' is a regular two-place predicate, and if we replace the variables with names, the resulting sentence relates the individuals concerned: for example, 'SoHo is like Hampstead' relates part of New York and part of London. But the sentence 'SoHo is like a village' does not relate anything to anything. It is

John Hyman

not comparable to 'The morning star is the evening star' or 'Cicero is Tully', but to 'The morning star is a planet' or 'Cicero is a statesman', the only difference being that it characterizes the place referred to by saying what it is like, rather than what it is. 'SoHo looks like a village' and 'SoHo resembles a village' are just the same.

It follows that although 'SoHo resembles a village' and 'John knows a fireman' are syntactically similar, they are logically different. If I tell you that John knows a fireman, you can ask me which fireman John knows, and if what I said is true, your question has an answer, even if I do not know what it is. In other words, we can add a namely-rider to the sentence 'John knows a fireman', for example, '… namely, the fireman who lives on Church Lane', or '… namely, Jim'.[6] By contrast, if I tell you that SoHo resemble a village, and you ask me 'Which village?', I can say that I did not mean to imply that it resembles any village in particular, and there does not have to be a namely-rider we can add to the sentence, in order to prove that what I said was true. 'SoHo resembles a village' normally means that SoHo has some of the salient characteristics of a village, without any village in particular being involved.

So, is resemblance a relation? If the idea is that the verb 'resembles' *sometimes* expresses a relation, then it is true. If it is that 'resembles' *always* expresses a relation, then it is false.

§3 I shall turn now to the philosophy of art. According to Robert Hopkins, one of the principal objections to the view that pictures invariably resemble the scenes or objects they depict is that resemblance is a relation between two particulars, whereas depiction is not.

> Resemblance is a relation between two particulars – one resembling the other. It is hard to make sense of resemblance between a particular thing and some, but no particular, item of a certain sort – a horse, say. […] there can be no resemblance between a picture and such a horse, and thus no prospect for understanding the depiction of a (no particular) horse in terms of resemblance.[7]

Hopkins's entry on depiction in the *Routledge Encyclopedia of Philosophy* contains a similar argument, but he adds the requirement that for two things to resemble one another both need to exist:

[6] The phrase 'namely-rider' was coined by Ryle. See G. Ryle, 'Heterologicality' repr. in *Collected Papers* II (London: Unwin Hyman, 1971), 250–57.
[7] R. Hopkins, *Picture, Image and Experience* (Cambridge: CUP, 1998), 10f.

For resemblance to hold, two things must exist – the thing resembling and the thing resembled. By contrast, depiction does not require there to be two things; one depicting, the other depicted. The picture alone suffices, since it may depict what does not exist. For example, it may depict a horse, but no horse in particular.[8]

Catherine Abell follows Hopkins closely:

For one thing to resemble another, both must exist. However many pictures depict things that do not exist. This is true of pictures [...] that depict objects of a certain type without depicting any specific particulars of that type.[9]

Interestingly, Hopkins does not appear to notice that his claim that 'resemblance is a relation between two particulars' contradicts the familiar idea that resemblance is a reflexive relation, which implies that true statements of resemblance may compare an object with itself. Even if this familiar idea is wrong, a person or place at one time can certainly resemble the same person or place at another time, and a kind of stuff in one place can resemble the same kind of stuff in another place. For example, the British Foreign Secretary William Hague famously looked the same at thirty-six as he looked at sixteen. Here we do not have two things, we have one thing at two different times. Again, Guinness in Tel-Aviv tastes the same as Guinness in Cork; and here we have one kind of stuff in two different places.

Neither Hopkins nor Abell says whether they believe that resemblances have to be between particular things that exist because this true of relations generally, or whether they think it is something special about resemblance. Be that as it may, it is not self-evident that when a statement of resemblance *does* relate two things, both need to exist in order for the statement to be true. And besides, as we have seen, true statements of resemblance do not always mention two particular things, to which the existence requirement can apply. I shall enlarge on these two points in turn.

When a statement of resemblance relates two things, must they both exist in order for the statement to be true? On the face of it, the answer is no. Reggie looks like Ronnie, Levin is similar in various ways to Tolstoy, Widmerpool resembles Malvolio, and Thor is like Zeus. At least these are things that we find it quite natural to say. It appears that a statement of resemblance can be

[8] *Routledge Encyclopedia of Philosophy*, Depiction, §1.
[9] C. Abell, 'Canny Resemblance', *Philosophical Review* **118** (2009), 186.

133

true whether both or one or neither of the individuals concerned exists.

Here is a simple theory which explains this. The mark of a fictional character, as the disclaimer that sometimes appears at the front of novels or at the end of movies attests, is that any resemblance to any actual person is coincidental (at the time of writing); it is not that none is possible, or that none exists. (The qualification 'at the time of writing' is needed for the reason Oscar Wilde famously pointed out: life can imitate art.)

If this is right, we can still insist that someone who uses two names to make a true statement of resemblance refers to something with each of the two names, as long as we are prepared to acknowledge that it is possible to refer to things – such as fictional characters – that do not exist.[10] Arguably, what the referring use of a name requires is that the speaker be able to identify whom or what she is referring to, which is not ruled out where fictional characters are concerned. On the contrary, fictional characters can be identified quite easily. For instance, Widmerpool is the character in *A Dance to the Music of Time* who marries Pamela Flitton and Malvolio is the character in *Twelfth Night* who wears yellow stockings with cross gartering.

If this simple theory is right, when a statement of resemblance compares two things, neither of them needs to exist in order for the statement to be true. Of course, this theory is not universally accepted and statements of resemblance involving fictional characters have been interpreted in various ways. But we should not assume that the simple theory is false.

The second point I said I would enlarge on is that statements of resemblance do not always mention two things, to which the existence requirement could apply. The reason I gave is that while there are many statements of resemblance in which two specific persons, places or things are mentioned, for example, 'SoHo is like Hampstead', there are just as many in which only one is, for example, 'SoHo is like a village'. Equally, there are many in which none are, for example, 'A kibbutz is like a village' and 'Margarine is like butter'. It is puzzling that philosophers writing about the resemblance theory of depiction uniformly ignore these kinds of statements, and repeat the canard that resemblances are necessarily between particulars, or specific things.

---

[10] On this topic, see Bede Rundle, *Grammar in Philosophy* (Oxford: OUP, 1979); Mark Sainsbury, *Reference without Referents* (Oxford: OUP, 2005), chs 2 & 6.

As we have seen, the supposed fact that resemblances are necessarily between pairs of specific things, both of which exist, is thought to pose a problem for resemblance theories of depiction, because a picture may depict a man or a horse without depicting any man or horse in particular. Here is the passage from the *Routledge Encyclopedia* again:

> For resemblance to hold, two things must exist – the thing resembling and the thing resembled. By contrast, depiction does not require there to be two things; one depicting, the other depicted. The picture alone suffices, since it may depict what does not exist. For example, it may depict a horse, but no horse in particular.

One thing that is puzzling about this remark is that if a picture depicts a horse, but no horse in particular, it surely does not depict something that does not exist. On the contrary, it depicts something, a kind of animal, that *does* exist, unlike a picture of a centaur, for example. A kind of animal is not a particular animal, of course. But the question whether the *particular* horse it depicts exists does not arise, since *ex hypothesis* it does not depict any horse in particular. Stubbs's portrait of Whistlejack depicts a horse that exists, or existed when he painted it; whereas Rubens's painting *Perseus and Andromeda* depicts Pegasus, a mythical horse, which never existed. But when a picture depicts a horse, but no horse in particular, there is no particular horse about whose existence we can enquire. Hopkins appears to confuse pictures with generic content and pictures with fictional content. I shall return to this confusion later.

The passages by Hopkins I have quoted seems therefore to combine two errors: first, the idea that resemblances are necessarily between pairs of specific things, both of which exist; and second, the idea that genre pictures – pictures with generic content – invariably depict things that do not exist, that is, they depict things that do not exist whether they depict centaurs (which do not exist) or horses (which do). I have said more about the first error so far. But the second error is equally important, because it illustrates a failure to think clearly about the relationship between the concept of a picture with generic content and the concept of a picture that portrays an individual, which is of fundamental importance in the theory of art, as I shall argue in a moment.

Where does this leave the traditional idea that representation in the visual arts in general, and depiction in particular, depends on resemblances in form and colour between works of art and the things they represent?

It is true that the verb 'depicts' is sometimes used to express a relation, and sometimes not. For example, 'It depicts a horse', '... a bridge', ' ... a river' can be read in either way. Read in the first, relation-involving way, the question 'Which horse?', 'Which bridge?', 'Which river?' has an answer, even if we do not know what it is, and the sentence can be continued with a namely-rider, '... namely, Whistlejack', '... namely, the Rialto', '... namely the Styx'. Read in the second, non-relation-involving way, the question 'Which ...?' and the namely-rider are out of place. It is useful to mark this distinction clearly in the language we use to talk about pictures, and to a degree we do: the verb 'portray' is biased towards the relation, whereas 'depict' is not.

But as we have seen, the verb 'resembles' has exactly the same dual use. Hence, the statement that a picture (or part of one) resembles a horse does not imply that there is a particular horse that it resembles, and the statement that it resembles a satyr does not imply that satyrs exist. Satyrs have a distinctive appearance, which it is easy to describe, and if something has the same appearance as a satyr, then it resembles one. The fact that satyrs are mythical creatures does not prevent this from occurring. In Plato's *Symposium*, Alcibiades says that Socrates looks like a satyr. This may have been unkind, but it was not absurd.

§4 I said that the relationship between the concept of a picture with generic content and the concept of a picture that portrays an individual is of fundamental importance in the theory of depiction, but neither the phrase 'picture with generic content' nor the word 'portrays' has exactly the right meaning. Perhaps the simplest way to capture what I have in mind is to take a picture of a specific person, place or object, whether fictional or real, and to consider what we can call, for want of a better pair of terms, its reference and its sense. The words 'reference' and 'sense' are the normal translations of the terms 'bedeutung' and 'sinn', which Frege used to distinguish between the object that an expression stands for or designates, and the way in which the expression presents that object, the 'mode of presentation' as he called it.

Frege introduced the distinction between sense and reference to explain how identity statements can be informative, without being about words.[11] Returning to the example I mentioned earlier, 'The morning star is the evening star' is not a statement about words, unlike the statement that the phrases 'the morning star' and 'the

---

[11] 'On Sense and Reference' in *Translations from the Philosophical Writings of Gottlob Frege*, ed. and trans. P. Geach & M. Black, third edition (Oxford: Blackwell, 1980).

evening star' refer to the same object, because the first statement *uses* these two phrases, whereas the second one *mentions* them. And it is not merely an instance of a law of logic either, like the statement that morning star is the morning star. 'The morning star is the evening star' can state an astronomical discovery, Frege explained, because the phrases 'the morning star' and 'the evening star' have the same reference, but do not have the same sense. Here is another example. The expressions '2 × 3' and '4 + 2' both designate the number six, but the first expression presents it as the product of two and three, whereas the second presents it as the sum of four and two So again these expressions have the same reference, but do not have the same sense.

Similarly, two portraits of the same individual may present him as dark-haired and seated, wearing a black smock (Kramskoy's 1873 portrait of Tolstoy), or as grey-bearded and standing, wearing a white smock (Repin's 1901 portrait). The analogy between expressions in a language and pictures is not exact. But it is helpful to think of each of these two portraits as designating, or standing for, same the same individual as the other, while differing in its 'mode of presentation' – in other words, as having the same reference, but a different sense. And we can use the same distinction to think about two pictures of the same fictional person – for example, Michelangelo's fresco of the creation of Adam on the Sistine Chapel ceiling and Piero della Francesca's fresco of the death of Adam in the church of San Francesco in Arezzo – or the same place.

I said earlier that the verb 'depicts' is sometimes used to express a relation, and sometimes not, and that sentences like 'It depicts a horse {… a bridge / … a river}' can be read in either way. We can see now that this distinction corresponds to the distinction between sense and reference. In the relation-involving use of the verb, the use where the sentence can be continued with a namely-rider, depiction corresponds to reference; whereas in the non-relation-involving use of the verb it corresponds to sense. We can also see that the kind of picture Hopkins and Abell are concerned about, a picture that depicts a horse, but no horse in particular, is a picture that has a sense – as any intelligible figurative picture must – but no reference, like the phrase 'the greatest integer' or 'the present King of France'. Henceforth, I shall use subscripts to distinguish between these two ways of using the verb 'depicts': 'depicts$_r$' for the use that corresponds to reference and 'depicts$_s$' for the use that corresponds to sense.

Together with the muddle about resemblance, the most important mistake philosophers have made about depiction is to confuse or amalgamate theories about the sense of works of art and theories

John Hyman

about their reference, or to assume that a theory of depiction is first and foremost a theory of reference – as it were, a theory of the portrait – and that a theory of sense can be developed from it, rather as Wittgenstein's theory of meaning in the *Tractatus* was developed from his conception of a name. Each of the two most influential theories of depiction during the last fifty years, Richard Wollheim's and Nelson Goodman's, makes one of these mistakes. Wollheim makes the first, while Goodman makes the second.

Wollheim argues that a picture is a marked surface, which is designed to cause a distinctive kind of visual experience, which he calls 'seeing-in'. Seeing-in, he explains, has two aspects or components:

> I am visually aware of the surface I look at, and I discern something standing out in front of, or (in certain cases) receding behind, something else.[12]

This kind of experience is not caused by pictures alone. It can also occur, for example, when we look at a damp-stained wall. The element of intention or design is what distinguishes pictures from other marked surfaces that have the same kind of effect. Representation occurs when a standard of correctness is imposed on the natural capacity of seeing-in, and the standard of correctness is set by the artist's intention. Thus a picture represents a specific person or place, or an object of a given kind, if, and only if, the artist successfully intends the view to see that person or place or that kind of object in its surface.

There are several well-known objections to this theory.[13] What concerns us here is that Wollheim ignores the distinction between the sense and reference of a picture. He talks indifferently about seeing Henry VIII or Charles Laughton or a generic bison in a picture. But this is logically naïve. It is like failing to distinguish between the sense and reference of a phrase such as 'the morning star', as if the philosophy of language could make do with a single idea of meaning or signification that includes both.

One result of Wollheim's failure to acknowledge this distinction is his claim that the standard of correctness, which determines whether the viewer has correctly perceived what a picture represents, is set by

---

[12] R. Wollheim, *Painting as an Art* (London: Thames and Hudson, 1988), 46.
[13] See M. Budd, 'On Looking at a Picture', in Jim Hopkins & Anthony Savile (eds), *Psychoanalysis, Mind and Art* (Oxford: OUP, 1992); J. Hyman, *The Objective Eye* (Chicago, Ill.: Univ. of Chicago Press, 2006), ch.7.

the intentions of the artist. This is normally true of a picture's reference, but not its sense. Wittgenstein was surely right when he said in the *Blue Book*: 'An obvious, and correct, answer to the question "What makes a portrait the portrait of so-and-so?" is that it is the intention.'[14] This is comparable to the question, What determines the reference of a proper name, in a particular instance of its use? For example, if I begin a letter with the phrase 'Dear George', what determines which of the myriad Georges in the world I am addressing? The answer is surely my intention.

But we cannot answer the corresponding question about sense in the same way, for there may be a difference between what a word or phrase I write or meant to utter means and what I meant to say. Similarly, a picture can depict$_s$ a man in the uniform of a midshipman when the artist intended to depict$_s$ a man in the uniform of an ensign, or it can depict$_s$ a spruce when the artist intended to depict$_s$ a larch. In both cases there are more general terms that apply to the depicted$_s$ object and conform to the artist's intentions, such as 'man' and 'tree'. But the divergence between intention and outcome remains, and this disproves the idea that an artist cannot produce a picture with unintended sense. As one might expect, inexpert artists are especially prone to do so. For example, most three-year-old children are no less capable of painting a picture that depicts$_r$ their mothers than Rembrandt or Whistler was, but drawings by three-year-olds tend to depict$_s$ arms growing out of heads.

Wollheim's error about the role of the intention is a result of his failure to distinguish between the sense and reference of a picture. He uses a single model to explain both what determines the reference of a portrait and what determines its sense or mode of presentation. But it is as elementary a mistake to overlook the difference between these questions as it would be to overlook the difference between the sense and reference of a descriptive phrase.

Goodman is a very different case. He does not overlook the distinction between sense and reference: he rejects it. The distinction he draws between a picture of a man and a man-picture is extensionally equivalent to the distinction between and picture that depicts$_r$ a man and one that depicts$_s$ a man, except that Goodman excludes the referring use of empty names. But the extreme form of nominalism he espouse reduces sense to reference, so we find the same failure to think about the sense of a picture, as opposed to reference, in his work. Thus his principal claim is that 'denotation is the core of

[14]   L. Wittgenstein, *The Blue and Brown Books*, second edition (Oxford: Basil Blackwell, 1969), 32.

John Hyman

representation' – denotation being a variety of reference – as if a portrait were the basic kind of picture.[15]

Both of these approaches are disastrous, because representation by pictures depends on a systematic relationship between the shapes and colours on the surface of a picture and its *sense* that does not exist between the shapes and colours on the surface of a picture and its *reference*. So if we amalgamate sense and reference, or if we regard the question of how pictures refer as fundamental, we are bound to miss the basic mechanism that explains how pictures represent.

Thus, if we imagine hanging Whistler's portrait of his mother (*Arrangement in Grey and Black No.1*, 1871) next to a child's portrait of its mother drawn at the age of three – admittedly different artists and different mothers – it seems obvious that there isn't a systematic relationship between the shape and colour of part of the surface of a portrait and the shape and colour of the individual it portrays. But if we turn from the reference of a picture to its sense, the situation is quite different. The case of a free-standing sculpture is simpler but similar to the case of a picture, so that is where I shall begin. (The qualification 'free-standing' will be omitted in the discussion that follows.)

§5 Consider the part of Michelangelo's Bruges Madonna that represents Jesus's head. What is the reference of this part of the scuplture, and what is its sense? Its reference is Jesus's head, and it presents it as having various features: thick locks of hair, chubby cheeks, and so on. These features, we may say, comprise the sense or mode of presentation of this part of the sculpture. But the sense or mode of presentation of a sculpture expressed in the most general terms is simply an object or arrangement of objects with a specific shape. And except in the unusual case of an anamorphic sculpture, which is designed to be seen from an extremely eccentric point of view, this shape is evidently the shape of the part of the carved block itself. This applies to Michelangelo's Rome Pietà in exactly the same way. The Rome Pietà refers to the same two individuals as the Bruges Madonna, but the *sense*, or mode of presentation, of Jesus's head is different because the shape of the corresponding part of the sculpture is different, and Jesus's head is presented as an object with this shape.

It follows that the fundamental difference between representation in sculpture and representation in words is not a matter of reference, it is a matter of sense. The simple rule about sculpture is that *what a sculpture represents has the same shape as the sculpture itself.* Another

---

[15]   Goodman, op. cit., 5.

way of making the same point would be to say that there is an exact resemblance in shape between a sculpture and what it represents. But by the phrase 'what it represents', I do not mean the sculpture's reference, I mean its sense. The rule does not relate two particulars, for example, the sculpture and the historical individual Jesus; it concerns a single particular, the sculpture, and its sense or mode of presentation. If resemblance were invariably a relation between two particulars, the rule would be incoherent; but as we have seen, this dogma about resemblance is a mistake.

The simple rule about sculpture should be obvious as soon as it is stated, so obvious that it seems trite. But notice that the rule is not conditional on the artist's intention; it does not involve a system of rules correlating symbols with the objects they refer to; it does not refer to any of the psychological states philosophers have postulated to explain how painting and sculpture represent; and it applies in exactly the same way to a Greek bronze figure of a generic horse from the Geometric period as it does to the Bruges Madonna or the Rome Pietà. The same is true of the equivalent rule for pictures, as we shall see.

I shall add four further observations, before discussing the rule for pictures. First, although the simple rule for sculpture can be stated in terms of resemblance it need not be. It is not a restatement of the theory that paintings and sculptures are iconic signs. That theory failed to distinguish between sense and reference, treated resemblance as a relation and was not limited to shape.

Second, the simple rule does not imply that a sculpture that represents Jesus resembles Jesus, or that a bronze figure of a horse resembles a horse. It says nothing about the reference of a sculpture, and nothing about its sense beyond its shape. It therefore combines naturally with the idea that reference is normally determined by the artist's intention, and with the idea that a viewer's ability to identify the sense or mode of presentation of a sculpture as a child's head or as a horse depends on her ability to recognize these kinds of objects by their shapes.

Third, the fact that the simple rule is not conditional on the artist's intention does not prevent the artist's intention from playing any role in the theory of representation apart from determining the reference of a work of art. The analogy with linguistic meaning suggests that it does play such a role. For acknowledging that the meaning of an utterance need not be the same as what the speaker meant to say is consistent with the idea that an utterance means nothing unless the speaker means something by the words he utters; and it is also consistent with the idea that a meaningful utterances cannot occur

John Hyman

except against a background that includes the custom of making utterances with the intention of saying something. Both of these ideas can be transferred to the case of painting and sculpture in a straightforward way; but neither implies that an artist cannot produce a representational work of art with unintended sense, as Wollheim's theory implies.

Fourth, as I have indicated, the simple rule that what a sculpture represents has the same shape as the sculpture itself combines naturally with various ideas philosophers interested in representation have proposed. It combines easily with John Kulvicki's recent defence of the role of bare-bones content in the theory of representation as well as claims about the role of recognition in explaining how works of art represent, such as those advanced by Flint Schier in his book *Deeper into Pictures* and Dominic Lopes in *Understanding Pictures*;[16] it is consistent with various ideas about the relationship between the concept of representation and the concept of intention or design; and as we shall see, it suggests that the concept of occlusion shape (outline shape) plays a central role in the theory of depiction, as Robert Hopkins and the author of this article have both proposed.

The equivalent rule for pictures is less straightforward than the rule for sculpture, because sculptures represent objects with the same number of dimensions as they have themselves, whereas pictures normally represent three-dimensional objects on a two-dimensional (i.e. flat) surface, or on a surface whose curvature is slight enough to be ignored. But it is not difficult to see what the rule for pictures is, if we think about how their two-dimensionality affects their sense.

The principal point is that we cannot discover different aspects of an object represented in a picture by moving around it and studying it from different angles, as we can in the case of a free-standing sculpture. That is why Van Dyke sent Bernini a triple portrait of Charles I: one referent, three modes of presentation. So whereas the sense or mode of presentation of a sculpture, expressed in the most general terms, is an object or arrangement of objects with a specific shape, the sense or mode of presentation of a picture is an aspect or view of an object or arrangement of objects – or several aspects or views, in unusual cases such as this one – relative to a line (or lines) of sight.

[16] John Kulvicki, 'Pictorial Diversity' in Catharine Abell & Katerina Bantinaki, eds., *Philosophical Perspectives on Depiction* (Oxford: OUP, 2010).

Now if we want to formulate a shape-rule for pictures analogous to the simple rule for sculpture discussed above, we shall need to identify a two-dimensional shape-property that an aspect or view of an object represented in a picture invariably includes, whether it is a shadow, a rainbow, part of the sea or sky, or a medium-sized specimen of dry goods. It is not difficult to identify this property if we think about an object with a simple shape, such as a coin. Consider a circular coin viewed along an oblique line of sight. The coin will look circular to a viewer as long as she can see its orientation. But the two-dimensional cross-section of the cone of light the coin subtends to the viewer's eye will be elliptical, and this is also a visible property of the coin. It is especially salient when an object is backlit, and appears in silhouette. It has been called a perspectival shape or outline shape or occlusion shape, it is two-dimensional, and of course it is relative to a line of sight. It changes as the line of sight changes. But relative does not mean subjective. The shape of a cross-section of the cone of light an object subtends to the viewer's eye is not merely a feature of the viewer's experience. It belongs to optics, not psychology.

I said a moment ago that the sense or mode of presentation of a picture is an aspect or view of an object or arrangement of objects, relative to a line of sight. This means that a picture invaraibly depicts$_s$ the occlusion shapes of objects. So suppose a picture depicts$_s$ a circular coin with an elliptical occlusion shape. What shape would the corresponding region of the picture's surface have to be? With the same exception as we noted in the case of sculpture – that is, an anamorphic picture, designed to be seen from an extremely eccentric point of view – the answer of course is that it would have to be elliptical, and the surface of the coin would be foreshortened.

But it would be a mistake to think that the occlusion shape is only represented when an object is foreshortened. For example, the shield in a painting on a kylix attributed to the Foundry Painter (Munich 2640, ca. 490 BC) is among the earliest examples of foreshortening in Greek art; whereas the hoop in a painting on a krater attributed to the Berlin Painter (Louvre G175, ca. 500 BC) is not foreshortened. This is not because the Berlin painter did not represent the hoop's occlusion shape. It is just that the line of sight in this case is perpendicular to the hoop, and the hoop's occlusion shape is therefore a circle. So whereas the simple rule for sculpture is that what a sculpture represents has the same shape as the sculpture itself, the shape-rule for pictures is that the shape of a region on a picture's surface is the same as the occlusion shape of the object it represents. In other words, there is an exact resemblance between these shapes. This applies to pictures of objects such as shields and hoops, but it applies equally to pictures that represent a rainbow, the sea or the sky.

It is reasonable to suppose that the simple rule for sculpture has always been understood by sculptors and their public, even if it is too obvious to be stated or written down. By contrast, the shape-rule for pictures has always been implicit in artistic practice, but the concepts used to state it precisely and to explain the idea of occlusion shape were first developed in Greek geometry and widely disseminated – in Europe – only in the Renaissance.

I have defended the claim that the idea of occlusion shape plays an central role in the theory of depiction and stated the shape rule for pictures in several earlier publications, most fully in my book *The Objective Eye*. The approach I took there contrasted subjectivist theories of depiction, which seek to explain how pictures represent by defining the kind of experience they are designed to produce in viewers, with objectivist theories, which proceed without attempting to define the experience. (Objectivist theories stem from Plato, subjectivist theories from Descartes.) The simple rule for sculpture and the shape-rule for pictures belong in the objectivist camp.

The principal justification for subjectivism has always been the evident dissimilarity between a picture or sculpture and the objects it represents. This is the point Descartes seizes on. He writes:

> Although they make us think of countless different qualities in [the objects they represent], it is only in respect of shape that there is any real resemblance. And even this resemblance is very imperfect, since engravings represent to us bodies of varying relief and depth on a surface which is entirely flat. Moreover, in accordance with the rules of perspective they often represent circles by ovals better than by other circles, squares by rhombuses better than by other squares, and similarly for other shapes. Thus it often happens that in order to be more perfect as an image and to represent an object better, an engraving ought not to resemble it.[17]

The shape-rule for pictures addresses both of the arguments in this passage. The first is that 'engravings represent to us bodies of varying relief and depth on a surface which is entirely flat'. But the only shape properties the shape-rule refers to are the occlusion shapes depicted$_s$ in a picture, and occlusion shapes are two-dimensional. The second argument is that the rules of perspective may,

[17] R. Descartes, *Philosophical Writings* I, trans. J. Cottingham et al. (Cambridge: CUP, 1985), 165.

for example, require an artist to represent a circle by means of an oval. But as we have seen the circular profile of a coin has an elliptical occlusion shape relative to an oblique line of sight. The dissimilarity between the physical shape of a circular coin and shape of the region on the surface of a picture that depicts$_s$ a coin is consistent with the rule.

Another justification that is sometimes offered for subjectivism is that the objectivist emphasis on resemblance embodies a bias in favour of realistic, literal or accurate representation and a narrow and stultifying programme for artistic work.[18] But this is confused. One might as well argue that regarding a language as a system of semantic and syntactic conventions or rules embodies a bias in favour of conventional literature, or literature that follows rules – a bias, say, in favour of Rupert Brooke over T.S. Eliot or Arthur Conan Doyle over James Joyce. It should be obvious that this would be a gross misunderstanding. The rule that the gerund in English ends in '–ing' does not limit the inventiveness of English writers, and it applies to Donne or Milton in exactly the same way as it does to lesser poets. Similarly, the simple rule for sculpture applies in exactly the same way to a geometric bronze figure of a horse, Donatello's *Gattamelata* and Marino Marini's *L'angelo della Città*, and the shape-rule for pictures applies to pictures irrespective of the style or tradition they belong to, their originality, or the artistic values they express. Both of these rules identify basic mechanisms of representation in the visual arts; they do not dictate or limit the forms artists create, the models they follow or the values they embody in their work.

However, the subjectivist position is not entirely without merit. For although the simple rule for sculpture and the shape-rule for pictures do not refer to viewers' experiences, their competence is limited in two ways. First, as we have noted more than once, the rules only provide an objective correlation – a correlation that is independent of the viewer's experience – between the shape of a sculpture or the shapes on the surface of a picture and the shape or occlusion shape of each object included in the sculpture's or the picture's sense. No specification of the sense or mode of presentation of a work of art beyond this can be 'read off' its non-representational properties in this way. Second, the parts of a picture that represent discrete objects or parts of a scene need to be distinguished from each other, and of course the rules cannot explain how this is done. Both of these limitations indicate ways in which psychological factors are

[18]   M. Podro, 'Literalism and Truthfulness in Painting', *British Journal of Aesthetics* **50** (2010).

essentially involved in defining the relationship between representational and non-representational properties of works of art.

As we have seen, there is a third limitation on the competence of the
two rules, which not provide a gap that subjectivist ideas can fill. It is
that they do not correlate the shape of a sculpture or the shapes on the
surface of a picture with its reference. Here, as in the case of language,
intentions and contextual factors are involved in complex ways that
are difficult to summarize or survey. I shall not attempt that task here.

§6 I said earlier that it is sometimes alleged that philosophers who
analyze the concept of depiction in terms of resemblance or occlusion
(outline) shape express a bias in favour of realistic or literal representation and offer a stultifying programme for artistic work. Michael
Podro makes this charge in his article 'Literalism and Truthfulness
in Painting'. These philosophers, he says, 'treat depiction as a
matter of mere visual representation', they pursue 'the project of
approximating depiction to an abbreviated equivalence of ordinary
environmental perception', and ignore the ways in which pictures
can 'transform our experience of the subject'. 'We need', he adds,
'to see how painting elaborates upon its underlying conditions as
poetry elaborates on those of language.'[19]

This is partly right and partly wrong. It is right to point out that defining the 'underlying conditions' is only part of the theory of art. The
foundations are part of the structure, not the whole of it. Artists exploit
the communicative possibilities inherent in the medium as such (i.e. its
'underlying conditions') with specific *materials, tools and techniques*,
to communicate *thoughts, feelings and perceptions* in a work of art.
Understanding art means understanding all three aspects of artistic
activity, both in themselves and in relation to each other. But it is
wrong to think that philosophical theories of depiction treat all pictures
'as a mere matter of visual representation', just as it would be wrong to
think that linguistics treats literature as a mere litany of facts. In fact it is
doubly wrong. It is wrong because philosophers need not mistake the
part for the whole – and to my knowledge they have not done so. And it
is also wrong because we cannot expect to understand how painting
'elaborates upon its underlying conditions' unless we know what
these 'underlying conditions' are.

For example, I said earlier that expressed in the most general terms,
the sense or mode of presentation of a picture is an aspect or view of an
object or arrangement of objects, relative to a line (or lines) of sight.
Several significant developments in the history of painting 'elaborate

[19]   Ibid., 457f.

upon this underlying condition' in ingenious ways. First, novel views of objects – views associated with novel lines of sight – can be introduced by combining views along established lines of sight. For example, quasi-frontal views were composed at different times in the history of painting by combining two profiles or oblique views, so that the composite image divides along a vertical axis. This is how the Andokides Painter produced a frontal view of a wrestler's face around 515 BC (Berlin F2159), with his oddly pointed head, projecting ears and thick neck; and it is how Giotto produced a frontal view of a mourner in his *Dormition of the Virgin* (ca. 1310, Staatliche Museen zu Berlin, Gemaldegalerie), with his broad shoulders (figs. 1 and 2).

Second, the lines of sight associated with distinct parts of a depicted scene can be coordinated or played off against each other. Thus, in an orthodox use of Renaissance perspective, the lines of sight associated with each part of the depicted scene are made to intersect, so that the entire scene is coordinated in relation to this implicit point of view. By contrast, in Masaccio's fresco of *The Trinity* (1425, S. Maria Novella, Florence), the architecture and the supporting figures are depicted as if seen from below, but the figures of the Father and the Son are depicted frontally, without any foreshortening at all.[20]

Third, the implicit line of sight can be associated with an implicit spectator. The idea of an implicit spectator was first used as a theoretical tool by Alois Riegl, in his analysis of Rembrandt's *The Staalmeesters* (1662, Rijksmuseum, Amsterdam). (Riegl credits the idea to Thoré-Bürger, who 'correctly presumed the presence of an unseen party in the space of the viewer, with whom the syndics are negotiating.'[21]) But the earliest examples are self-portraits, because here an implicit spectator can be introduced by accident, without being intended as a narrative device. For example, Dürer's drawing known as *Self-Portrait with a Cushion* (1493, Robert Lehman collection, Metropolitan Museum of Art, New York) shows the artist absorbed in the act of drawing himself, and so the view of the young man it depicts is necessarily represented as his own.

[20]   There is a good discussion of the use of single and multiple vanishing-points as organizing principles in fifteenth-century painting in J. White, *The Birth and Rebirth of Pictorial Space* second edition (London: Faber & Faber, 1967), 196ff.

[21]   A. Riegl, *The Group Portraiture of Holland*, trans. E.M. Kain (Los Angeles: Getty Research Institute, 1999), 285.

John Hyman

Figure 1. Andokides Painter, Amphora, ca. 515 BC, detail.

Of course other equally significant developments in the history of painting depend on other factors, and failing to understand in general terms how pictures represent is unlikely to impede the work of art historians interested in the impact of the Council of Trent or the supply of paint in tubes. But the inventions I have mentioned involve more abstract concepts, and the cost of misunderstanding them can be high. The theoretical debates about Renaissance perspective in the twentieth century are an embarrassing episode in art history for precisely this reason. Everyone understood that perspective is a geometrical system that enables artists to control the occlusion (outline) shapes and relative occlusion sizes of the objects represented in a picture, but misunderstandings about these properties inherited

Figure 2. Giotto, *Dormition of the Virgin*, ca. 1310, detail.

from philosophy and optics led art historians from Panofsky onwards into pointless controversy and needless confusion.[22]

In summary, the simple rule for sculpture and the shape-rule for pictures define part of the basic mechanism on which representation in the visual arts relies. (I have not discussed colour here. In *The Objective Eye*, I argue that analogous rules for colour can also be defined without referring to the experiences sculptures and paintings cause in viewers.) Alongside these rules, a comprehensive theory of representation in art will also refer to psychological factors, to the artist's intentions, to customs and conventions, and to other factors. But if we wish to adjudicate between the traditional view that representation in the visual arts depends on resemblances between works of art and the objects they represent and the theories of representation defended by Goodman and Wollheim and their followers, who reject this view, we are, I believe, bound to conclude that

[22] On this topic, see *The Objective Eye*, ch.10.

John Hyman

the traditional view is right. It was not eclipsed for fifty years because it is philosophically naïve or artistically stultifying, but because some exceedingly simple and well understood ideas in logic have been misunderstood or routinely ignored: first, resemblance is not invariably a relation between particulars; second, we need to unpack the general idea of representation and distinguish between sense and reference in order to understand how pictures represent.

The Queen's College, Oxford
john.hyman@queens.ox.ac.uk

The Problem of Perfect Fakes[1]

M.W. ROWE

Fakes fall into two categories: copies and pastiches. The first is exemplified when someone paints a reproduction of Manet's *The Fifer* with the intention of selling it to you as the original. The second is exemplified when someone paints a picture in the *style* of Manet – although not a reproduction of one of his actual works – with the intention of selling it to you as a picture *by* Manet.

However, not all – or even most – copies and pastiches are fakes. There can be many reasons for painting a copy (you might want a token of this type on your wall); and the same applies to painting a pastiche (you might want to explore the original artist's technique). Of course, both kinds of painting can be pressed into service as part of a fraud or hoax, but I shall assume that a painting is only a fake or forgery (two words I use interchangeably) if it is was created in order to deceive. There can be a number of motives for such deceptions: for fame, for revenge, to make money, to demonstrate the virtuosity of the faker, and so on.[2]

A copy or pastiche is not necessary of inferior aesthetic or monetary value to the original. Rembrandt's copies of Pieter Lastman are more valuable in both senses than the works he copied; and Chatterton's pastiches of fifteenth-century poetry are often of greater artistic interest than his stylistic models. It's also quite common for an artist to paint a number of different copies of the same painting

---

[1] This paper was originally written as a popular lecture, and I have not tried to remove all stylistic traces of its origin.

[2] There can also be more complicated cases. For example, someone can deliberately misattribute an existing work to Rubens, or he can also touch it up to make it look more like a Rubens' painting. In addition, a forger can exploit a work's close causal connection with Rubens: he can claim, for example, that a picture is by Rubens when he knows it to be entirely the work of Rubens' school; or he can claim it is by Rubens when the master himself added only a few details to the face. But, as in the case of most copies and pastiches, the majority of touched-up paintings and misattributions are not intended to deceive. A painting can be touched up as part of a restoration process or in order to make an older picture look more fashionable; and most misattributions are the results of ignorance.

doi:10.1017/S1358246112000240   ©The Royal Institute of Philosophy and the contributors 2013

(Leonardo's copies, for example, of the *Mona Lisa*) and these can often be of similar aesthetic and monetary value.

Forging is often a dubious moral practice, but I don't intend to say anything further about its ethical aspects here. My interest is rather in the aesthetic value of copies and pastiches, and these pose a more delicate theoretical problem for the aesthetician than fakes and forgeries do for the moralist. The only reason I am focusing on fakes is that they raise the issue of the aesthetic value of copies and pastiches in a particularly dramatic, public and emphatic form. Moreover, I am largely interested in the aesthetic values of copies and pastiches, not for their own sakes, but because they illuminate some profound issues in the metaphysics of normal art: about the nature of art's ontology; and the roles genre, originality and intention legitimately play in our aesthetic responses.

My debts to previous aestheticians who have thought about these and related topics – Walton, Danto, Currie and Lamarque amongst others – will be obvious throughout.[3]

I

Let me begin with three examples. The first is reported by the *Daily Telegraph*:

> A half-man, half-goat sculpture, which was attributed to Post-Impressionist artist Paul Gauguin and took pride of place at the Art Institute of Chicago for a decade, has been declared to be a forgery created by a British family. The Museum admitted that the Faun sculpture is not by the nineteenth-century French artist but is the work of the Greenhalgh family who swindled an estimated £1.5 million from museums, galleries and auction houses. A private dealer bought the sculpture at Southeby's London, for £270,000 in 1994. The Art Institute purchased it from the dealer three years later. Eric Hogan, the director of public affairs at the Institute said: 'Everyone who bought and sold the work did so in good faith.' Shaun Greenhalgh, 47, who was jailed earlier this month on fraud

[3] Kendall L.Walton, 'Categories of Art,' *Philosophical Review* **79** (1970), 334–67; Arthur C.Danto, *The Transfiguration of the Commonplace* (Cambridge, MA: Harvard University Press, 1981); Gregory Currie, *An Ontology of Art* (London: Macmillan, 1989); Peter Lamarque, *Work and Object: Explorations in the Metaphysics of Art* (Oxford: OUP, 2010).

charges, created it at his parents' home in Bolton, Greater Manchester.[4]

The second example is taken from the *Guardian*.[5] David Lassman, the director of the Jane Austen Festival in Bath, had had his own novel, entitled *Freedom's Temple*, rejected by a number of publishers. Feeling somewhat aggrieved, he openly speculated with friends about whether Jane Austen herself would have trouble finding an agent or publisher today, and decided to put matters to the test. He typed up the first three chapters of *Northanger Abbey*, changing the book's name to *Susan*, and the heroine's name from Catherine Moreland to Susan Maldorn. Then, signing himself Alison Laydee,[6] he sent off the chapters to a number of leading publishers and agents. None spotted the hoax; all recipients rejected the manuscript, and Bloomsbury reported that, although they had read the chapters 'with interest,' the book would 'not be suited to their list.'

He then performed a similar operation with *Persuasion*. Again, none spotted the hoax; all recipients rejected the manuscript, and J.K. Rowling's agent, Christopher Little, said this was because he was 'not confident' of being able to place it. Finally, Lassman doctored *Pride and Prejudice* – changing the title to *First Impressions*, the central family's name from Bennet to Barnet, and so on – and sent it off in his normal manner. One publisher did spot the hoax this time – the opening sentence provided a helpful clue – but otherwise Lassman received the usual flood of rejections. Penguin consoled him by saying that his work 'seemed like a really interesting and original read.'

This is a rather unusual example of forgery; perhaps it is better described as a hoax. In the usual kind of case, a forger claims that his own modern work is an older work by an acknowledged genius. In the Lassman case, a hoaxer claims that an older work by an acknowledged genius is a modern work of his own.

A number of people found different reasons for being disheartened by the Lassman story. One reason was that so many publishers simply rejected work without looking at it; another was that, when the work was read, so many publishers' readers failed to recognise some of the most famous novels in English. But the really interesting case, and the one relevant to this article, is when an intelligent publisher's reader

4   *The Daily Telegraph*, 13/12/2007, 2.
5   *The Guardian*, 19/7/2007, 9.
6   Lassman's modifications of Austen's texts usually make some allusion to her life or art. For example, *Susan* was a title for an early draft of *Northanger Abbey*, and 'Alison Laydee' is a play on Austen's *nom de plume* (if it can be called that) 'A Lady.'

fails to recognise the work, reads the manuscript conscientiously, and then decides the work is not of sufficient quality to publish.

My third example is older and better known. Fritz Kreisler was one of the greatest violinists of the twentieth century. When he was in his twenties, he began to write a series of encore pieces in various antique styles, announcing them in his programmes as free arrangements of works by a number of obscure composers – Pugnani, Popora, Dittersdorf, Francoeur, etc. – whose names he had found in reference books. His motive for the deception, he said, was to avoid his own name appearing immodestly often in the programme notes for his concerts.

The ruse allowed Kreisler a certain amount of private amusement. On one occasion, he gave a recital in Berlin which included a group of three of his own compositions: the *Caprice veinnois* announced in his own name, and his *Liebesfreud* and *Liebesleid* described as transcriptions of posthumous waltzes by the nineteenth-century Austrian composer, Joseph Lanner. For this, he received a verbal reprimand from Dr Leopold Schmidt, the critic of the *Berliner Tageblatt* for daring to include his own 'insignificant' composition in the same group as some Lanner 'gems'. Schmidt expanded his criticisms in print: 'A feeling slightly akin to bad taste was engendered by the somewhat daring juxtaposition of Kreisler's 'Caprice veinnois' – to be sure a charming offering – and the dances of Lanner, these delightful genre creations filled with Schubertian melos and reflecting the good old Vienna days, for which encores were enthusiastically demanded.'[7] Similarly, after a recital including Kreisler's own *Praeludium and Allegro* (billed as being by Pugnani), the violinist was approached in his dressing room by the French composer Vincent D'Indy, who pointed an accusing finger and said: 'Pugnani would not have played the Allegro in that tempo[!]'[8]

Kreisler did not guard the secret terribly closely, and finally, in 1935, he instructed his publisher to remove the pseudonyms and advertise the pieces as his own compositions. Before the new catalogue was published, however, his secret was discovered and made public by the chief music critic of the *New York Times*, Olin Downes, who had made a diligent and unsuccessful search for Pugnani's original *Praeludium and Allegro* while researching a lecture-recital. Kreisler was thoroughly amused, remarking: 'The name changes, the value remains.'[9]

[7] Louis P. Lochner, *Fritz Kreisler* (London: Rockliff, 1951), 292.
[8] Lochner, *Kreisler*, 293.
[9] Lochner, *Kreisler*, 298.

II

There is something very enjoyable about such cases, largely because we feel that someone with pretensions to knowledge has been shown up. In the Greenhalgh case, the most obvious candidates are the experts at Southeby's and the Chicago Institute of Art; in the Lassman case, the publishers' readers; in the Kreisler case, the music critics. Some feel, however, that the people shown up are the artists whose names have been attached to such frauds. Gauguin can't be much good if even the greatest experts can't tell the difference between a Gauguin sculpture and something Shaun Greenhalgh, 47, knocks up in Bolton; Jane Austen's reputation can't rest on more than one literary type telling another that she's wonderful, if an educated reader, presented with a manuscript he takes for just another romantic novelette, cannot spot the difference. Of course, the interpretation which suggests that artists are shown up in such cases also tars the experts and professional readers, because they too must either lack discernment, or have played along with – and thereby helped sustain – a groundless reputation.

Most critics shared Kreisler's amusement when his hoax was revealed, but Ernest Newman, music critic of *The Times* and distinguished Wagnerian, was furious. 'In the case of paintings,' he wrote, 'a purchaser can proceed at law against anyone who sells him a picture which is not by the artist to whom it is attributed. [...] It would be interesting to see what would happen if someone were to claim damages from Kreisler and his publishers on the ground that he had been induced to purchase a score of a certain concerto on the representation that it was by Vivaldi, whereas Vivaldi on Kreisler's own admission had nothing whatever to do with it. [...].[10] He was also in no doubt as to what Kreisler's hoax had shown up:

> The average concert-goer no doubt feels that those hateful fellows the critics have had their ignorance shown up and been made to look foolish. On the contrary, what is shown up is the falsity of current judgments upon certain types of old music and the absence of any real critical standard where music in general is concerned.
>
> The simple truth is that a vast amount of seventeenth and eighteenth century music was merely the exploitation of formulae, the effective handling of which is within the scope of an ordinarily intelligent musician to-day. From one point of view Kreisler

[10]   Lochner, *Kreisler*, 297.

has not gone nearly far enough in the excellent work of clearing up the world's muddled thinking on these points: for my part I wish he had "discovered" some Bach and Handel manuscripts as well. In so far as Bach and Handel merely sat down in perfectly cold blood and ground out their morning's ration of music according-to–the-recipe [...].[11]

He excepts Bach's *Aria*, Handel's *Largo*, and the first movement of Mozart's G minor symphony[12] from his strictures, but one can only be impressed, even so, at the level of theoretical destruction he feels Kreisler's hoax ought to bring about.

In this article, I want to argue that neither the critics, nor the publishers' readers, nor the artists whose names are attached to fraudulent works, nor their entire eras, are shown up by these kinds of hoaxes. In fact, the only people shown up by fakes, are people who think that anyone is shown up by fakes.[13]

III

Wollheim[14] argues that works of art are either physical objects or types: Strawson[15] counters that the distinction is only contingent and depends on our currently primitive reproductive techniques. If we had a machine that could produce molecule-for-molecule reproductions of Leonardo's *Lady with an Ermine* as easily as a printing press can run off Beethoven's *Moonlight Sonata*, then we would soon start to think of your copy of Leonardo's picture as just as authentic as your copy of the *Moonlight Sonata*. I accept Strawson's amendment: all works of art are necessarily manifest types, patterns, designs that are potentially infinitely reproducible.

---

[11]   Ernest Newman, 'The Kreisler Revelations – Debit and Credit', in *The Sunday Times*, February 24th 1935. Quoted in Lochner, *Kreisler*, 295–6.

[12]   He probably means the second movement, 'Air,' from Bach's Orchestral Suite No.3, in D minor, BWV 1068; the aria, 'Ombra mai fui' ('Never was shade') from Handel's 1738 opera *Serse*; and Mozart's symphony number 40 in G minor, K.550.

[13]   I am referring only to excellent fakes; clearly, an expert can be held accountable for overlooking a *crude* forgery.

[14]   Richard Wollheim, *Art and Its Objects* (Harmondsworth: Peregrine Books, 1975), 17–28, 90–100.

[15]   P.F. Strawson, 'Aesthetic Appraisal and Works of Art' in his *Freedom and Resentment and Other Essays* (London: Methuen, 1974), 178–188, esp.183–4.

However, the reason most people think that fakes show up experts and artists is because they implicitly believe in what I shall call the 'manifest type-theory'.[16] This says that if two works of art share a manifest type – where a manifest type is defined in terms of a work's perceptible and potentially perceptible features – then they will actually be two *copies* of the *same* work of art; and they will have the same aesthetic qualities, and the same aesthetic value. To put it another way, if a work of art and its manifest type are one and the same, sameness of manifest features is both necessary *and sufficient* for sameness of work. On this view, the identity of a work of art has nothing to do with either history or evaluation.

It follows from the manifest type-theory, that if you want to say that an original is aesthetically much more valuable than a perfect copy, then this can only because you are – perhaps through snobbery and pretentiousness – hallucinating certain aesthetic virtues or vices, or confusing aesthetic with historic interest, or valuing the associations of the object not the object. These are exactly the kinds of errors and attitudes which people believe are shown up so satisfyingly when what was once taken to be a masterpiece is revealed as a forgery.

In fact, the manifest type-theory is wildly at variance with the way everyone – literary critics, musicians, dance historians, auction houses, the general public – treats and responds to works of art. For example, even wonderful copies of important paintings and sculptures command only a fraction of the price – often 1% or less – of the original, and they tend to be removed from gallery walls once discovered; despite being repeatedly reminded that there's a

---

[16]   For me, all works of art are types which are identified by their physical properties and the history of their production. But a type is different from what I here call a 'manifest type', which is just the actual or potential appearance of a work or several works. The phrase 'potential appearance' is designed to show my opposition to Goodman's theory as a complete account of fakes. He thinks that if an original and a fake look exactly alike, but we know that the copy is in some way different physically from the original, then this could lead to our eventually *seeing* that the original and the fake are not identical. This is why, according to Goodman, it is important to distinguish between originals and fakes, even though they currently look identical. (See Nelson Goodman, *Languages of Art: An Approach to a Theory of Symbols* (Indianapolis: Hackett, 1976), 99–123). He does not consider a case where the original and the copy are molecule-for-molecule identical because this, for him, would mean that they actually *are* the same work of art. By contrast, I argue that there need be no actual or potential perceptual difference between two paintings for them to be different works; they need only have different histories.

significant difference between the man who suffers and the mind which creates, the public still feels that light is shed on literature by reading biographies of the people who wrote it; and literary critics will keep talking about intention and historical context despite theorists telling them that only *the words on the page*[17] should be the object of their studies.

I want to argue that the practices of experts and the general public are correct; and that it is the manifest type-theory which needs to be abandoned. Sharing a manifest type is certainly necessary for two works to have exactly the same aesthetic properties, or to be the same work, but it is by no means sufficient.[18] Two or more works can share the same manifest type, and yet have wildly dissimilar aesthetic properties and be of completely different aesthetic values. To begin my demonstration of this, I want to consider our attitudes towards human languages and gestures.

IV

How much can you learn about a word, phrase or sentence by looking at it very carefully? To show that the answer is 'not much', consider the following example. You are standing outside a seminar room where group of literary critics have just finished discussing Milton. When you go into the now deserted room, you find the following words written on the blackboard:

PAIN FORMIDABLE

The word order and sense are slightly puzzling, but it might be reasonable to assume that a critic has been discussing how Milton is inclined to place his adjectives after nouns ('curses deep') and that this particular example refers to terrible pain. However, when you mention these thoughts to the next person who enters the room, he smiles and tells you that in fact all the Milton critics were next door; the last group in this room was a small convention of French bakers ... which makes the inscription on the board suddenly look very different.

---

[17] See Wimsatt and Beardsley, 'The Intentional Fallacy,' the *Sewanee Review*, Vol.**54** (1946), 468–88.
[18] It would be misleading to describe two such works of art as 'copies' – they might not be copied from originals, other works, or each other. 'Counterparts,' or Danto's term, 'indiscernibles,' might be better.

In the same way, a woman who has parked in a Scandinavian shopping precinct might be upset and alarmed to discover, on returning to her car, that a piece of paper has been placed under her windscreen wiper containing – in large letters – the words:

TOTAL SLUT

But it should not take long to discover that the paper is a flier for a closing-down sale, and that the inscription above, in Swedish, means 'completely closed'.[19]

To discover the meaning of these phrases, we have to find out who wrote them and in what context. However, it is clearly not enough to know about the native language of the person who wrote the two inscriptions described above. The Milton critic may have been trying out his French; the French baker may have been experimenting with Miltonic English; the Swedish shopkeeper may have intended to convey an insult in English. Intention is all important, and it is strange how intentionality can imbue an inscription so deeply that it can never be removed. If there are two inscriptions of PAIN FORMIDABLE, one meaning *terrible pain* the other meaning *wonderful bread*, and they are muddled up so no one can tell which is which, they would both retain their original meanings whether anyone knows which is which or not.

In the case described immediately above, each inscription has a meaning although we cannot tell what it is. But in some cases, exactly the same inscription will have no meaning at all. Let us suppose that there is no God, and no intentional purpose in nature, and yet one day, a stream deposits some pebbles in the pattern PAIN FORMIDABLE on a small sandbank.[20] Usually, the reason we have difficulty in determining what an inscription means is because we have difficulty recovering the intention with which it was written. But in this case, the difficulty is not that we cannot know what was originally intended, is that there was no original intention to discover: the pattern is entirely accidental and meaningless.

---

[19]   I would like to thank Karin Moses for bringing this example to my attention, and to Elisabeth Schellekens for confirming the translation.
[20]   I base this example on the famous seashore case in Steven Knapp and Walter Benn Michaels, 'Against Theory,' in W.J.T.Mitchell (ed.), *Against Theory: Literary Studies in the New Pragmatism* (Chicago: University of Chicago Press, 1985), 11–30.

M.W. Rowe

Of course, we can entertain ourselves by projecting various meanings on to it – an Englishman will be inclined to suppose it means *terrible pain*, a Frenchman *wonderful bread* – and we soon realize it could have an infinite number of possible meanings in an infinite number of possible languages. But projecting a meaning – usually of a phrase the pattern reminds you of in your own language – is not a reliable way of establishing what ordinary written languages mean (translation would be an easy business if it were), and it is no more effective for establishing the meaning or meaninglessness of natural objects. In the pebble example, every projected meaning – including every contradictory meaning – is as good as any other, and where everything is the correct answer, nothing is the correct answer.

Gesture is another useful object of comparison for works of art. How much can we learn about a gesture from looking at the position or movement of a body part? The 'V'-sign made with the first two fingers of the hand can either be a gesture of abuse or it can symbolize victory. Which is which depends again entirely on the context and intention with which it is used. Showing the feet in Thailand is thought to be deeply offensive, but in Western Europe the gesture is without particular significance. Whether it is offensive or not depends once again entirely on context and intention. The same considerations apply to less formalized actions. Going clubbing is just a normal activity in youth; it causes comment and alarm in the middle-aged. Wearing a twinset and pearls expresses perhaps good taste and conservatism in the older woman; the outfit would have a different meaning if I were wearing it now.

The moral of these considerations is that you cannot begin to understand a segment of language or a gesture when you do not know its origin and context. If someone is shown a picture of a hand, foot or inscription, and is asked to assess the meaning and significance of what is shown, then it would not be at all surprising if he made errors. In addition, if the person showing the pictures found these errors wildly funny, it would be him – rather than the person trying to interpret the pictures – who'd be thought foolish.

I am not claiming that works of art are gestures or form part of a language, but I am claiming that both comparisons can help loosen the grip of the analogy between works of art and natural objects. However, I think it's true to say that both words and works of art possess what Searle calls 'secondary intentionality', where objects in the world become imbued by, and become natural extensions of, thought.[21]

[21] See his *Intentionality: An Essay in the Philosophy of Mind* (Cambridge: CUP, 1983), 160–79.

V

Let me move closer to the issue of fakes by saying something about the role of conventions in art and art appreciation.

In the Zion and Bryce canyons in Utah, there is a rock which, through millions of years of weathering and erosion, has come to look like the elderly Queen Victoria. Let us suppose, for the sake of example, that the rock in Zion-Bryce is molecule-for-molecule identical to an undistinguished statue of Queen Victoria, erected towards the end of her reign in some remote corner of London. Can we ascribe the same aesthetic properties to the rock that we can to the statue? Clearly not.

One thing which I can say about the statue which I cannot say about the rock is that it depicts Queen Victoria. The rock may resemble Queen Victoria, it's true, but resemblance isn't enough for depiction. To begin with, resemblance is a symmetrical relation whereas depiction isn't. If the statue resembles Victoria then Victoria resembles the statue; but if the statue depicts Victoria then it does not follow that Victoria depicts her statue.

Similarly, many things resemble one another which do not depict one another. One identical twin resembles the other identical twin, but one twin does not depict the other. There may also be many people who resemble the statue more than Victoria does, but this does not entail that the statue depicts them rather than Victoria. And it's probably true that every statue of Victoria more closely resembles every other statue of Victoria more than any of them do the Queen, but the fact remains that each depicts the Queen rather than all the other statues. For depiction – as opposed to straightforward representation – some degree of resemblance is necessary, but it is by no means sufficient.[22]

Even more obviously, we can ascribe many more particular properties to the statue which we cannot ascribe to the rock. For example: the statue is staid, conventional, smug, naturalistic, conservative, old fashioned, flattering, sentimental, influenced by Donatello, unironic, ineptly posed, cluttered, High Victorian, unimaginative, grovelling, boldly realized, skilfully modelled, and a tribute to Millais. In addition, we might say it expresses the confidence of Empire, captures her ordinariness, is a virtuoso exercise, or shows no understanding of its medium. None of these things can be truly predicated of the rock.

---

[22] Most of these arguments are found in Goodman, *Languages of Art*, 1–43.

M.W. Rowe

The rock and the statue are identical *objects* because they share a manifest type; but only one of them is also a *work*.[23]

VI

Given the example above, it is not difficult to see that there can be a difference between two *works* even though they share a manifest type and have identical objects.

Art is heavily convention-governed, and unless you understand the conventions in play, you do not understand the work you are contemplating. Let me elaborate on one of Kendall Walton's examples.[24] Imagine, on your left, a very large marble portrait bust of a Roman senator the nose of which has been damaged in the course of time. Now imagine, on your right, another work, made by a ludic, postmodern artist, perhaps to highlight and make fun of the conventions of portrait busts. Both objects, needless to say, are molecule-for-molecule identical; if their positions were reversed over night, then it would not be possible to discover, just from examining the objects themselves, which is which. And yet these objects could be vehicles for, could realize, utterly different works.

The statue on your left is a larger-than-life depiction of a normal sized man; a normally coloured man; a living man who can move; a man with a normal nose. Perhaps it has a title: *Valarius Maximus*. The one on your right is a life-sized depiction of a giant; a mottled albino; severed below the shoulders, dead and immobile, with a mutilated nose, impaled on an ornate spike. It too has a title: *Dead Mutilated Albino Giant Severed Below the Shoulders and Impaled on an Ornate Spike*. Because each work has different representational qualities, they have different aesthetic qualities including those which contain an evaluation. The work on your left is conventional, staid, solemn, and straightforward. The one on your right is original, grotesque, witty, cruel, irreverent, ironic, self-conscious and allusive. As works they are very different; and yet no two objects could be more alike.

This example is clearly drawn from the realm of theory, but mistakes about artistic conventions occur in real life, and sometimes they can vitiate a judgement. I remember once attending a concert whose second half ended with a very crisply executed performance

---

[23] I take this terminology from Peter Lamarque, 'Work and Object' in his *Work and Object*, 56–77.
[24] Walton, 'Categories of Art', 147.

of a *concerto grosso* by Handel. As we were leaving, a man behind me said to his companion that he thought the performance had been pretty poor: 'The sound kept coming and going', he said, 'and the orchestra wasn't together.' The only possible explanation for this was that he didn't realize that much of the interest of a *concerto grosso* depends on the contrast between the agility and lightness of a small group of soloists, and the weightier sound of the full body of strings. The man behind me, it would seem, had heard (in some sense of 'heard') a scrappy account of a string serenade or something similar, where most of the players weren't up to the technical demands of their parts.

What determines which conventions apply to a particular object? It is quite clear that they are determined not by those who see, hear or otherwise perceive it, but by the person who made or adapted the object. Indeed, the title an artist gives his work can have an enormous impact on our response. We can see this if we imagine a post-modern artist who decides to re-make and re-title some acknowledged masterpieces. Suppose Rodin's *The Kiss* were re-made as *Incest*; suppose Cézanne's *Still Life* were re-painted as *Poisoned Fruit*; suppose Goya's *Shootings of the 3ʳᵈ May* were re-painted as *A Night at the Opera*. Wouldn't our responses change out of all recognition, despite the fact that the earlier and later work in each case share a manifest type?

VII

In choosing the examples described above, I have clearly tried to pick cases where discovering that an object has one origin rather than another, or conforms to one set of conventions rather than another, has a decisive and obvious effect on our understanding. Clearly a fake is a case where the forger tries to preserve the conventions governing the genre he fakes, but I shall argue, nonetheless, that exposing something as a fake has a legitimate effect on our approach and attitude.

Consider again Lassman's Jane Austen hoax. How did Austen's original readers respond to her work? One thing stuck all of them: her novels contained virtually nothing that readers had come to expect in a novel. For example in May 1813, Annabella Milbanke (later Lady Byron) wrote:

> I have finished the Novel called *Pride and Prejudice*, which I think a very superior piece of work. It depends not on any of

the common resources of novel writers, no drownings, no confla-
grations, nor runaway horses, nor lapdogs and parrots, no cham-
bermaids and milliners, nor rencontres [duels] and disguises. I
really think it is the most *probable* I have ever read. It is not a
crying book, but the interest is very strong, especially for Mr
Darcy. The characters which are not amiable are diverting, and
all of them are consistently supported.[25]

This set of observations was endorsed by William Gifford two years
later:

I have for the first time looked into *P. and P.* and it is really a
pretty thing. No dark passages; no secret chambers; no wind-
howlings or long galleries; no drops of blood upon a rusty
dagger – things that should now be left to ladies' maids and sentimental washerwomen.[26]

Equally absent, are depictions of the upper ranks of the nobility, plots
turning on mistaken identities, hidden then rediscovered wills, virtuous maids fighting off male sexual predators, abductions and rapes,
protracted and pathetic scenes of illness, extended declarations of pas-
sionate love, violence of any kind, plots based on mistaken parentage,
politics, foreign intrigues and travel.[27] Sir Walter Scott summarizes
the revolution in the novel Austen largely brought about in his
review of *Emma*:

[*Emma*] belongs to a class of fictions which has arisen almost in
our own times, and which draws the characters and incidents introduced more immediately from the current of ordinary life
than was permitted by the former rules of the novel [...]
copying nature as she really exists in the common walks of life,
and presenting to the reader, instead of splendid scenes of the
imaginary world, a correct and striking representation of that
which is taking place around him.[28]

[25] Annabella Milbanke, letter, 1st May 1813, to her mother, in *Lord
Byron's Wife*, Malcolm Edwin, 159. Quoted in B.C. Southam, *Jane
Austen: The Critical Heritage*, vol.1, 1811–1870 (London: Routledge,
1968, 2 vols), 8.
[26] William Gifford, letter September (?) 1815, in *A Publisher and his
Friends*, ed., Samuel Smiles, vol.1, 282. Quoted in Southam, *Jane Austen*, 8.
[27] See http://www.pemberley.com/janeinfo/janeart.html accessed 25/
10/2010
[28] Sir Walter Scott, unsigned review of *Emma*, *Quarterly Review*, dated
October 1815, issued March 1816, XIV, 188–201. Reprinted in Southam,
Jane Austen, 59 and 73.

Early readers were so dazzled by this accomplishment, that they tended to overlook equally revolutionary aspects of Austen's art: the development of an ironic narrative voice, the extended use of free indirect discourse, and depictions of conversations where characters talk over and ignore one another.

Now suppose you are an intelligent and well informed publisher's reader who is suddenly presented with three chapters and a synopsis of *Northanger Abbey* disguised as a new novel. If you do not recognize the typescript, what would your reaction be, and how would this differ from that of the original readers?

To begin with, I imagine you would realize that what you are being presented with is a *pastiche*: a fiction purporting to be written in the late eighteenth or early nineteenth century. This of course did not strike Austen's original readers, who found the style utterly up to date and contemporary. In addition, the modern reader is more than familiar with novels that deal with the common affairs of daily life – they have themselves become absolutely commonplace - whereas early readers, as we've seen, were dazzled and occasionally baffled by anything so startling and original.[29]

Secondly, I imagine you would soon realize that the book has a satirical target – the late eighteenth-century Gothic Romance, such as Mrs Radcliffe's *The Mysteries of Udolpho*. A comment Austen makes just before Catherine Moreland's journey to Bath would alert you to this: '[...] The parting took place and the journey began. It was performed with suitable quietness and uneventful safety. Neither robbers nor tempests befriended them, nor one lucky overturn [of the coach] to introduce them to the hero.'[30]

On reading this passage, the modern reader may well ask why, of all the things the writer could have satirised, he has lighted on the eighteenth century Gothic romance. Certainly, many clichés of that genre have been absorbed by modern romantic films and fiction, but these

[29] The question of how two physically indistinguishable texts can embody completely different aesthetic qualities was, of course, first raised and explored in Jorge Luis Borges, 'Pierre Menard, Author of the Quixote,' in *Labyrinths: Selected Stories and Other Writings*, eds, Donald A. Yates and James E. Irby, trans., James E. Irby (Harmondsworth: Penguin Books, 2000), 62–7.

[30] Jane Austen, *Northanger Abbey and Persuasion*, ed., John Davie, textual notes and bibliography by James Kinsley (Oxford: OUP, 1975), 16. In my quotations, I have left the names of Austen's heroine untouched. Readers who want completely to recreate the experience of Lassman's publishers' readers will need to substitute 'Susan' and 'the Maldorns' for 'Catherine' and 'the Morelands'.

M.W. Rowe

commonplaces have been satirised many times before (not least by Jane Austen); and is the eighteenth-century Gothic romance so prominent in our culture as to require novel-length satire? Why choose this dusty object when so many other and more necessary targets offer themselves? Again, this reaction would not be shared by the original readers: the Gothic Romance, as the reactions of Milbanke and Gifford show, was omnipresent and oppressive, and corrective satire both appropriate and necessary. In writing a novel early in her career attacking its conventions, Austen is self-consciously and explicitly clearing a space for herself and her art.

Other aspects of the typescript's satire will be harder to understand. Just before the journey to Bath, Catherine takes leave of her sister Sally:

> It is remarkable, however, that she neither insisted on Catherine's writing by every post, nor extracted her promise of transmitting the character of every new acquaintance, nor a detail of every interesting conversation that Bath might produce. Every thing indeed relative to this important journey was done, on the part of the Morelands, with a degree of moderation and composure, which seemed rather consistent with the common feelings of life, than with the refined sensibilities, the tender emotions which the first separation of a heroine from her family ought always to excite.[31]

If the target here is the behaviour of heroines in modern film and prose romances, then it's difficult to see the point of this passage; after all, most modern romantic heroines don't seem to spend long periods of time writing letters. You will have to assume that the target is the kind of exaggerated closeness between sisters sometimes found in romantic novelettes; or perhaps romantic *professions* of closeness and undying love. But to Jane Austen's first readers, the main target of the satire was obvious. Many eighteenth-century novels were in epistolary form, and one artificiality of the genre is that the heroine, as well as surviving shipwrecks and fighting off male predators, has to spend an inordinate amount of time writing letters. (Many have wondered, for example, how Richardson's Clarissa Harlowe, in addition to writing two million words, finds the time to undergo the experiences she's writing about.) But the epistolary novel is no longer a standard form for modern novelists, and to spend time guying its awkwardness in a modern novel seems perverse.

---

[31]   Austen, *Northanger Abbey*, 16.

166

VIII

We now return to the aspect of Austen's art which struck early readers most forcefully: its clear-eyed naturalism, its low-key probability, its careful observation of people and their manners. But reading a Regency novelist observing the manners and foibles of her own age is one thing; reading a modern novelist describing the manners and foibles of how he *imagines* the Regency period to be is quite another. The work of the modern novelist can only be a matter of laborious and quite possibly inaccurate reconstruction; so why not simply turn to the work of Regency novelists themselves, who were in a much better position to know what life at this period was like, and who have more than covered this ground already? In addition, the average modern reader will not find a portrayal of eighteenth century foibles interesting if those foibles disappeared with the eighteenth century; he will only be gripped if we continue to suffer from these foibles now. But if we continue to suffer from them now, why not show that this is the case by using a contemporary setting?

The reason many modern novelists turn to the early nineteenth century is that it seems to offer opportunities for romance and adventure that the twentieth century lacks: the absoluteness of class boundaries; the sense that much of the world was not properly explored; the splendours of dress; the camaraderie and terrors of life on board a wooden fighting ship. Different genres of the historical novel exploit different distinctive aspects of the period. The Georgette Heyer variety exploits the clothes, manners and class distinctions; while the Patrick O'Brien variety exploits the suspense and heroism of warfare in Nelson's navy. Moreover, there are serious novels which use other features of the period: William Golding's *Rites of Passage*, written in pastiche early nineteenth-century prose, explores the psychological effects of the confinement and excitement of a voyage to Australia lasting many months. We understand quite well why these novelists chose this period.

But how do Lassman's typescripts exploit the distinctive features of their chosen period? The opening chapters of *Northanger Abbey* present an account of the tedium of Regency Bath; the opening chapters of *Persuasion*, show a genteel family having to economize. It's not at all clear that topics this low-key and commonplace warrant setting a novel 200 years in the past: how exactly is the setting being exploited? What does this period have to show about social tedium and genteel economizing that the modern period cannot?

Oddly, modern novelists choose the early nineteenth century precisely because it offers all the things Jane Austen largely abjured – Romantic settings, dare-devil escapes, ostentation, hand to hand combat, pirates, betrayals, and so forth. Consequently, when critics want to point to twentieth and twenty-first century novelists who write like Jane Austen, they do not point to Heyer, O'Brien and Golding and other novelists who use early nineteenth-century settings, but to Anita Brookner or Barbara Pym, novelists who write carefully observed fictions about the less dramatic features of contemporary life. Jane Austen now would have every reason for not writing like Jane Austen then.

When it was first written, *Northanger Abbey* was intended to be read largely by middle-class provincial women on whom time hung heavy; and it was also intended to be read against the background of the sprawling *Mysteries of Udolpho* and – Jane Austen's favourite – Richardson's *Sir Charles Grandison*. In this context, Austen's performance can only seem light, sparkling, rapid, delightful. But a modern novel – as Lassman's is – cannot, for good commercial reasons, be intended to be read only by people who want to take months in reading it. And it is read against the background, not of Richardson and collections of sermons, but Philip Roth, *Pulp Fiction*, Twitter, and so forth. For the modern reader, who is not primed to make allowances, Lassman's typescript can only seem painfully slow and laborious.

The typescript is also likely to seem puzzlingly coy and prudish. Clearly, the modern historical romance can portray the steamiest sexual details, and the reader might well wonder why this resource is not better utilized, or what this self-denial signifies. But no original Jane Austen reader found her prudish or her reticence puzzling: she was simply following the conventions and laws of her own time, and, as such, roused no comment at all.

Lastly, the modern reader is likely to think the typescript is learned and accurate pastiche but that it pushes its erudition rather beyond the range of the average modern reader. Consider the following:

> Her mother was three months teaching her only to repeat the 'Beggar's Petition;' and after all, her next sister Sally, could say it better than she did. Not that Catherine was always stupid, – by no means; she learnt the fable of "The Hare and many Friends" as quickly as any girl in England.[32]

One is not in a position fully to comprehend the significance of this information until you know what the 'Beggar's Petition' and 'The Hare and many Friends' are. Are they prose works? Are they both

---

[32]   Austen, *Northanger Abbey*, 2.

fables? Are they poems? Are they songs? How difficult or lengthy are these works, and are they both of about the same length and difficulty? After all, if 'The Hare and his Friends' is a much longer or more difficult work than the 'Beggar's Petition' then this will go some way towards overturning the evidence that Catherine is rather stupid.

You will not be able to answer these questions fully unless you are familiar with the 'Beggar's Petition' (a frequently reprinted didactic poem from the Revd Thomas Moss's *Poems on Several Occasions* from 1769), and 'The Hare and his Friends' (from John Gay's *Fables* of 1727).[33] Once, no doubt, these poems were utterly familiar to any novel-reader, but now their obscurity stands as an obstacle to the modern reader's understanding and enjoyment. Of course, one can take some educated guesses, but the examples seem ill-judged in a modern historical novel: why not chose some simple eighteenth-century poems or fables which are still familiar? – the choice is wide enough.

Jane Austen was faced with one set of options, and the significance and wisdom of the choices she made must be judged against the options available to her. The modern novelist is presented with another set of options, and the significance and wisdom of the choices he makes must be set against the options available to him. It is thus not surprising that a set of ordered words in one period should be an important novel, and the same set of ordered words in a later period should not be considered publishable. After all, the inscription TOTAL SLUT seen against the options available in Swedish, is very different from TOTAL SLUT seen against the options available in English.

In sum, whereas the original readers found Austen's work focused, witty, intelligible, contemporary, racy and revolutionary; the modern reader, faced with Lassman's hoax, is liable to find the same words in the same order arbitrary, unmotivated, unoriginal, dated, slow, esoteric and coy; no more than a satirical pastiche whose satirical targets have long faded from view.[34] Lassman presented a work

---

[33]   Austen, *Northanger Abbey*, 473.

[34]   *Northanger Abbey* was probably written in 1798 or 1799 and it was sold to a publisher called Crosby in 1803 for £10. He did not publish the novel and was only willing to let Austen enter a contract with another publisher if she returned the money he had paid for it. Eventually, the novelist's brother, Henry, bought back the manuscript from Crosby in 1816, and it was finally published in 1818, a year after Austen's death. The relevance of this story to the topic of the present paper is how concerned Austen

which shared the same manifest type as *Northanger Abbey* – he presented an identical *object* to his readers – but he presented a wholly different *work*.

I now turn to Kreisler and Greenhalgh whose cases can be treated more briefly.

IX

Let us suppose that Kreisler's *Leibesleid* and a waltz by Lanner share a manifest type. Are we justified in responding to them in different ways once we know one is by Kreisler and the other by Lanner? I think the answer must be 'Yes'.

Joseph Lanner (1801–43) is a minor composer but his music is nonetheless attractive, distinctive and innovative. He was one of the composers who is largely responsible for turning the triple-time German Dance and Ländler, used by Mozart and Beethoven, into the modern Viennese concert waltz. Composing for his own orchestra, he introduced richer harmonies, sweeping melodies, and greater use of minor keys. Above all, he assisted in the development of three features which are now thought distinctive of the modern Viennese waltz: a marginally quicker tempo than the Ländler;[35] a slight delay on the second beat of the bar; and the utilization of syncopated melodies.

Although it was the older Strauss, in about 1830, who developed the common format of the modern Viennese concert waltz – a sequence of five waltzes with an introduction and coda – it was Lanner who developed the waltz's introduction (by introducing different tempi and time-signatures), and made the coda more clinching climactic by exploiting themes already used in the main body of the work. He was also one of the first composers to *name* his waltzes, a practice taken up and made familiar by the older and younger Johann Strauss.

---

was by the delay: she clearly felt that the vogue for Gothic novels had waned, and that a book published after 1816 which satirizes a fashion of the late 1790s had missed its moment. She herself may well have contributed to the waning of this vogue. (*Northanger Abbey*, vii–xiv). Presumably, she would have felt even less sanguine about the commercial and artistic prospects of a work with the same manifest type published for the first time in 2007.

[35] Kreisler does not imitate this particular innovation of Lanner's: the speed indication for *Liebesleid* is 'Tempo di Ländler'.

When we listen to Lanner's work we should also bear in mind its cultural and political milieu. Metternich's Vienna was run on totalitarian lines, and estimates of the number of police informers vary between six and ten thousand. Accommodation was in short supply and medical conditions were appalling: there were regular epidemics of typhus and cholera, and nearly half of the adults who died were under twenty. The dance halls where Lanner and the elder Strauss ran their orchestras were patronized by people from middle classes backgrounds, but the majority of their clientele came from the working classes.[36] Such gatherings inevitably raised the spectre of disorder for the authorities, a spectre made worse by the evident and shocking sensuality of the new waltzes. One contemporary writer turns the dance into a kind of *Totentanz*:

> As soon as the women are touched by the man's arm, a feverish thrill passes through them. They put their head on his shoulder, their breast close to his, and let themselves be swept about. In this voluptuous posture, and to this lascivious music, they imbibe his every movement. Imploringly innocence flees, terrified from the hall; femininity throws herself beseechingly at their feet; and death stands in the corner and laughs up his sleeve.[37]

In consequence, we should hear Lanner's work as innovative, radical, inventive, a stepping stone between Schubert and Johann Strauss the younger; and an invitation to sensual release that offered working people some relief from the oppressive conditions of pre-1848 Vienna. Kreisler's work, on the other hand, is none of these things: it is middle-class music, deeply nostalgic, backward-looking and conservative, that is in some sense *about* an image of old Vienna – but a lilac-tinted confection that never existed in reality. My objection to Dr Schmidt is not that he misidentified a Kreisler piece as one by Lanner – this was perfectly reasonable, he had been told it was by Lanner and it sounds like Lanner – but that, with his talk of delightful Schubertian melos and the good old Vienna days, he falsifies how Lanner should be heard.

Of course, if we are asked to judge blind, we cannot tell the difference between Kreisler's work and the hypothetical work by Lanner; but the same is true of the two inscriptions of PAIN FORMIDABLE meaning *terrible pain* and *wonderful bread*, the Roman senator and the

[36] Alice M.Hanson, *Musical Life in Biedermeir Vienna*, Cambridge Studies in Music (Cambridge: CUP, 1985), 168.
[37] Hanson, *Vienna*, 163. Translation revised.

albino giant, the rock and the statue. We must not confuse epistemology with ontology.

X

We have Gauguin to thank for Western art's turn away from the immediate everyday world of the Impressionists – with their parks, picnics, rivers, stations and beach scenes – towards the primitive. One aspect of this primitivism is his engagement with medieval art. He helped develop the technique of Cloisonism – where perspective is in abeyance, and thick black lines surround unshaded blocks of colour – and this is clearly influenced by stained-glass techniques; and we can see further medieval influence in his use of symbols, visions and distortion. Another aspect of his primitivism is the way his paintings from Tahiti not only extend painting's geographical range, but introduce animal totems, exaggerated bodily proportions, and vibrant colours into western art.

If we read through his letters, we find that the discovery of his own voice and style was agonizingly slow, and that the journey was beset by disappointments, cul-de-sacs, misjudgements and personal sacrifices. However, the way he turned art away from focusing on western civilization, and, in particular, his use of geometrical blocks of two-dimensional colour, are major influences on twentieth century culture, especially on the work of Picasso and Matisse, and the designs for the *Ballet Russe*.

In contrast, Shaun Greenhalgh did not spend years of disappointment and self-sacrifice discovering a personal style; he was not responsible for Western art's turn towards the primitive, and he did not influence Picasso and Matisse. The work he produced represents a faun just as Gauguin's might have done; and it follows the conventions of sculpture in just the way Gauguin might have done. But what Greenhalgh cannot put into his work is the originality, insight, discovery and innovation Gauguin put into his; and consequently Greenhalgh's achievement cannot approach Gauguin's.

XI

To repeat a witty remark is not to be witty; to transcribe a report of a scientific discovery is not to make a scientific discovery; and, in the same way, to copy a work of art or a certain style of art, cannot approach the achievement of creating a work of art or discovering a style.

It is for these reasons that we place the achievements of the *pasticheur*, forger and mimic, below that of the original artist. The forger often has a splendid technique and a chameleon-like talent for imitation, but what he lacks is individual vision, inspiration and originality. On the other hand, there are many artists who lack some aspects of conventional technique (perhaps Berlioz as harmonist, Chopin as orchestrator) and yet they overcome these deficiencies, and became acknowledged masters, precisely because of their individual vision, inspiration and originality.

If we want to write a good pastiche, we know the work we must study, the critics we must read, the features we must examine, and the kind of trial and error we must engage in. Producing copies and pastiches is a *technical* problem: everyone knows how to set about solving it. But founding an influential movement in art, seeing the world in a wholly new way, developing a unique personal style, is not a technical problem. We do not know how to go about solving it; we do not know where to look for a solution. This is what makes being an artist so much more difficult than being a *pasticheur*.

XII

The argument of this paper, means that sameness of manifest type is not enough for sameness of work, otherwise Kreisler and Lanner, Austen and Lassman would have produced the same work. Instead, a work is not only identified by its manifest features, but also by the non-manifest features of its context, history and the intentions with which it was made. This means that one work may differ from another in the way that a fake of a known work differs from a perfectly innocent copy: physically the latter pairing may be indistinguishable and the relevant difference may only reside in the different intentions with which they were created. Ultimately, discovering a work of art's identity means tracing the appropriate causal chain back from the scattered tokens to the relevant intentions of the person who conceived it. These intentions will only become comprehensible when we understand the choices and conventions the artist confronted, and these in their turn will only become comprehensible when they are placed in their historical context. In other words, a work's historical context is *part of the work*; we cannot detach works of art from art history.

This means Kreisler was quite wrong to say of discovered fakes, 'The name changes, the value remains'. The change of name means a different person, and this often means a different place and a different time. This entails a different set of options; possibly a different set of conventions; and this ensures the choices made will have different meanings. These factors in their turn can create a new set of aesthetic qualities, and these will often affect a work's aesthetic value.

To try and detach works of art from the making of art is like trying to sunder gestures from gesturing, or words from speaking, because when gestures and words are completely understood they are recognized to embody the intentions which lead to their creation. It would be quite false to think these intentions are just distant causal events which are left behind in the past, because they continue to suffuse and imbue a work as long as the work exists; and this is true whether or not anybody now knows about them. A work is immanent in its token patterns, and those tokens contain and embody the history and context of their creation. This is the truth, I think, in the old Idealist claim that works of art are in some sense mental: they cannot exist but for human intentions, and works cannot be recognized for what they are unless we recognize these intentions.[38]

Consequently, if you are asked to judge the quality of a work when you do not know whether it is by Kreisler or Lanner, Gauguin or Greenhalgh, then the correct response is to decline because the important non-manifest qualities of the work have been withheld from you. There used to be a programme on the BBC's Radio 3 called *The Innocent Ear*. This played pieces of music without telling the listener what they were or who they were by; the implication being that knowing these things before judging was in some sense guilty or suspect. But knowing what a work of art's non-manifest features are is a prerequisite for knowing what the work of art's aesthetic qualities are – it is often the only way you can tell if a work is straight or ironic, satirical or non-satirical, clever or commonplace, original or unoriginal, realistic or fantasy, genuine or pastiche – and to try to judge in the absence of this information is like trying to judge a colour picture from a black and white photograph, or a novel which has its first chapter missing.

I've encountered two main objections to the view I'm proposing here. The first is that it's snobbish. It means you can't just look at paintings or listen to music; you have to be educated and know things about the works you contemplate. I think the reasoning here is true. You can get a certain amount out of just experiencing a work's manifest features, but sometimes the manifest features alone

---

[38]   On aesthetic Idealism, see R.G. Collingwood, *The Principles of Art* (Oxford: OUP, 1977), 139–151, and Wollheim, *Art and Its Objects*, 51–61.

will be inert or misleading. Of course, I don't accept that this makes my view snobbish. It may require a certain level of knowledge to understand the text on a seed-packet, but nobody thinks asserting this fact is snobbish; and artistic knowledge is open to all in exactly the same way that horticultural knowledge is open to all.

The other objection comes from the opposite direction. 'Aesthetic pleasure,' it runs, 'should be autonomous and unalloyed: unsullied by gossip about political history, society, artistic trends, details about artists' personal lives, and so forth. Art requires that we detach an object from its quotidian background, and surrender ourselves to pure and thought-free contemplation.' There is also a certain amount of truth in this view – while contemplating works of art we should concentrate on the work and put immediate practical projects and bias into abeyance – but it can give no account of why a response to a Victorian statue is inappropriate to a virgin rock in Utah.

In the end, both objections should cancel one another out, and leave us not with a highbrow view or a lowbrow view, but with complex and sobering truth.[39]

University of East Anglia
Mark.Rowe@uea.ac.uk

[39]   I would like to thank Clive Ashwin, Stephen Everson, Marie McGinn, Anthony O'Hear, Catherine Osborne, Anthony Price, Beth Savickey, and audiences at UEA, the Welsh Philosophical Society, and the Royal Institute of Philosophy, for discussions of this paper.

Music, Metaphor and Society: Some Thoughts on Scruton[1]

ROBERT GRANT

Roger Scruton's 530-page blockbuster *The Aesthetics of Music* was published by Oxford University Press in 1997.[2] A paperback edition followed two years later. Neither received more than a handful of notices, a few appreciative, but some grudging and some actually hostile. As its quality has come to be recognized, and as the resentments it provoked have either died down or found newer targets, the book has gradually achieved a certain canonical, even classic, status. Students of the subject now seem to feel that, however unpalatable some of its conclusions may have been, it can no longer safely be ignored. The questions, it appears, are the right ones, even if we don't care for Scruton's answers. (Thus far the pop critic Simon Frith, who said as much from the start.)[3]

The book actually covers more than aesthetics, being nothing less than a complete philosophy of music. There are some major omissions: of non-Western music, for example. But they are justifiable, given that Scruton's project is analytical rather than documentary. Some extra-aesthetic matter is inevitable, since it is scarcely possible to deal in isolation with any art form's purely aesthetic element (assuming there really could be such a thing). But with music Scruton casts his net wider even than he did in his early *The Aesthetics of Architecture* (1979). In *The Aesthetics of Music* he extends his inquiry to virtually every aspect and ramification of the phenomenon in question. (His book *Sexual Desire* [1986] aspired to a similar comprehensiveness regarding matters still more elusive and even less tractable.)

One reason for the present work's greater scope is presumably that Scruton has not so far numbered the practice of architecture among

---

[1]   I am most grateful to Roger Scruton and Guy Dammann for their comments on the penultimate version of this article. They are not to blame for any remaining inadequacies.

[2]   References to this work are indicated henceforth by unprefixed page numbers in the main text.

[3]   'Sound and Fury', *Prospect*, no. 26, January 1998.

doi:10.1017/S1358246112000173

his accomplishments (though he has built, in polychrome brick, a most aesthetic pigsty). Over and above the theoretical discussions in *The Aesthetics of Music*, the book's sheer density of technical detail testifies to a serious practitioner's interest (there are 250 musical quotations). Scruton makes no great claims for his own compositions, but once or twice quotes from them in illustration of some minor point. He has written a couple of chamber operas in broadly tonal, semi-Brittenesque idiom, one of which, *The Minister*, has been performed several times at home and abroad. As he says, he cannot compete in this respect with another philosopher, Rousseau, whose opera *The Village Soothsayer* drew praise from Gluck himself, and had 400 performances. Nevertheless, in the generous words of his critic and rival in aesthetics Jerrold Levinson, Scruton's musical culture is 'simply astounding'. Even if, like Levinson, one dissents (as I do not) from Scruton's 'phenomenological-idealist' assumptions,[4] one might still agree with him that *The Aesthetics of Music* is not only 'the most valuable work to date on the subject', but also 'an advanced primer in the appreciation of music, one worthy to be set alongside those of distinguished predecessors such as Copland, Bernstein and Tovey'.[5]

A reader familiar with Scruton's other works, which include two witty fictions in mock-Platonic dialogue – *Xanthippic Dialogues* and *Perictione in Colophon*, both containing much about music[6] – will soon perceive that *The Aesthetics of Music* follows the general drift. I do not mean that Scruton simply clamps the same ideological grid over every topic he treats and then reads off the approved answers. On the contrary, he always begins with the phenomenon as generally experienced, and works back to the underlying principles. A radical anti-reductionist, Scruton has never tried to hypostatize those principles into a catch-all theory. If they converge, that

---

[4]   It is hard to see, in fact, how one could dissent from them while continuing, with Levinson, to treat music as music rather than as a purely acoustic or sensory event, which seem to be the only realist alternatives. (Deryck Cooke's exhaustively-documented claim that music is substantially a language, with an established vocabulary, is surely not 'realist' in any strict sense.) This is not to say that 'phenomenological-idealist' assumptions must be valid across the entire range of human experience. Only a post-modernist would think them applicable (e.g.) to science.

[5]   *The Philosophical Review*, Vol. **109**, No. 4 (October 2000), 608–614.

[6]   Calling itself a 'discourse on music', the first half of Ch. 10 of *Perictione in Colophon* (South Bend: St Augustine's Press, 2000, 208–223) illustrates many of the main ideas behind *The Aesthetics of Music* in dramatically vivid and compressed form.

testifies less to a one-track mind on his part than to his having uncovered a genuine, common reality, one no less objective for being founded, not in physical nature, let alone in the supernatural, but in historic human experience, which is 'objective' in the qualified sense of simply being shared.[7] If Scruton persuades us, that is for no fancier reason than that we recognize that this, in fact, is the way things seem. Ours is a world of seeming, not being; or rather, since there is no escape from it, seeming, for all practical purposes, *is* being.

All Scruton's thinking is humanistic, in the sense that it postulates a clearly-demarcated, definitively human 'world' or *Lebenswelt*, whose values, pursuits and conceptions are to be understood first and foremost in their own terms. Such things are not to be explained from outside, as simply passive functions, products or epiphenomena of the underlying material processes – political, economic, physical, biological and so on – on which they may variously depend. Further, unlike other brands, Scruton's humanism is neither sentimental, nor anti-religious, nor incompatible with religion, at least in his own largely non-doctrinal understanding of it. For him religion is definitively and uniquely human, as are music, morals and the erotic.

All these things are unknown in the animal world. The higher animals manifestly have immediate, action-guiding beliefs (at least to judge by their behaviour), but neither religious beliefs, nor any beliefs they could articulate. To attribute *opinions* to an animal – that is, settled beliefs regarding categories of events both actual and possible, independently of particular instances (though applicable to and ideally generalized from them) – is absurd or comic, and quite literally the stuff of fable (for example, Chaucer's cock Chauntecleer learnedly discussing dream interpretation). Animals make decisions, but on the spot, not self-consciously, and certainly not in the light of ethical conceptions, as we do. They are not moral beings, and are therefore not answerable for their actions. They have no duties, and their so-called rights are merely our shorthand for the importance we attach to their welfare. They have sexual urges, as they have affections, but not erotic experience, since that involves not the mere conjunction of organs, but the mutual disclosure and embodiment of selves. Often more acutely than we, animals hear and can discriminate between sounds; birds 'sing', as lions roar, apparently with communicative intent, but, however pleasing the

---

[7] Mass delusions are shared too, but concern objective states of affairs from which they are distinct, and against which they can be measured. The experiences of which I speak are themselves the objective state of affairs.

Robert Grant

result, their song is not, in Scruton's terms, music, any more than a hyena's so-called laugh testifies to its sense of humour.

It is plausible to conclude, with Aristotle and others, that animals' limitations in the foregoing respects are due to their lack of self-consciousness, and that that in turn is due to their lack of language. For language alone can capture whatever lies beyond the moment – self, past, future, projects, ideas, possibilities, imaginary or hypothetical situations, other selves – and hold it suspended in contemplation. (That, however, is not to equate music directly with language, as we shall see.)

Scruton's key distinction in this book, from which all else stems, is between sound and tone. Very little work has been done on the metaphysics and ontology of sound, as the comparative sparseness of Scruton's references in Chapter 1 indicates. This chapter contains some exceedingly novel, interesting and true observations, such as that sounds, unlike most visual objects, are not opaque, so that one sound does not occlude another.[8] Further, sounds, unlike colours, are not qualities or properties, but objects, albeit 'secondary objects', like smells and rainbows. They are 'pure events',[9] conceptually isolable from their material sources, and constituting their own independent 'sound world'.

The sound world, Scruton claims, is a quasi-spatial order, in which we detect both position (high and low, i.e. pitch) and consequently movement (for example, 'up' and 'down'), though those things, like much else under consideration, are what he calls 'indispensable metaphors',[10] an expression which, as we shall see, has caused much (to my mind) superfluous trouble. We might add that although Scruton speaks of position and movement as applying to pitched tones and sequences thereof, they apply equally well to noise. Consider the Doppler effect, to the ears of a stationary listener, generated by a fast-moving noise-emitting object, a train, say, or a projectile. Or the see-saw, indeed hee-haw, undulations of a siren or a car alarm. Even noise can be high or low, and thus appear to move 'up' or 'down'.[11]

---

[8] Scruton, *The Aesthetics of Music*, 13, 338
[9] Scruton, *The Aesthetics of Music*, 12, 10
[10] Scruton, *The Aesthetics of Music*, 19ff. etc.
[11] When an actual *tone* is made to 'slide' up or down, it seems as though we cannot continue to call it a tone (since we think of tones as having fixed pitches). So what are we to call it? Glissandi in music are sometimes virtual, being no more than very rapid runs (e.g. on the harp, or when swiped with a thumb- or fingernail on the piano), in other words a blurred succession of

Though it belongs to the sound-world (in other words, *is* sound), tone differs from sound in general in being one step – a crucial one – further removed from the realm of primary objects, substances and the rest, viz. in being a 'tertiary object'.[12] Sounds might seem 'material' in comparison to tones, but they are immaterial (and thus 'secondary') in comparison to their physical source (a flute, an explosion) and description (audible pressure waves or vibrations induced in a suitable medium by a flute, an explosion, etc.).

Tone is a 'tertiary' phenomenon in that it belongs exclusively to the intentional realm, which is to say, the human or self-conscious order, the world of deliberate meanings and purposes. It is not a question merely of pitch, or of a singular, identifiable frequency (concert A, say). In the natural world there are not many pure pitches, but such as there are, are not in themselves musical tones, though they may be acoustically identical. (I am elaborating somewhat on Scruton here.) A pitched sound only becomes a musical tone when deliberately brought into relation with others,[13] that is, sounded alongside them, either successively or simultaneously, in what we

---

tones. But there are true glissandi too, where the initial tone is made to increase or decrease in frequency without a break, as with a slide trombone, a violin, or even a clarinet, as at the beginning of *Rhapsody in Blue*. 'Sound', though it is a sound, will hardly do for such an effect. I think we must call it a note, as distinct from a tone. (Or is that insufficiently distinct? The distinction does not exist at all in German, where *Ton* serves for both, and *Note* only for the written sign.) Both true and virtual glissandi exhibit 'movement' from one discrete pitch to another. Vibrato, however, because it oscillates about a central pitch, is named for that pitch (tone). (The latter is actually sounded, unlike the mean pitch between the two tones of a trill. For some reason this unheard mean pitch is not imaginatively 'deduced' or 'averaged out' from them by the mind's ear.) On the other hand (but consistently), we generally speak of a note's, rather than a tone's, being 'bent', e.g. by an acoustic guitarist's sideways finger pressure, or an electric guitarist's 'whammy bar'. (As in jazz we speak of a 'blue note', not a blue tone, in the melody. This, though it may be accurately described, and written, as fully flattened in relation to the the equivalent note in the harmony – E flat as opposed to E natural, where the key is C major, say, and the instrument one of fixed pitches, such as the piano – is still somehow perceived as being 'bent' away from its normative pitch, and not as a separate, named tone in its own right.)

12 Scruton, *The Aesthetics of Music*, 160ff.
13 By this criterion one might have to concede that the chimes of a clock or electric doorbell were musical tones, though hardly that the result was music.

respectively call melody and harmony. Pitches, or notes, and their duration, volume and so on have a physical description (or at least formula: e.g. concert A has a frequency of 440 Hz), but melody, harmony, movement and the rest do not. These, as it were, are emergent patterns or *Gestalten* – melody, incidentally, being a paradigmatic example of *Gestalt*,[14] according to the founders of *Gestalt* psychology – which we perceive in the sonic surface, just as the composer who specified that sonic surface (and the patterns perceived in it) meant that we should; and indeed much as, looking at a picture, we recognize a face in what are literally only patches of pigment; as we detect a certain expression on a real or pictured face; or as we see now a duck, now a rabbit, in Wittgenstein's celebrated duck-rabbit figure.

All three examples are Scruton's, and he has repeatedly used the 'face' examples in other contexts. The duck-rabbit analogy, I think, works well enough, but only up to a point, and perhaps the same is also true of the whole 'seeing-as' and 'seeing-in' scenario (alias 'aspect perception')[15]. We don't, subjectively, hear the sound *as* music, or hear the melody *in* the succession of notes. Unless we make a deliberate effort to do so, we hear neither the sound *qua* sound nor the notes *qua* notes; what we hear, and all we hear, is the music (the melody, harmony, etc.), rather as, in language, we hear the words themselves, not the sounds of the words.[16] (That is, we

---

[14]   Scruton, *The Aesthetics of Music, 87*, etc.

[15]   A *Gestalt* is defined *inter alia* as 'an organized whole', or as one that, presented to our perception, is more than, and different from, the sum of its parts (i.e. is supervenient). See, e.g. Christian von Ehrenfels, 'On Gestalt-Qualities' (1932): 'The theory of Gestalt-qualities began with the attempt to answer a question: What is melody? First and most obvious answer: the sum of the individual notes which make up the melody. But opposed to this is the fact that the same melody may be made up of quite different groups of notes, as happens when the self-same melody is transposed into different keys. If the melody were nothing else than the sum of the notes, different melodies would have to be produced, because different groups of notes are here involved.' (*Psychological Review*, Vol. **44** [1937], 521–524.) See also Wolfgang Köhler, *Gestalt Psychology* (London: G. Bell and Sons, 1930), 165, 212, 223 etc. As can be seen at a glance from his index, Scruton leans heavily on the *Gestalt*-idea, his use of it being admirably summarized and clarified by Alison Denham on 415 of her outstandingly conscientious review article concerning *The Aesthetics of Music*. See A.E. Denham, 'The Moving Mirrors of Music', *Music and Letters*, Vol. **80**, No. 3 (August 1999), 411–432.

[16]   In an interesting, sympathetic review of *The Aesthetics of Music* (*Music Perception*, Vol. **15**, No.4 [1998], 412–422), the experimental psychologist Bruno H. Repp notes that 'the purely auditory properties of

182

normally hear not two things, but one, that being only as much as is immediately necessary to the communication of the 'meaning', anything more being cognitively diseconomical.) Though all depends on perception, let me add, an intended pattern is quite different from an unintended pattern, such as when children 'see' pictures in the fire, or when Hamlet ironically invites Polonius to see a whale or a camel in the clouds. Both kinds of perception require imagination, but for the event to be meaningful as music is meaningful, there has, as with language, to be utterance as well as perception (which then becomes reception). In other words, although the thing perceived is imagined, and although it may lack an exhaustive physical description or explanation, it is not 'imaginary', as pictures in the fire are. It is really, objectively there; and it is there because somebody put it there, with the intention that it be both recognized (identified), and recognized as having been put there with that intention. The circuit of communication is completed when both recognitions take place. The philosopher H.P. Grice famously, and in my view persuasively, accounted for linguistic meaning in terms of the reciprocal recognition of intentions, and a similar anatomy of musical communication would, I think, be equally plausible.[17]

As in language – though the analogy cannot be pressed indefinitely – every item in the tone-world, be it single (a note) or composite (a key, a phrase, a theme, a melody), derives its meaning, identity and direction from its fellows, which collectively summon into being, and inhabit, what Scruton calls a 'field of force'.[18] Tone, and thus music, which (for Scruton's purposes) is composed entirely of sounds heard as tones, can be perceived and understood only by

---

speech sounds ... are less important and partially inaccessible in the context of coherent and meaningful speech' (414). I was puzzled as a child (and still am) by the curious fact that, try as one will, one cannot see a printed word simply (or even) as – what it is – a series of black marks on a white background, but is invariably compelled not only to see it as that word but even to 'hear' it in one's head. (By contrast, as I remark in both this and the following paragraph, and though we normally hear music simply as music, we do seem also to be able, at will, to hear it purely as sound.)

[17] H.P. Grice, 'Meaning' (1957), reprinted in Paul Grice, *Studies in the Way of Words* (Cambridge, MA: Harvard University Press, 1989), 213–223. This is not to say, of course, that what is 'communicated' in music is anything like a declarative utterance (i.e. propositional), let alone a piece of emotional autobiography ('this is how I feel'), though it may well resemble (e.g.) fictional utterances.

[18] Scruton, *The Aesthetics of Music*, 17

Robert Grant

rational beings.[19] Again as in language, and even though we are here obviously dealing in metaphor (or something like it), only rational beings can identify musical 'statements', 'questions', 'answers' and the like. We may need instruction in how to do this, which indicates that, unlike their secondary counterparts, 'tertiary' phenomena and perception fall to some extent into the province of will.[20] Except by blocking my ears, I cannot choose not to hear a given sound; but I am able, and up to a point can choose or not, to hear it as exhibiting these or those musical features, or not, as may be. (It is possible, for example, by suppressing one's normal diatonic expectations, not to hear atonal music as discordant, and also possible, as I have already suggested, to hear it, or any music, not even as music, but rather as 'sound-art', a series of abstract sound-patterns.)

The ability to perceive the *expressive* features, or content, of a piece of music is similarly responsive to instruction; though whether or how far one is actually free to perceive them this way or that, as one may switch *ad lib.* between 'duck' and 'rabbit', may be doubted. The philosopher Nietzsche was no musical ignoramus, but a highly accomplished musician. Yet it is certainly possible, as he did, to miss the retrospective irony in the Prelude to Wagner's *Die Meistersinger* (especially, one might add, in its pompous opening theme) – Nuremberg's musical tradition, Wagner subsequently implies, could well do with Walther's radical challenge to it – and to lay its expansive burgherly self-importance directly at Wagner's (and Germany's) door.[21] But such a mistake is not based on a misapprehension or mischaracterization of the actual *music*, such as would be involved in sincerely describing that particular theme as (say) '*Angst*-ridden', or 'vivacious', or 'delicate'. In fact, aberrations of the latter type are surely so gross as to be inconceivable.[22] We

---

[19]   Scruton, *The Aesthetics of Music*, 16, 17, 39, 94, etc.
[20]   Scruton, *The Aesthetics of Music*, 44, 90, 94
[21]   See Nietzsche, *Beyond Good and Evil*, §240. He calls the Prelude 'a piece of magnificent, gorgeous, heavy, latter-day art', but of course that is exactly how Wagner *means* us to regard the Mastersingers' theme with which it opens. Later in the paragraph Nietzsche seems visited by a fleeting suspicion to this effect, but ignores it and ploughs on with his denunciation regardless.
[22]   They would also be inconceivable among the genuinely tone-deaf, whose misfortune it is to be unable to perceive a theme as expressing anything very much, since they cannot clearly distinguish the pitches, and sometimes not even the general 'upness' or 'downness', of its component notes. (Tone-deaf people, however, are often responsive to rhythm, which plays an important part in expression.)

should, however, distinguish such aberrations from confusing the mood of the music *in itself* with its dramatic effect, which (as just noted) may not be the same thing. At the Vienna premiere of Gluck's *Orfeo* in 1762, the Venetian ambassador's wife acutely observed that Orpheus's aria 'Che farò' ('What shall I do without Eurydice?') was 'too light-hearted for a man who wants to kill himself'.[23] That is (we might say), it would be more appropriate to a reunion with Eurydice than to her irretrievable loss. So perhaps here it is the *dramatic* context which makes the aria pathetic, Orpheus's loss being all the more poignant for being rendered in the accents of a past happiness (a happiness shortly to be recovered in their miraculous, unexpected reunion).

Let us return to Scruton's account of metaphor in music, which, as I have said, has caused much trouble to Malcolm Budd and other perplexed commentators, and indeed probably more than it is intrinsically worth.[24] For even if Scruton is right about metaphor's

[23]   Diary of Comte Charles de Zinzendorf et Pottendorf (Staatsarchiv, Vienna), Tuesday 5th October 1762: 'L'ambassadrice trouva la musique de l'air *Che farò senza Euridice?* trop gaie pour un homme qui veut se tuer, elle dit cependant que l'ensemble faisoit un fort beau spectacle.' (Quoted in Bruce Alan Brown, *Gluck and the French Theatre in Vienna* [Oxford: Clarendon Press 1991], 369. I am grateful to Dr Guy Dammann for tracking this distantly-remembered reference down for me.) The point was later picked up by the French writer Pascal Boyé, as reported by Hanslick: 'At a time when thousands were moved to tears by the air from *Orpheus* ... [quotes 'Che farò' in French, and the music in piano score] ... Boyé, a contemporary of Gluck, observed that precisely the same melody would accord equally well, if not better, with words conveying exactly the reverse' (Eduard Hanslick, *Vom Musikalisch-Schönen*, Ch. 2, in E.A. Lippman, ed., *Musical Aesthetics: a Historical Reader* [New York: Pendragon Press, 1986-], Vol. II, 275–6). Boyé's essay (1779) is aptly summarized in its title, 'L'Expression musicale, mise au rang des chimères', the burden being that expression is not intrinsic to the music but is essentially a feature of performance. An extract is given in Lippman, Vol. I, 285–294, the comment on 'Che farò' being on 290. As part of his proto-Hanslickian argument, Boyé claims that because, according to him, music cannot express hate or rage, neither can it other emotions. He had not the advantage of having heard the episode in Act 1 of *Götterdämmerung* known as 'Hagens Wacht', nor the Prelude and first scene of Act 2 (Hagen's subliminal visitation from Alberich), nor the Prelude to Act 2 of *Parsifal* (introducing Klingsor).
[24]   See, e.g. Naomi Cumming, 'Metaphor in Roger Scruton's aesthetics of music', in Anthony Pople, ed., *Theory, Analysis and Meaning in Music* (Cambridge: Cambridge University Press, 1994), 3–28; Paul Boghossian, 'On Hearing the Music in the Sound: Scruton on Musical Expression',

Robert Grant

centrality to the musical experience,[25] if I am right nothing very much follows from it, despite the fact that it could be true and is certainly interesting. (I am taking up a suggestion once made to me by Dr Guy Dammann, who said – perhaps provocatively – that to him a tune's going 'up and down' was no more or less metaphorical than a thing's going up and down in the air.) The fact, I suspect, is that when we hear (for example) a melody going 'up' and 'down', or lines of counterpoint 'converging' or 'diverging' (as in staff notation they visibly do), or a leading note (as its name implies) somehow 'striving' towards the tonic or keynote, and so on, we do so not metaphorically but literally, *as those terms are applied in the context of music*. We forget – if it had occurred to us, as it might never have done, even to musicians of the highest competence – that 'up', 'down', 'tension', 'resolution' and the rest were ever metaphors at all, since their musical meaning seems to us more or less continuous with their other meanings, and, for all practical purposes, just as literal. They have become so habitual, so useful, or, as Scruton says, so 'indispensable' in their musical application as virtually to have borrowed their 'literal' meaning from their origins.[26] A

The *Journal of Aesthetics and Art Criticism*, Vol. **60**, No. 1, Winter 2002, 49–55; Malcolm Budd, 'Musical Movement and Aesthetic Metaphors', *British Journal of Aesthetics*, Vol. **43**, No. 3, July 2003, 209–223; Roger Scruton, 'Musical Movement: a Reply to Budd', ibid., Vol. **44**, No. 2, April 2004, 184–7. Naomi Cumming's essay is based on Scruton's earlier musical aesthetics, as expounded in his *The Aesthetic Understanding* (Methuen, 1983), but is equally relevant to *The Aesthetics of Music*, into which they are largely incorporated. If these commentators are perplexed – as who is not? – it is due as much to the slipperiness of metaphor as a concept, as to Scruton's treatment of it. (An example of such slipperiness: 'length' is predicated of both space and time, and sometimes of both at once, as in 'a long journey'. Unless we are students of rhetoric, do we ever ask ourselves which usage, the spatial or the temporal, is metaphorical and which literal? Does it really matter? If so, how would we set about deciding the issue? Could each perhaps be 'half-and-half', or is that idea ridiculous? Cannot both be literal? And so on.)
[25] Scruton, *The Aesthetics of Music*, 80–96, 239, etc.
[26] Words such as 'harmony', 'consonance' and 'dissonance' possess a literal meaning in their own right. Those were musical terms to start with, and, so far from being metaphors themselves, are the source of metaphorical applications outside music, as in 'harmony' to mean peace or agreement, and 'dissonance' conflict, as in the expression 'cognitive dissonance'. In Greek *harmonia*, for musical harmony, actually is a metaphor, the word literally meaning 'joining' or 'fitting together'. But in English the first recorded

186

metaphor so constantly employed as to be indispensable or inelimin-
able might just as well be no metaphor at all. Some writers have
claimed that all literal usages are in fact dead metaphors; others,
such as Nietzsche and Derrida, that metaphors never really die.
The first group could be right; the second are demonstrably wrong.[27]

A further point, not made by Scruton, is that we use such metaphors all the time in non-musical contexts without considering
how far they actually are metaphors. There is nothing special about
their application to musical phenomena. It is both true and interesting, as Scruton says,[28] that when we say the music, or the melody,
moves up or down, nothing, or nothing physically measurable,
moves at all.[29] The individual notes stay exactly where they are relative to each other, and it is only their being played sequentially which
gives the appearance of movement. If the notes themselves don't
move, what is it then that we think *does* move?[30] We speak, outside

---

use of 'harmony' is in the musical sense. See *OED*, 'harmony', etymology
and senses 4 and 5.

[27] Derrida himself admits that 'to read within a concept the hidden
history of a metaphor is to privilege *diachrony* at the expense of system',
i.e. is etymologically deterministic and thus illegitimate (*Margins of
Philosophy*, tr. Alan Bass [Brighton: Harvester Press, 1982]). 215). It is
current, not past, use that determines meaning. If I use, say, the words *con-
cetto* or *Begriff* in their everyday senses, while being quite unaware of their
roots in a (presumably) once-live 'grasping' metaphor, then I am not speaking metaphorically. Moreover, neither am I doing so even if I use them
knowing their derivation: 'It is use in discourse that specifies the difference
between the literal and the metaphorical, and not some sort of prestige attributed to the primitive or the original' (Paul Ricoeur, *The Rule of
Metaphor*, trans. R. Czerny [London: Routledge and Kegan Paul, 1978],
291).

[28] Scruton, *The Aesthetics of Music*, 49ff

[29] The observation seems to have originated in Viktor Zuckerkandl,
Sound and Symbol: Music and the External World (Princeton: Princeton
UP, 1969), 83.

[30] An impressive attempt, from the standpoint of 'conceptual metaphor', to answer this and related questions comes to my attention just as I
submit the present piece in typescript. It is '"Something in the Way She
Moves" – Metaphors of Musical Motion', by the philosopher Mark
Johnson (co-author with George Lakoff of *Metaphors We Live By*) and
the musicologist Steve Larson, in *Metaphor and Symbol*, Vol. **18**, No. 2
[2003], 63–84. They conclude that movement in music is both real *and* metaphorical, and 'no less real for being a product of human imagination' (77).
It is also grounded, they say, in our experience of physical movement.

music, of a 'flight' of steps (notice, by the way, that the musical term 'scale' derives from the Latin *scala*, meaning a ladder or staircase). Yet nothing flies, and the steps are stationary. The path 'leads to' the castle, and beyond the castle the ground 'falls away' into the gorge. In builders' jargon, the waste pipe has a 'fall' of 1 in 40. But the path does not take us by the hand and physically conduct us to the castle, and no part of either the ground or the pipe changes its vertical position. Since these expressions, once you think about it, are manifestly not literal, they must be metaphors (or so it seems at first sight). But we use them, quite unconsciously, and without the imaginative effort involved in understanding a 'live' metaphor, *as if* they were literal, and no harm or confusion comes of it. We know what we mean, and so do our hearers. More strikingly, they do apply literally (or near enough), not to the original items falsely credited with motion, but to other things which are potentially part of the scene, waiting in the wings as it were. The steps do not move, let alone 'fly'; but when I mount them, if I do not exactly fly, I certainly rise. The ground itself does not 'fall', but if I drop something, that thing may literally fall down the slope. The pipe doesn't literally fall, but the waste entering it does. And so on.

Now, I, the thing I have dropped and the waste are all quite as tangible as the stationary objects – the steps, the path, the ground and the pipe – which we metaphorically, and thus falsely, credit with movement. It is the first group of things which actually move, and they are not different in kind from those to which the predicate of motion is transferred. In music, however, the thing which is alleged to move, the melody (say), though it can certainly be described, has no physical description, or even physical existence, unlike the notes of which it is composed. Yet it is no less real and no less objective for that. So I would suggest that it does indeed move, and is perceived to move, and that movement is the core feature of its description. It (or something in it, perhaps analogously to a pencil point inscribing a figure) moves in just the same way as it exists, that is, non-physically, as melodies do. If you want to protest that what we are really talking about is 'virtual' movement or 'the appearance of' movement, that's fine. The entire world of tertiary objects and their associated qualities is a world of appearance, and as Scruton pointed out thirty-odd years ago in his notorious book *The Meaning of*

Astonishingly, they make no reference to Scruton, with whom they have so many points of contact.

Conservatism, those are the things that really matter to us. That is what he there meant by his key phrase 'the priority of appearance'.[31]

I have suggested that movement, position and other musical terms have grown so familiar as virtually to have become literal, and therefore effectively to have lost whatever metaphorical status they may once have had. This means, in effect, no more than that the supposedly prior, literal, pre-metaphorical meanings of certain terms are plausibly extended into new areas without losing their explicit link with the original meaning. And that may be to say that the newer meanings were never genuinely metaphorical at all.[32] This seems obvious when the music has a narrative or illustrative function, as in opera, song, ballet, film scores and 'programme music', when music exemplifying the extended, allegedly metaphorical meaning is used to suggest or accompany something exemplifying the original, literal meaning. The beautiful Grail theme (as it turns out to be) with which the Prelude to Act I of Wagner's *Lohengrin* opens (indeed, of which it almost entirely consists), enters in an ethereal, almost inaudibly high string register, redolent of innocent angelic voices and heavenly, other-worldly things. Its so-called 'bass' part is actually located far up in the treble, so that there is no 'earthly' component in the harmony. The (supposedly) metaphorical altitude of the scoring is clearly meant to suggest the imagined but still quite literal height of the heavens above us and their distance from earthly concerns. In Beethoven's *Ode to Joy* (the final, choral movement of the Ninth Symphony) the chorus asks the world whether it

---

[31]   *The Meaning of Conservatism* (Harmondsworth: Penguin, 1980), 36–38, 98.

[32]   As any dictionary entry shows, words acquire new applications by what looks like metaphorical extension. But, proper nouns apart, since a word's original application already covers a diversity of particulars perceived nevertheless to possess enough in common to deserve the same name, there is nothing anomalous about bringing further phenomena under the same semantic umbrella whenever it seems appropriate to do so, whether we call the process metaphorical or not. An ordinary designation flatly assumes or asserts the similarity *pro tanto* of the various items it denotes, whereas metaphor, rather, invites an imaginative perception of similarity. The object, at least of the first, is to give us a handle on specifics, more especially to enable us to communicate them, by successively narrower qualifications of items within an agreed general category. (Not just 'a table', but 'the new pine table in John's kitchen'; not any old cat, but 'the black cat we saw in the garden yesterday'.) The system of reference in language is (let us hazard) not unlike that used in a library, and has a similar purpose, of enabling us to locate things.

senses its Creator ('Ahnest du den Schöpfer, Welt?'). Accompanied by whispered exhortations to seek him beyond the *Sternenzelt* ('tent of stars'), the orchestra then settles into a prolonged, widely-spaced (or 'hollow') chord consisting of Grail-textured, mysteriously ambiguous diminished seventh harmonies right at the top, pulsing and twinkling in tremolando triplets like the said stars, nothing much in the middle registers, and the whole underlain by a deep throbbing bass in cross-rhythmic quadruplets on the dominant A (thus revealing the high diminished seventh chord, containing a B flat, to be part of an all-inclusive minor ninth chord), all this suggesting the awesome, inscrutable presence of God spanning both the furthest heights and the profoundest depths of the vast cosmos. Here again high (or, if you prefer, 'high') notes suggest height, while added to them are deep notes suggesting depth. I am sorry if all that sounds childishly crude, but what I am trying to de-scribe is anything but, as those familiar with the passage will know. At all events, one could give endless examples, but in those just given the music, being paired with a narrative, can fairly easily be said to have a kind of literal meaning (or even reference, since it accompanies one). It would be no surprise, therefore, if such associations persisted even in music with no narrative content. Conversely – who knows? – such musical effects might be deployed in narrative contexts precisely because of the associations they already bore.

In sum, if, by everyday consensus, so-called 'high' notes can never-theless suggest, even signify, *literal* height (and so on), it is not clear that the 'up' and 'down' we associate with relative pitches and the 'movement' of a melody, nor such 'movement' itself, really are meta-phors in any full-blooded sense. There are many and conflicting the-ories of metaphor, from Aristotle to Goodman, Davidson and the present, but most agree that metaphor, to be intelligible, invites us to perceive at least some similarity or basis of comparison between two or more disparate things.[33] Not for the first time in his writings,

---

[33] So does simile, but the rhetorical logic differs. Simile says that X is *like* Y, which may be true; metaphor, in effect, says that X actually *is* Y, when it is literally and manifestly not. The imaginative force, or so-called 'truth', of a successful metaphor may derive from its literal falsehood. It is a kind of exaggeration to say that X *is* Y, when it is only *like* Y, but the hy-perbole, as in other contexts, lends emphasis. Further, a simile is an asser-tion, to be accepted or rejected; but a metaphor, being literally untrue, and understood to be so by both speaker and listener, demands interpret-ation, a cognitive effort which may well prove more enlightening than a mere statement of resemblance.

Scruton gives a striking example from Rilke,[34] in which a bat's zigzag flight through the dusk is 'seen as', or (as Scruton would say) fused with the image of, a crack running through porcelain. There is doubtless more involved, but it will surely be admitted that the core of the metaphor is an implied resemblance. When we ask, however, in just what respect a 'high' note is actually *like* a literally (i.e. physically) high object (the heavens, say), we find ourselves at a loss for an answer. It certainly doesn't *sound* like one. And to say 'it vibrates at high frequency' merely displaces the problem, for how, any more than its corresponding pitch, or a price, or a number, can a frequency *literally* be 'high'? It seems, on reflection, that there is no similarity at all between high pitch and physical altitude, except for the facts that we (and others) call them both 'high',[35] and that the first, in a musical context, is generally understood (when appropriate) to suggest or represent the second. So 'high' and 'low', when used of sounds, tones and other immaterial things, appear to exclude what would normally be thought a key feature of metaphor, namely resemblance. At the same time, this non-resemblance to physically high or low things (if we regard those meanings as primary) means that 'high' and 'low', in non-physical matters, cannot be unambiguously literal, even though in musical or other specialized applications (e.g. quantitative ones, such as 'high prices') we unthinkingly employ them as though they were. So if such usages, and the associated conceptions, are neither strictly metaphorical nor strictly literal, what are they? While agreeing with Scruton that they are indispensable, if (as I think we must) we are to understand music as virtual movement from and to somewhere, I should incline rather to call them quasi-metaphors, though I admit this looks pretty much like – in fact, is – a capitulation in the face of the inexplicable.

Let us return to the question of meaning in music. Despite the examples given earlier, of music's ability to illustrate, reinforce or suggest extra-musical ideas, a literal meaning, in general, and strictly construed, is just what music doesn't have. This is because, again in general, and unlike language, music doesn't refer to anything. (Music *is*, rather than *means*.) However, neither does literature have a straightforwardly literal meaning, despite being composed of words which do, and, despite inviting us, though it is admittedly fictional,

---

[34]   Scruton, *The Aesthetics of Music*, 86
[35]   There seems to be some evidence that 'height' and 'depth', as applied to pitch, are universal human usages, independently of cross-cultural influence, and thence effectively 'natural'. (Not that this explains anything. Rather, it demands explanation itself.)

to imagine people and situations sufficiently close to real life, even in fairy tales, to be believable.[36] Literature is often said to be symbolic, and 'symbolism' in the orthodox literary-critical sense is part of its stock-in-trade (there was once a literary and pictorial movement called Symbolism, though it was unclear just what was being symbolized),[37] but, though largely representational, literature and literary language are not symbolic in the same way as declarative discourse, where words are presumed to relate directly to the so-called 'real' world (i.e. to 'stand for', or represent, things in it).

Music is not symbolic in *any* sense, for the same reason as it is not truly representational, and even though it may serve as an adjunct to narrative. It cannot systematically denote or refer, because, unlike language, literature and pictures, it is not finally separable from the things it might be thought to refer to or depict if it could. (Reference implies a generic distance, or category distinction, between sign and referent.) Those are not typically items in the external world (though they may very occasionally be), but rather mental and emotional states, gestures, attitudes and processes.[38] Because music is inseparable from such intangibles, it cannot be said to

---

[36] It may be asked in what sense Schiller's *Ode to Joy* is 'fictional', since, although people do not normally speak in verse, this is pretty clearly the poet speaking in his own person. The 'thought' contained in the poem is evidently not *entertained*, as in fiction generally, but *asserted* (to use Scruton's distinction on pages 88–9). The poem is a kind of manifesto, like Wordsworth's *Immortality Ode*. But I cannot pursue this question here.

[37] The point was, through symbolism, to make apprehensible something thought to exist but to be apprehensible by no other route. See, in general, Edmund Wilson, *Axel's Castle*, Ch. 1: 'What the symbols of Symbolism really were, were metaphors detached from their subjects.' A near-perfect illustration is Kafka's *The Castle*, in which, though something is clearly being allegorized, it is not quite clear what. (Who is the elusive castellan? God? And so on.) Contrast this with *The Pilgrim's Progress*, which is generically very similar, but in which Bunyan even tells us, through their names, what his symbols mean: Giant Despair, the Slough of Despond, Doubting Castle, etc.

[38] Though he gave each movement of his most pictorial composition a programmatic title, Beethoven himself said of the so-called *Pastoral Symphony* that it was 'more the expression of feeling than painting in sound'. His titles for the two outer movements stress the 'feeling' element, an element which, to the listener, predominates even in the storm scene (4th movement), despite its striking 'realism'. (By 'realism' I mean that even without the programme one might easily guess that the music was intended to suggest a storm, with rain, wind, thunder, lightning, etc.)

symbolize them. We usually say that what it does is *express* them. Obviously emotions and mental states (and so on) exist independently, but music is not typically a *means* or *vehicle* for their transmission. It is not a receptacle into which they are poured and from which they are subsequently dispensed to a grateful audience. In other words they are not *first* experienced (or rather, conceived as experiences), *then* symbolized in music, *then* reconstituted as the listener's experience. The thing expressed, rather, is identical with its expression. (It was for some such reason that Schopenhauer thought that music was not an oblique *representation* of the Will, i.e. was not mediated via ideas, concepts, images or symbols, but was rather its direct emanation, reality itself as he conceived of it.)[39]

Sadness, happiness, doubt, resignation, determination, triumph and despair all exist independently of music, as I have said, and are also expressible in music; but what an actual piece of music expresses, here and now, is a particular and complex bundle of emotions, gestures and mental states which can be fully expressed, or if you like embodied, in no other way. A piece of music ideally considered (that is, so-called absolute music) *presents* something rather than *represents* it,[40] even if it can also suggest or allude to things outside itself, including other pieces of music. In the latter case, of course, it is not – so to speak – breaking musical ranks. A striking example, which I mention more for its interest than its strict relevance (since there is a narrative dimension), is found in Schubert's viscerally gripping song *Der Zwerg* ('The Dwarf', D. 771). The poem is a frankly lurid Romantic *Schicksalslied*, or song of fate, in which a remorse-stricken young queen willingly submits to being murdered by her dwarf (her ex-lover), for having betrayed him by marrying the king. (There is even a hint that she drops dead of grief before he can strike the fatal blow.) In its bass line the piano accompaniment, first rhythmically and then melodically, mimics, develops and distorts the ominous opening motto from Beethoven's 5th Symphony, stretching it at

---

[39]   *The World as Will and Idea*, Vol. I, Book 3, §52. One need not accept Schopenhauer's metaphysics to see that these few pages contain some remarkably profound, detailed and informed reflections on the least readily explicable of the arts (yet also, as he rightly observes, the only one which is immediately and universally understood). It should however be added that if music, as Schopenhauer claims, is either the Will itself or a 'direct copy', it can hardly deliver us from our blind servitude to it, in the manner alleged of the other arts, viz. through aesthetic contemplation. (How far, then, can it really be called an *art*?)

[40]   It would not be unreasonable, however, to claim that the representational arts also 'present' something, but do so *by means of* representation.

the climax across a horrible tritone interval. Schubert must certainly have known that Beethoven had characterized this motto as 'Fate knocking at the door'. (Perhaps, since the trail of allusion here ends in a concept, Schubert was breaking musical ranks after all. Or maybe Beethoven was, or both were. Though Schubert's musical allusion would have been effective even if Beethoven had never given the 'fate' motto a name.)

But to return: if the musical content or experience is inseparable from its expression, how are we to describe it, perhaps because we wish to discuss it? And what are the consequences of our responding to a piece of music as directly and immediately as it is presented to us, so that we effectively become one with it?

An obvious answer to the first question, how we can describe musical experience, is via our old friend metaphor, which will naturally not be a perfect fit. The same is true, in lesser degree, of any artistic experience. It is just that in painting or literature exposition is given more of a handle, because there the work's content is already couched in symbolic terms. Even so, the only genuinely exhaustive characterization of any work of art would be to duplicate or repeat it. The New Critics of the 1940s used to condemn 'the heresy of paraphrase'. If a work of art really could be fully translated into declarative terms without remainder, then one could presumably dispense with the actual work and content oneself with the description. But, since it would lack the imaginative dimension – which is to say, there *would* be a remainder – this would seem peculiarly pointless. To hear a thing described is quite different from *living* it, which is what art makes us do. (As, in its way, does metaphor.)

Music criticism, as distinct from from pure formal analysis, depends overwhelmingly on metaphor. Some of the most vivid and suggestive criticism is contained in metaphorical one-liners, such as Schumann's brilliant characterization of Chopin's polonaises as 'cannons buried in flowers', or Debussy on Grieg's *Lyric Pieces* for piano: 'pink bonbons stuffed with snow'. Or, with equal brilliance, and an analytical bonus, here is Scruton himself[41] on Bach's great D minor Chaconne, which he movingly and truthfully describes as being:

> … one of the most noble and profound utterances for solo violin in the history of music, and a remarkable study in implied harmony. Its effect of titanic strain, as of a giant Atlas, bearing

---

[41]   Scruton, *The Aesthetics of Music*, 452

the burden of the world's great sadness, is inseparable from the the way in which the performer must stretch across the four strings of the instrument, to provide as many voices as can be produced by it, and to imply as many more. The performer's effort must be heard in the music, but heard too as *part of* the music. The brilliance of Bach's writing was precisely to achieve that effect: to make the difficulty of the piece into a quality of the music, rather than a matter of virtuosity.

Such illuminations are rare in critical prose. They are not so rare, however, in music teaching, particularly practical, hands-on instrumental teaching. Béla Bartók was a great pianist as well as a great composer. But according to the late Sir George Solti,[42] one of his piano pupils (one, moreover, who revered him), he was a terrible teacher, probably (one supposes) on account of his famous, almost neurotic reticence. Solti would play a passage, and Bartók would say simply, 'No, you must play it like this,' and then do so himself, without explanation. A good teacher, by contrast, will occupy himself (or herself, of course) with the minutest details of interpretation, alongside matters of execution. He will insist on tiresome scales, arpeggios and exercises, since intrepretative competence is useless until there is sufficient technique to realize it. But typical explanations will be small-scale, local, and limited to what the performer can hope to make a listener hear. With what delight a child, say, might greet the teacher's pointing out Arthur Sullivan's clever, gratuitous and in the context really quite cheeky imitative swapping of vocal lines between the tenor and treble parts in the first eight bars of 'Onward, Christian Soldiers'. And with how much more delight he would learn to recognize, and to bring out, similar devices in less utilitarian compositions such as the easier of Beethoven's late piano bagatelles.

At the core of this kind of instruction is ostension or demonstration, which is not to say that verbal encouragement and explanation are superfluous. Maybe demonstration is what Bartók thought he was providing; but maybe he was also cutting corners or just not very good at it. Where understanding is sought, and analysis and metaphor have proved inadequate, ostension – literally, pointing out – is our last (but not inferior) resort. (It was ideally F.R. Leavis's literary-critical approach: you interpret a passage, says Leavis, you show it to your interlocutor, and say, 'This is so, isn't it?' And he

---

[42]   In a TV interview broadcast during his lifetime, whose details I have tried in vain to retrieve. Someone other than I will remember it, and doubtless them too.

replies, 'Yes, but ...'. And so on.)[43] Suitably guided, and perhaps after lengthy trial and error, the novice eventually sees the point or masters the skill. To be sure the process resists description, and is thus far 'ineffable', like its object, and also (it is said) like God; but in fact there is nothing mysterious, still less mystical, about it, and it is quite familiar, especially to skilled tradesmen and manual workers, as we know from books such as George Sturt's *The Wheelwright's Shop* and Matthew Crawford's recent (and brilliant) best-seller *Shop Class as Soulcraft*. Scruton likens our understanding of music to the philosophers' 'knowledge by acquaintance',[44] and, like Gilbert Ryle's 'knowledge how', it may be effectively a practical accomplishment, despite its subsequent rationalization in theory. Indeed, in some musical traditions, such as jazz or Indian music, one learns entirely by apprenticeship, or total immersion. That this is not 'knowledge by description', and therefore cannot be written down or got out of books, does not make it any the less knowledge. The mechanical principles behind riding a bicycle are readily intelligible to an adult; but no abstract familiarity with them in advance can teach you actually to ride one, something which many an ignorant five-year-old can do.

And so, perhaps, with music. The early 20th-century musicologist Heinrich Schenker thought he had detected hierarchical, hugely extended formal structures underlying masterpieces in the tonal tradition, all, though masked by various disguises and displacements, reducible in the end to the familiar harmonic progression ('I-V-I') from tonic to dominant and back.[45] This suggestion has a certain plausibility, in that in most musical compositions we normally sense something like a circular A-B-A pattern, one jointly signalled, exemplified and reinforced by harmonic sequence; but Schenker's cadential *Ursatz*

---

[43]   Leavis's original formulation of this principle (which some would deny that he himself consistently observed) was in his notorious Richmond Lecture 'Two Cultures? The Significance of C.P. Snow', first printed in the *Spectator*, March 9th, 1962, and subsequently reprinted elsewhere.

[44]   Scruton, *The Aesthetics of Music,* 362, 376

[45]   *The Aesthetics of Music* contains some lengthy, highly technical discussion of Schenker's theories (see esp. pages 313–329). In music theory the Roman numerals I, IV, V etc. represent standard triads (three-note chords made up, when in so-called 'root position', of two stacked thirds) built on the corresponding degrees of the diatonic scale, so that in the key of C major (the piano's white notes) I = C-triad, V = G-triad, and so on. Capitals are used for major triads, small letters for minor, so the D-triad is ii and the E-triad iii, because their harmony (on the white notes) is minor.

(fundamental structure), otherwise 'background', is unlikely to fire any learner's or performer's imagination,[46] since it is on the auditory surface, in the Schenkerian 'foreground' – that is, in the elaborations of the supposedly latent *Ursatz* – that our primary interest lies, rather than in the *Ursatz* itself. The latter (the I-V-I sequence), being the commonest of musical building blocks, and thus (on unwitting Schenkerian assumptions) underlying not just masterpieces, but all tonal music, is almost bound to be banal, if harmlessly so.[47] Similar reductions were performed by Freudians, for whom in the end everything stemmed from unconscious inner conflicts (notably the Oedipus complex); by Marxists, for whom socio-cultural (or 'tertiary') phenomena were all 'in the last analysis' (as Engels put it) economic in origin; and by literary formalists (e.g. Propp, Greimas), for whom all narratives were effectively large-scale variations upon the classic sentence-pattern of subject, verb and object.[48] If such all-embracing theories are true, then nothing really remains to be learnt, since all is known in advance, and our immediate objects of concern, the individuating details and differences in which we had taken the significance of things to reside, are after all trivial. But a theory which does not engage with or illuminate

[46]   I am informed by Guy Dammann, however, that 'Murray Perahia swears by Schenker, although he is unusual' [in so doing].

[47]   An analogy: suppose the theme, by the publisher Anton Diabelli, of Beethoven's towering, sublimely inventive *Diabelli Variations* had been lost, but (impossibly) that some brilliant musicologist such as Schenker had accurately reconstructed it from Beethoven's variations, and was then vindicated by its subsequent discovery. It would still be the mere 'cobbler's patch' that Beethoven described it as being, despite the wondrous things, like gold from straw, that Beethoven had spun out of it. And similarly, perhaps, for the *Ursatz*, even if, like Schenker, we see it as the fundamental structure of the finished work rather than, like Scruton, as an *a posteriori* abstraction from it (Scruton, *The Aesthetics of Music*, 321–4). Of course, Diabelli's clunky but robust little waltz really does 'underlie' Beethoven's piece, by definition – that is what variation form is 'about' – and, if you like, constitutes its 'fundamental structure'; but even so, the whole point of the work (again, as with any variations) is not the theme, but what the composer has made of it. As Diabelli himself modestly observed, its sheer ordinariness only makes Beethoven's achievement the more spectacular.

[48]   The post-modernist twist on this is (perhaps one can now safely say 'was') that since everything is a 'narrative' – unsurprisingly enough, given that every thought, sentence and proposition has a narrative structure – everything must also be a fiction (except, presumably, post-modernism itself). Of course this is a total *non sequitur*, due to assimilating all narratives to the literary kind, which *are* fictional.

Robert Grant

our immediate concerns is not true in any sense that matters. It is not they, but the theory, that is trivial. As Dr Johnson said, that book is good in vain, which the reader throws away.

Such small-scale, practical, detail-based explication and instruction as I have been commending may be compared with what Karl Popper and many of his fellow-Austrians favoured in politics, viz. 'piecemeal engineering' and the avoidance of grand, or overarching, theory. So-called grand theory is like the *dirigiste*, over-centralized government which is actually needed to put it into practice. Both are disconnected from the reality of everyday existence (the *Lebenswelt*), which is a myriad of dispersed individual acts, desires and predicaments, and their constant mutual adjustments and accommodations. In musical interpretation, however, the lack of a central explanatory principle is no great matter. As we have seen, music tends to elude any non-figurative description, other than the purely formal (which may be correct but uninteresting). But this is not necessarily disadvantageous to musical understanding. Because music comes to us unmediated by concepts, our encounter with it (to exaggerate only slightly) is like a face-to-face encounter with a person, an 'I-Thou' relationship, to use Martin Buber's term. The 'other' (music) requires no introduction, because one already knows him sufficiently well and (metaphorically, if not literally) he speaks one's language. Already semi-transparent, the relationship is potentially intimate, and may proceed to friendship on the basis of shared experience and common sympathies.

Like many thinkers since antiquity, especially, though not exclusively, those of a conservative stamp, Scruton comes on strong regarding the solidarity-inducing qualities of music.[49] However, and like the other arts, music has always been conscripted for political use by regimes of every stripe, some of them very nasty. It may well foster solidarity, but the question is, of what kind? If, as Dryden tells us in his 'Song for St Cecilia's Day', music can both raise and quell any passion, the sympathy it excites among its listeners can be diverted to a variety of ends, some good and others not.[50] In this respect music is like any art, which, if it can ennoble, can also deprave. The idea that a shared emotion creates a common identity among the sharers resembles R.G. Collingwood's even more radically

[49] Scruton, *The Aesthetics of Music*, 338-9, 354ff., 438-9
[50] In Dryden, however, that true classicist, even the baser passions – fury, anger, jealousy – once expressed in music, are raised to a certain dignity. (As, one might add, is the horrific, irresistible lust of Racine's Phèdre for her innocent stepson.)

198

idealist notion that since a mind is indistinguishable from its contents, then minds sharing a single thought effectively become a single mind (so that to read Plato is temporarily to *become* him). Of course, if the shared thought is this, that I am utterly separate from all these other people, then that must create problems for the single-mind hypothesis, even if it also throws some light on the role of pop music in at once provoking and alleviating adolescent *Angst*. So must it if the shared thought is that we are all incorrigible egoists. But I shall come to all that. The point is that a shared thought, or a shared emotion, is not necessarily virtuous simply because it is shared, nor necessarily productive of social harmony.

The solidarity that, according to Scruton, music (or rather, 'good' music) engenders in us begins less in unmediated emotion – though that, in the end, is of the greatest importance – than in the comparatively technical areas of harmony, polyphony and collective music-making, perhaps particularly when choral (the 'voices' there being literally human). This recalls Thomas Mann's rambling pro-German polemic from the First World War, *Reflections of a Non-Political Man*. Mann, then very much the conservative, quotes Luther, who was famously musical, as saying that music is 'a semi-discipline and taskmaster that makes people softer and more gentle, more moral and more reasonable', and himself goes on to say that the great German fugal tradition represents the 'powerfully polyphonic joining of self-will and subordination' and is 'the artistic-spiritual reflection of German life itself'.[51] It is certainly true that there could be, and is, an implicit 'politics of music', or at least of group music-making, just as there is an implicit politics of team sports, which require precisely Mann's combination of individuality and self-subordination. Scruton also alleges that our response to music is partly informed by an underlying impulse to dance.[52] There is something

[51]   Mann, *Reflections of a Non-Political Man* (1918), trans. Walter D. Morris (New York: Ungar, 1987), 231–3. Mann's somewhat bellicose nationalism at this period, his 'organicist' musical notions, his anti-Enlightenment Francophobia, and his scornful polemical bluster were all shared, incidentally, by Schenker. (See, e.g. Schenker's 'Rameau or Beethoven? Paralysis or Spiritual Life in Music?', Ch. 3 of his *Das Meisterwerk in der Musik*, 1930, reprinted in Lippman, cit., Vol. III, 71–86.) None of those things, I hasten to add, is found in *The Aesthetics of Music*, except the postulated and very plausible connection between a society's musical and its general culture.

[52]   Scruton, *The Aesthetics of Music*, 338-9, 355-7, 391, etc.

in this, but it cannot apply to all music.[53] Nietzsche likened music of
the classical era to dancing, with its precision, courtesy and grace. But
he likened Wagner's music to swimming (and, he half-suggested,
drowning).[54] And, though Wagner called Beethoven's Seventh
Symphony 'the apotheosis of the dance',[55] there is much in
Beethoven that is not even remotely dance-like, but prayerful,
inward and meditative. At all events, in dancing we become our
bodies (and they us), rather than merely inhabiting them, and
dancing, of the kind Scruton favours, is a communal activity, requir-
ing spontaneity, to be sure, but within a formal framework of discipline and co-operation. And here of course, there is a tenuous link
not only to politics but also to sex, because in both dancing and
erotic experience I actually become incarnate in my body.

The implications of this complex of ideas are suggestive but not
altogether clear. The combined individuality and community exemplified by co-operative music-making may well be a model of desirable social relations, especially since the activity is voluntary, being
driven only by each participant's desire to participate, and the
product being an end in itself. (This is true even of professional musicians: except for star performers, the remuneration, as in academe,
is too paltry, on its own, to count as a serious career incentive.) But the
quality of the music thus produced could in principle be entirely irrelevant. The close harmony of a barber-shop quartet is pleasing, or
at least tolerable, in small doses (e.g. while waiting to get one's hair
cut), while the performers' timing, polyphonic virtuosity and dramatic vocal interaction often surpass anything found in 'serious'
music-making. In its socio-political implications, barber-shop is un-
improvably Scrutopian (to use Nick Zangwill's amusing expression).
The music itself, however, is usually banal, sometimes extremely so,
and, when so, worthless except as a vehicle for the performance. So
why should we prefer serious music to barber-shop? Indeed,
should we? Would Scruton himself? Do we even need the music?

---

[53] Nor (he reminds me) does Scruton positively claim that it does. What
he seems to suggest (*The Aesthetics of Music*, 357) is that the 'latent dancing'
in our response to some music indicates 'a sublimated desire to "move with"
the music' generally, whether it 'dances' or not. In this way, as doubtless in
others, we identify ourselves with it and make it our own.
[54] *Nietzsche contra Wagner*, III ('Wagner as a Danger'), §1 (an extract
from *Human, All-too-Human*).
[55] In his Communist pamphlet *The Art-Work of the Future* (1849), II,
§4.

Wouldn't Busby Berkeley, or synchronized swimming, do just as well, with the sound turned off?[56]

Kant called music 'a mere playing with sensations'[57] and was notoriously insensitive to it, except as regards the annoyance it caused to neighbours (notably himself). But many other intelligent people, such as Dr Johnson, Jane Austen and Evelyn Waugh, have also disliked it, and some, as it seems, have resented its threat, not to their physical, but to their emotional, peace and quiet.[58] That, of course, is an unconscious tribute to its power, and is prompted, perhaps, by a fear of 'losing control'. (There is something of this in many people's violent dislike of Wagner, which is the obverse of others' near-worship of him.) Simply as a practical matter, successful group music-making obviously requires a common understanding among the players; but the same sympathy, projected on to society as a whole, is also intimated in the dynamic interactive relationship between the written parts (this is Mann's point, I take it, about polyphony and German-ness). In Scruton's highly plausible view an audience, even a solitary person listening to a recording, actually does participate empathetically in the performance, much as (again according to Scruton) the music prompts him subliminally to rehearse bodily movements which are never translated into actual motion. Such a performance need not be brain-teasingly polyphonic or German. And even more fundamental is the situation in which the listener identifies himself simply with the music itself, which is to say with the entire ensemble of work, composer, performer and real or imagined audience. Here all, and by definition the listener himself, become both a single thing and a virtual community. In *The Dry Salvages* T.S. Eliot speaks, profoundly, of 'music heard so deeply /

[56] After writing those sentences I listened to the world barber-shop champions, The Acoustix, on YouTube. Their performance (or perhaps I should say 'act') was so breathtakingly brilliant that I really didn't care whether the actual music was any good, or even notice what it was. (Hence, perhaps, the appropriateness of their name.)

[57] *Critique of Judgment*, Book II, §53 ('Comparative estimate of the aesthetic worth of the fine arts').

[58] The novelist L.H. Myers (1881–1944), a man of exceptionally scrupulous and demanding tastes, had nevertheless such an aversion to music that he forbade his wife, a first-rate pianist – and also, it is said, the model for Henry James's Maggie Verver – ever to play when he was in the house. (Needless to say, he was also something of a domestic tyrant.) Latterly, however, his daughters persuaded him to listen to, and to tolerate, the late Beethoven quartets. (See 'The Case of L.H. Myers' in my *Imagining the Real* [Basingstoke: Palgrave, 2003].)

That it is not heard at all, but you are the music / While the music lasts',[59] and embellishes the insight with all kinds of religious and semi-religious images and suggestions, most notably to the effect that the experience resembles the Incarnation, in being 'the intersection of the timeless with time'.

What of the idea that music takes you out of yourself, that this is what you seek and find fulfilling, and above all, that it must be good, both for you and for the community at large? Must it? The foregoing reflections would seem to say, yes. But could there be a another sense, in which to be 'taken out of oneself' was a bad thing? In his book of 1921, *Group Psychology and the Analysis of the Ego*, Freud suggests one answer, which we may contemplate simply as a fable, without buying into his overall vision. He introduces the concept of the ego-ideal (later renamed the superego), an internal monitor, originally modelled on an external figure (typically a parent), which activates the mechanism of repression. By this means unsafe, socially undesirable, or what the unscientific call 'immoral' impulses are (allegedly) excluded from consciousness and either blocked completely or diverted to proxy gratifications.

The ego-ideal, in short, is the moral conscience. Freud speculates how this programme might have operated at the dawn of mankind, in what he calls the 'primal horde'. Rather than what we would call a society, the primal horde is essentially a human herd, united under a single powerful, charismatic leader (an 'alpha male', in modern ethological parlance). Social solidarity and co-ordinated action, Freud suggests, are secured by each follower's transferring his ego-ideal to the leader, or (to put it another way) introjecting the image of the leader in the place of his ego-ideal,[60] so that the

---

[59] One might adduce these lines to support the point made earlier concerning '*x*-ing *in*' and '*x*-ing *as*' (where *x* = hear, see, etc.), and how one hears not the sound of the words, but the words themselves (and so on). One can become so absorbed in a sensorily-mediated experience that the medium itself, the sensory component, drops out of consciousness, leaving one face-to-face simply with the experience, or even identical with it. Cf. *Perictione in Colophon*, 212: 'To Archeanassa's ears it [Perictione's novel polyphonic composition, prefiguring "Western" music by two millennia] was more like thought than sound, and seemed to echo within her as though she herself were producing it.'

[60] It is unlikely, to say the least, that there could have been any 'ego-ideals' properly so called to be found in the primal horde, and not merely because the leader had engrossed them all to his own use. One might accuse Freud of anachronism, were the whole story not so speculative to start with.

leader's command is now the follower's moral conscience, and the follower himself is relieved of all responsibility except for obedience, in fact, in exchange for obedience. The consequence, Freud says, is that the followers effectively become a single ego or consciousness, united under the absolute authority of the leader.

This may or may not have been true of the primal horde, if it ever existed, but it is certainly prescient of the fascist and communist regimes looming on the horizon as Freud wrote, with their personality cults and murderous ruthlessness. (There are not many laughs in fascism; but the final article of the official Fascist Decalogue is one of them, and illustrates Freud's point to a T: '10: Mussolini is always right.')[61] If to be taken out of oneself means this, to surrender one's moral judgment to a dictator and submerge oneself in an amorphous mass of indistinguishable others who have done the same, and in so doing to be redeemed from one's loneliness and powerlessness, it is clearly not to be encouraged. But in liberal societies, such as our own, where it is neither compulsory nor the principle of political order, it, or something structurally very similar, is both encouraged and embraced, only in spheres other than politics, viz. football, celebrity culture, and pop music. Being 'taken out of oneself' in this way is – perhaps not invariably, but often – an abnegation, not of self, but of the power of choice and self-direction, which is central to one's 'real' self. It is a kind of voluntary slavery, and, appearances notwithstanding, profoundly selfish. The moral, responsible self that should be fulfilled is surrendered in favour of the timid, hedonistic self seeking only temporary security and shallow gratification, things which, because they can be withdrawn at the slightest sign of nonconformity, imprison the subject in perpetual infantile dependence. If significant numbers in a free society still choose such a shrunken existence, it suggests that totalitarian societies were not as unpopular as they seemed to be, and that the grotesque travesty of social membership that they offered was evidently better than nothing.

Real social membership is not easy to anatomize. But let me note that there is nothing intrinsically wrong with football, popular music, or even an interest in celebrities. No doubt this is my timid, hedonistic self speaking, out of fear of brickbats to come, but football, like other team sports, demands courage, skill, dedication and

---

[61] During the public protests of December 2011 concerning the Russian parliamentary elections, the chairman of the electoral commission, Vladimir Churov, was widely reported as having said, in an interview with *Kommersant* magazine, that his 'No.1 law' was that 'Putin is always right'. (See Google.)

Robert Grant

endurance, and also has many sensible, mild-mannered devotees, probably the majority, who rightly admire those things about it and take no interest whatever in the vicarious life it offers to its more deluded fans or in the tabloid squalor in which its luminaries seem permanently sunk. Even celebrity culture is neither new (remember Mr Guppy in *Bleak House*?) nor as stupid as it may often seem. Like soap operas, gossip, and even the great Victorian serial novels, it provides an arena for the exercise, exchange and development of our moral ideas. Not everyone interested in celebrities necessarily approves of them. It is often said that the world of celebrities, like reality TV, resembles a zoo. But did anyone ever watch the admirable, and now banned, chimpanzees' tea party expecting to learn table manners from it, except negatively?[62]

As for pop music, well, there is pop music and pop music, as well as popular music in the old sense, a category to which some pop music still belongs, and of which Scruton approves, unlike Theodor Adorno, the high-minded and frequently insufferable Frankfurt School Marxist. Adorno could have got away with it, indeed did so at the time, being on the Left, but nothing recent has earned Scruton more opprobrium than his attacks on contemporary pop, unless it be his strictures (contrary to Adorno) concerning serialism and the avant-garde. No matter how wholesome your intentions or accurate your aim, if you take simultaneous potshots at both the market-supplied proles and the taxpayer-supported toffs, you can expect trouble.

Despite the offence they have caused, Scruton's by no means blanket criticisms of pop occupy only a couple of pages in *The Aesthetics of Music*, though he has expanded on them since. They and his objections to serialism and the like[63] centre on the proposition

[62] The spectacle is nowadays reckoned to have been injurious to the animals' dignity, but, at least to my childish perception at the time, that never worried them greatly, or at all.

[63] By 'serialism and the like' I mean Modernist music that, whatever its structural principle, is radically atonal. Much Modernist music from *The Rite of Spring* onwards, including works as different as Honegger's *Pacific 231* and the first movement of Bartók's *Music for Strings, Percussion and Celesta*, is atonal in the sense of being in no particular key, either locally or overall; but there is always a centre of gravity, a particular note, say, around which the composition rotates and on which it typically converges and comes eventually to rest. In both the Bartók and the Honegger we sense what the final note – we might call it the virtual tonic – must be some time before it arrives, and are harmlessly pleased when our expectation is fulfilled. Almost uniquely for an atonal and authentically Modernist work, then (1923) or subsequently, *Pacific 231* achieved worldwide

that neither genre is really music, as both philosophy and common sense (not always allies) conceive of it, since both, in essence, have reduced music proper to mere sound. That in itself might not matter, we might reply, since not all 'sound-art' is worthless, any more than the natural sounds of wind and waves are worthless or un-pleasurable. But pop of the bad sort is bad anyway, Scruton thinks, not just because it is intrinsically anti-musical, nor just because such real musical expression as survives in it is feeble, monotonous and uninventive. Techno music in particular, he says, has become little more than a tonally incoherent, electronically-generated noise, driven not by melody or harmony, which are vestigial at best, but by an external, purely mechanical beat, accompanying a tuneless de-clamatory gabble of fragmentary, nihilistic word-clusters.[64] Such head-banging stuff intimates no real renunciation of the self or its ex-pansion into true community, but only, and at best, an extinction almost to be welcomed.

It is as difficult to say what is good about good music as it is to define the good society and relate it to music. But here goes. In aesthetic as in ethical matters, the very word 'good' signifies a communal, shared, so far objective and even compulsory dimension. (If a thing really is good, rather than merely desired, be it an object, an artefact, an action or a person, then you and I are somehow, if obscurely, 'obliged' to see it as good, and to do so at first hand, not on others' say-so.) It is not so much the shared nature of an experience that makes it valuable, though that is necessary, as its quality, and – which is the same thing – the quality of the selves who share it. Is it a genuine community, a *Gemeinschaft*, bound by a selfless love of each for the others, and of all for the community thus composed, or a purpose-driven *Gesellschaft* or association, another kind of sharing, to which each sub-scribes basically for what he personally can get out of it, and whose

---

popular success, doubtless for the 'wrong' reasons (its brilliant sound effects, imitative of a steam locomotive), but one shouldn't look a gift horse in the mouth, and it is a fine piece about which much more could be said.

[64] Scruton has written many magazine articles in this vein. Here are two: 'Youth Culture's Lament', *City Journal*, Autumn 1998; 'Soul Music', *The American*, 27th February 2010. Both are readily available online. In 'Soul Music' he notes 'the collapse of music into sound... both in the world of pop and in the concert hall' (www.american.com/archive/2010/february/soul-music).

subscription may lapse as soon as the association fails to deliver?[65] There is nothing wrong with *Gesellschaft*. It is the root of commerce, it puts clothes on our backs and food on the table, it makes *Gemeinschaft*, duty and charity affordable, and it is copiously overwritten with *Gemeinschaft* anyway (as when I use this shop rather than a cheaper, because I like the proprietor, and his children go to school with mine). But a life lived exclusively under its banner – 'materialism', in short – would not be fully human.[66]

Scruton occupies himself at some length with the problem of sentimentality,[67] which we might call fake *Gemeinschaft* or bogus altruism. Courage, stoicism, generosity, charity, self-sacrifice, compassion, modesty and even humility: all are both broadly altruistic and difficult of achievement, given the universality, and even up to a point the necessity, of egoism. But, unlike egoism, they are admired, and admiration is something everyone wants and even needs, whether he deserves it or not. The easiest route to it, therefore, in one's own eyes as in others', is to simulate such virtues (especially compassion) whilst concealing even from oneself the underlying purpose, which is to look good, or, failing that, feel good, as cheaply as possible. When we all do this, united by a collective self-interest rather than by any real sympathy, we agree to keep up the common pretence and band together to wreak the severest vengeance on any outsider who points out its hollowness.

Real sympathy is different, and stems from strength, not weakness. I surrender to the music because I can afford to, and I lose nothing by doing so except my egoism. I abjure neither my autonomy nor my self-respect. I do not seek my private joy or sadness in the music; instead, for so long as I listen, I make the music's joy or sadness my own, and return to my mundane existence refreshed and revivified by this glimpse of a life which, while like mine, is not mine, and is the better for not being mine. Nor is it the composer's, for his egoistic concerns are no more interesting than my own or anyone else's, and if he fills his music with his own joys and sadnesses that leaves less room for the joys and sadnesses that we all feel, and which bring us together in our common sympathy. As Wilfrid

---

[65] At the risk of superfluity, perhaps I should mention that the distinction was first explicitly drawn by the pioneering German sociologist Ferdinand Tönnies (*Gemeinschaft und Gesellschaft*, 1887).

[66] 'Without *It* man cannot live. But he who lives with *It* alone is not a man.' (Martin Buber [1923], trans. R. Gregor Smith, *I and Thou* [London: Continuum, 2004], 32.)

[67] Scruton, *The Aesthetics of Music*, 485ff.

Mellers wrote of that least self-absorbed, least self-regarding, least self-dramatizing and consequently most truly dramatic of artists, concerning his G minor Symphony, no. 40: 'The suffering is not ours, or Mozart's, but all mankind's.'[68]

University of Glasgow
robert.grant@glasgow.ac.uk

[68] I am quoting, from memory, an article by Mellers in *Scrutiny* which I have tried, but failed, to locate. A later, less resoundingly-phrased formulation of the same idea can be found in Alec Harman and W.H. Mellers, *Man and his Music* (London: Barrie and Rockliff, 1962), 626.

Brilliant Performances

AARON RIDLEY

I am generally unsympathetic to the project, pursued by many recent philosophers of music, of attempting to specify the identity conditions for musical works – of attempting to specify the conditions that something, typically a performance, must satisfy if it is to count as an instance of this or that work. Call this the identity-project. Elsewhere, I have suggested that any such project is fundamentally misconceived.[1] Here, however, I want simply to explore a couple of the difficulties with which the identity-project is confronted, and to point out some of the costs that are likely to be incurred in trying to overcome them.

I

I begin with Nelson Goodman, whose *Languages of Art* did much to spark recent enthusiasm for the project that I have mentioned. His basic idea, it will be recalled, is that a musical work is 'defined' by the score in which it is notated: 'complete compliance with the score', he says, 'is the only requirement for a genuine instance of the work', so that even 'the most miserable performance without actual mistakes [counts] as such an instance, while the most brilliant performance with one wrong note does not'.[2] Goodman's reason for making this hugely counter-intuitive claim is that, if we allow the brilliant performance with one wrong note to count as a genuine or legitimate instance of the work, then, by transitivity of identity – through a succession of further wrong notes – we can get all the way to the thought that 'Three Blind Mice' counts as a genuine or legitimate instance of, say, Beethoven's Fifth Symphony; which is, as he remarks, absurd.[3]

To most of Goodman's readers, however, the absurdity of counting 'Three Blind Mice' as a legitimate instance of Beethoven's Fifth has not seemed self-evidently greater than that of refusing to count, say, Furtwängler's 1937 performance of it, fluffed horn-notes and all, as

---

[1] Ridley 2003; for a fuller version of the suggestion, see Ridley 2004: ch.4.
[2] Goodman 1968: 178 & 186.
[3] Goodman 1968: 187.

doi:10.1017/S1358246112000239   ©The Royal Institute of Philosophy and the contributors 2013
Royal Institute of Philosophy Supplement **71** 2013

such an instance; and so the tendency, post-Goodman, has been to try to build enough wiggle-room into the initial identity conditions to allow the latter, but not the former, to count as a genuine instance of Beethoven's work.[4] (I'll return to the issue of wiggle-room shortly.) The tendency, then, has been to accept that while Goodman's position does perhaps state a sufficient condition of a performance's being a genuine instance of a work – i.e. that it be in complete compliance with the score – it does not state a necessary condition. And, for the time being, I think we should go along with this.

II

Before moving on, though, I want to take a closer look at Goodman's position. The first thing to notice about it is how admirably explicit he is in distinguishing between identity-related issues – or, as one might call them, ontological issues – and evaluative issues. A performance can be a fully legitimate instance of a work despite being 'the most miserable' imaginable; whereas, on the other side, a performance can be altogether 'brilliant' while failing to be such an instance. This insistence, that ontological and evaluative issues can be treated completely separately, is an article of faith that Goodman's successors have endorsed, perhaps for the good- or obvious-seeming reason that one wouldn't, with one's ontological hat on, want to appear to be ruling putative instances of works in or out merely because one admired or thought ill of them.

The second thing to notice is how asymmetrical Goodman's apparently very symmetrical formulation is likely to strike one as being. The 'most miserable performance without actual mistakes', he says, counts as a genuine instance of a work, 'while the most brilliant performance with one wrong note does not'. Purely intuitively, it seems to me, we are likely to accept the first half of this without demur. We are all familiar with workaday, competent renditions of works – performances that linger in the memory not one jot – while never once having had it occur to us that they might not in fact *be* performances or instances of the works in question. (Our reasons, here, are closely related to the ones that we have for not resisting the application of the term 'music lessons' to what are given in most primary schools, despite the recognition that nothing especially musical is likely to feature in or result from them.) Whereas the second half of

[4]   See, e.g., Dodd 2010: 33.

Goodman's formulation is apt to strike us as outrageous. Surely, we will protest, if *anything* is a legitimate instance of Beethoven's Fifth Symphony then Furtwängler's 1937 performance is, the odd wrong note notwithstanding. It's quite brilliant! How can the occasional stumble affect *that*?! And so on.

But we don't need to appeal to intuition in order to grasp an asymmetry here. For there is a conceptual asymmetry in Goodman's formulation too. The first half of it – the half about miserable performances – appears to make perfect sense. There seems to be nothing problematic in understanding the claim that an uninspired and uninspiring, but accurate, performance of Beethoven's Fifth counts *as* a performance, *as* a genuine instance, of it, however drab. But the second half – that 'the most brilliant performance with one wrong note' does not count as such an instance – is far thornier; is, indeed, or so I suggest, strictly unintelligible. We cannot, that is, attach any real sense to the claim that Furtwängler's 1937 performance doesn't count as a genuine instance of Beethoven's Fifth Symphony, as Goodman would have us do. And this is because we cannot say what it counts as *instead*.

Perhaps, it might be suggested, it counts as an *il*legitimate instance of the work. But, if so, Goodman's initial problem simply resurfaces: for, by transitivity of identity, we can get all the way from there to the thought that 'Three Blind Mice' is an illegitimate instance of Beethoven's Fifth; which is absurd, since 'Three Blind Mice' is no sort of instance of that work at all. So it appears that Furtwängler's 1937 performance can be regarded as neither a legitimate nor an illegitimate instance of Beethoven's Fifth, since either alternative would license, it seems, counting 'Three Blind Mice' as an instance of that work too. It appears, that is, that the Furtwängler cannot be *any* kind of instance of that work. But then in what sense might it be said to be a 'brilliant performance'? Of *what*?

There would seem to be two possibilities here. One is that Furtwängler's performance is a brilliant performance of something *else* – of a work that is very like, but is distinct from, Beethoven's Fifth Symphony. But this seems wildly implausible. On Goodman's schema, after all, it would appear to be a condition of a performance's counting as a legitimate instance of a work that it be produced in (complete) compliance with the score that defines that work. Yet the score that Furtwängler and his orchestra were attempting to comply with was that of Beethoven's Fifth Symphony, not of some other work similar to it.

We might, perhaps, meet this objection by claiming that a performance can be *of* a work without having been meant to be a performance of it. So here, we might say, Furtwängler and the Berlin Philharmonic, although intending to comply with the score that defines Beethoven's Fifth, actually produced a performance that conformed with another, closely similar score – and so was in fact a performance of *that* instead. But we must resist this suggestion, for at least two reasons. The first is rather Kantian in flavour. Just as Kant insisted that, in order to be moral, an action must be done out of respect for – or, as we might say, in compliance with – and not merely in conformity with, the moral law, so we should insist that, in order to be recognizably a performance *at all*, a given sound-event must be produced in compliance with, and not merely in conformity with, a score. For, in its ordinary sense, 'performance' is an intentional notion – a fact that Goodman's use of the term 'compliance' appropriately picks out; and we should be reluctant, in the absence of compelling reasons to the contrary, to abandon that sense, and to allow that performances can be given by accident.[5] The second reason to resist the present suggestion is that, if we were to grant that what Furtwängler's performance is a performance of is a work that is very like, but is distinct from, Beethoven's Fifth, we could no longer make sense of the idea that it contains 'wrong note[s]'. For, by hypothesis, the score that Furtwängler's performance in fact conforms to is perfectly realized in the sound-event that he and the Berlin Philharmonic produced.

The other possible way out might be to suggest that the term 'performance' should be understood here in one of its other ordinary senses, perhaps as meaning, simply, 'something done' – as when we speak of agents 'performing' actions – or as meaning 'something done showily' – as when we might describe someone's way of leaving the room as a 'performance'. Construed in one or the other of these ways, we might say that Furtwängler's 1937 performance was a performance in the sense, merely, that it was something done, perhaps showily, with an orchestra – maybe indeed something brilliant (certainly the sounds that we hear are thrilling enough), but not to be understood in terms of its compliance or non-compliance, or even its conformity or non-conformity, with any score. But this is unconvincing. First, it breaks the rule of charity that states that

---

[5]   It is not a counter-example to this claim to note that, e.g., for many years performers believed that they were giving performances of Purcell's *Trumpet Voluntary*, when the work was in fact by Jeremiah Clark (see Davies 2001: 163–166 for discussion). For here the mistake did not concern the *work* – i.e. what the performance was *of* – but rather its correct attribution.

agents should, wherever possible, be understood as in fact doing what they take themselves to be doing – and there is no question here but that Furtwängler and his orchestra took themselves to be performing Beethoven's Fifth Symphony, and, indeed, that they took themselves *not* to be, merely, making orchestral noises, showily or otherwise. And, second, it makes it wholly obscure what might be meant by the idea that their 'performance' contains wrong notes. Wrong by what standards? Why pick out just *these* notes as mistakes? I can see no way of answering such questions.

The upshot of the foregoing is that there really is no plausible sense that can be attached to Goodman's invocation of the 'brilliant performance with one wrong note': either the performance turns out not really to *be* a performance, brilliant or otherwise, or else its notes turn out not to be wrong. So there is, I think, no properly strict interpretation of Goodman's formulation that makes sense of it – and it does need to be strict, if we are not, by transitivity of identity, to find ourselves in 'Three Blind Mice' territory. Which suggests that there is something deeply the matter with what he is trying to do. I shall try to say presently what I think that is.

III

As a first step in that direction, let's look more closely at the idea that legitimate performances are those produced in complete compliance with a score. This idea is, in one obvious sense, very exacting – a feature of it that, as we have seen, leaves Goodman with nothing sensible to say about whatever it was that Furtwängler and his orchestra brought off in 1937.[6] But it should also be noted that, in another sense, the idea is actually quite accommodating, for it allows that a potentially indefinitely large number of readily distinguishable sound-events should *all* count as legitimate instances of a work. In part, we can see this from Goodman's own almost gleeful admission that 'the most miserable performance' might, according to him, count as such an instance: for so, evidently, might a less miserable performance, or an average performance, or indeed a brilliant one, so long as none of them contains 'actual mistakes'; and these differences in quality are respects in which the relevant sound-events differ from and are distinguishable from one another. But it can

---

[6] He can say, of course, what they were *trying* to do: they were trying, but failing, to produce a performance of Beethoven's Fifth.

Aaron Ridley

also be seen from the familiar observation that scores underdetermine performances.[7]

Depending on the style and period of the music in question, scores prescribe more or less closely what a performer is to do. Some scores (from, e.g., the early baroque) give only a figured bass, leaving it to the performer to decide what melodic material to place on top; some scores specify the instruments to be used, while others do not; some scores contain detailed prescriptions concerning dynamics (Alban Berg's, notoriously, distinguish *f* not only from *ff* but also from *fff* and *ffff*), while others contain none; some scores are very specific about tempo, and changes in tempo, while others say nothing; and so on. But no matter how prescriptive a particular score might be, and along however many dimensions, there will always be some latitude, and so always an indefinitely wide range of ways of complying with it. So, for example, your performance of Berg's piano sonata might, at its loudest, be much louder than mine, and someone else's might be louder still. But so long as we are all playing our *ffff*s louder than our *fff*s, and are playing both of these louder than our *ff*s (let alone our mere *f*s), we are all complying with the dynamics that the score prescribes.

It follows from this that Goodman's account, although it demands that a performance be *completely* compliant with the score, also permits much latitude, whether that latitude is taken voluntarily – as by a performer determined to play his *pianissimo*s as softly as possible – or not – as by someone whose *andante* is at the slow end simply because he cannot play the piece any faster. Thus Goodman construes scores as *sets of instructions*, where those instructions underdetermine the performances that comply with them. And, to this extent at least, what he says seems unproblematic.

IV

Things only become problematic, it seems, when a performer exceeds the latitude permitted by Goodman's demand for complete compliance with the score – when the performance includes 'actual mistakes' or the odd 'wrong note'.

Goodman speaks as if all fallings short of complete compliance consisted either in playing non-prescribed notes by accident or in accidentally failing to play the notes prescribed. And of course many

---

[7] For a very thorough discussion of this observation, see Davies 2001: 116–123.

departures from a score have precisely this character – for example, Furtwängler's 1937 performance of Beethoven's Fifth: the fluffed horn-notes are clearly both non-prescribed and inadvertently produced. But, just as complete compliance with a score can be achieved by deliberate as well as by non-deliberate occupation of the latitude that a score permits, so departures from a score can be deliberate as well as not. Such departures can, moreover, involve many more things than playing the wrong notes or failing to play the right ones. Depending on the period and style of the work in question, scores can prescribe – and hence departures from them are possible – along at least six different dimensions: these are, crudely, the dimensions of melody (or pitch), harmony, rhythm, dynamics, tempo and timbre. So we must suppose that, for Goodman, departures along any of these, whether inadvertent or otherwise, count as non-compliance: the second half of his formulation, that is, should state – albeit less punchily – that 'the most brilliant performance with one departure from the score' does not count as a legitimate instance of a work.

We have been assuming, for the sake of argument at least, that Goodman's demand for complete compliance with a score represents at most a sufficient – but not a necessary – condition of work-identity. And its non-necessity is shown, we have been assuming, by a performance such as Furtwängler's, which is 'brilliant' but contains notes not prescribed by the score. Furtwängler's performance departs, inadvertently, from Beethoven's score along the melodic dimension, the one dimension that Goodman explicitly acknowledges. And we can probably agree with Goodman that, even if this does not disqualify it as a performance *of* Beethoven's Fifth, it does constitute a blemish in it. We can probably agree, that is, that Furtwängler's performance would have been in some sense *better* had it been in complete compliance with the score – had the brass section not had its dodgy moments. For those moments, we can probably conclude, add nothing to the performance that we should actively prize.

There are other cases, however, in which we might want to say something different – even when these involve, as in the Furtwängler case, nothing but non-deliberate departures from the melodic dimension of what a score prescribes. I have in mind examples such as Sviatoslav Richter's 1960 performance of the Liszt piano sonata, in which, as a more or less inevitable side-effect of the driven, demonic quality of its delivery, the occasional wrong note features; or Jacqueline du Pré's accidental pizzicato in the second of the big ascending scales in the first movement of Elgar's cello concerto (the version conducted by Barbirolli). In these cases, it seems to me, we might well prize the performers' departures from the score, resulting from and testifying to, as both do, the quite extraordinary intensity of their playing – and, in the Richter case at least, testifying also to the work's ultra-virtuousic demands coupled with his own determination to take no prisoners in meeting them. We might not want to say that these performances are *better* for departing from the relevant scores in their respective ways; but nor, it seems to me, would we have much inclination to say that either performance would have been better for *not* departing from the score in the way that it does.

Two things are worth noting about examples of this kind. The first is that they strengthen the assumption that Goodman's identity-condition is at most sufficient, rather than necessary. For, if what I have said is plausible, it seems that some departures from a score are not even to be regarded as blemishes in the performances that include them – i.e. are not to be regarded as moments that, unlike those provided by Furtwängler's errant horns, we might, *ceteris paribus*, wish were otherwise.[8] The second thing to note is that what I have just said is true *only* on the assumption that the departures in question are accidental. If we were to find, for instance, that Du Pré had planned her very distinctive glitch, or had decided, once she had inadvertently made it, to include it on future occasions, we would regard the performances in question not as thrillingly intense, but as contrived, as merely affecting intensity, and would think the worse of them for it.

V

But now consider another sort of case, in which non-compliance with the score is perfectly deliberate. A good example can be found in performances of the closing bars of the passacaglia finale of Brahms's Fourth Symphony, whose score indicates no deviation at this point from the tempo already prescribed. Brahms *could* have indicated such a deviation: he was fully cognizant of *accelerando*s and *rallentando*s, and was not averse to using them. So the absence from his score of any instruction to speed up or to slow down is, in effect, the instruction to do neither, but to play these closing bars in tempo. And yet: two of the most celebrated performances that have been given of Brahms's symphony depart, and depart entirely intentionally, from the score in just this respect. The ones that I have in mind are Toscanini's 1935 performance, which decelerates markedly

---

[8]   For a denial of this claim, see Davies 2001: 241–253.

in its final bars, and Furtwängler's 1943 performance, which does the exact opposite. And both are brilliant.

It is quite difficult, from a perspective at all like Goodman's, to make sense of this. One can imagine that a follower of Goodman might attempt to accommodate the Richter and Du Pré examples by saying that *the intention* to comply completely with a score is a condition of the resultant performance's counting as a legitimate instance of a work: this would be one way of trying to build in the sort of 'wiggle room' that I mentioned earlier. But that move clearly cannot work here. For it is quite evident that what the Toscanini and Furtwängler performances evince is a fully premeditated intention to *depart* from Brahms's score, to *not* comply with it.

One possibility here would be to suggest that the two conductors were proposing *revisions* to Brahms's score, or even *corrections* to it. But neither suggestion is attractive. The latter implies that Brahms's Fourth Symphony is something independently and antecedently existent which Brahms, in his score, failed to transcribe accurately: and even if one were in the grip of the sort of metaphysical picture that would make this suggestion so much as passingly plausible – as no one, surely, should be – it cannot account for *both* performances' being corrections to Brahms's score, since they 'correct' it in mutually exclusive ways. Nor is the other suggestion, that Toscanini and Furtwängler were proposing revisions to Brahms's score, any better. Its effect is just to multiply the number of works at issue, so that we have Brahms's Fourth Symphony, Brahms's Fourth-as-revised-by-Toscanini and Brahms's Fourth-as-revised-by-Furtwängler. Neither conductor, on this conception, is actually performing Brahms's Fourth Symphony – although both took themselves to be doing so; and neither is departing in any way from the score of the work that, in fact, he is performing, since, by hypothesis, the score of Brahms's Fourth-as-revised-by-Toscanini prescribes a deceleration in the final bars, while that of Brahms's Fourth-as-revised-by-Furtwängler prescribes the reverse.

Another possibility would be to draw on the distinction that is sometimes made between interpretation and performance.[9] According to this, an interpretation is a *way* of performing a work, so that many different performances can count as instances of the same interpretation. Here, then, we can think of Toscanini as performing *his* interpretation of Brahms's Fourth and of Furtwängler as performing *his*. This has the advantages of introducing nothing metaphysically extravagant; of construing Toscanini and Furtwängler

[9]   See, e.g., Hermeren 1993.

as doing nothing at odds with what they took themselves to be doing; and of keeping the number of works at issue down to one – Brahms's Fourth Symphony – which is where it should be. But it secures these advantages only at the cost of not moving anything on. For it just reintroduces the original problem at the level of interpretation rather than performance. How are we to make sense of the idea that an interpretation which deliberately departs from the score of the work that it interprets is, still, an interpretation *of* that work? Or, to put things in a more overtly Goodman-like way, how are we to block the move which might, by transitivity of identity, take us all the way from the thought that Toscanini's interpretation of Brahms's Fourth, say, is a legitimate instance of it to the thought that so-and-so's interpretation of Brahms's Fourth, a performance of which is identical to 'Three Blind Mice', is also a legitimate instance of it?

VI

But these suggestions – that we're dealing with revisions, or with corrections, or with interpretations – are actually only red herrings, prompted by our willingness, or so I'll suggest shortly, to follow Goodman even as far as we have done. The question we should really be asking is what we should say about Toscanini's and Furtwängler's performances of Brahms's Fourth if we set Goodman aside entirely for the moment, and wear only our listeners' hats.

We would say, I think, that both are brilliant, that both depart from the score, albeit in opposite ways – but, also, that both depart from the score *to very similar effect*. For both bring out the fact that Brahms's symphony ends tragically, that it ends in a way that is both fated and fateful. In the Toscanini, the effect is like that of watching a train hurtle into a rock-face; in the Furtwängler, the hurtling is also headlong, but is into the abyss. In both we hear the catastrophe. And this, I think, would make us want to say that these performances are just *better* than any performance which, while wholly compliant with the score, did not allow us to hear this. Indeed, for what it's worth, I have never heard the close of the passacaglia played to such devastating effect in any performance that *does* stay in *tempo*. Barbirolli's 1967 performance (with the Vienna Philharmonic) comes close; so, too, perhaps, does Celibidache's 1959 Milan performance: both have the right air of ineluctability about them. But neither conductor, to my ear at least, does *full* justice to the ending of Brahms's symphony, as Toscanini and Furtwängler do.

What this brings out is the unsurprising fact that there is *more* to a musical work than can be indicated in a score. And this, in turn, brings out the inadequacy of saying, as I did earlier, that scores un-underderdetermine the performances that comply with them. For, if we take seriously the idea that a score is a set of instructions, we should at once note that, in the case of almost all sets of instructions, there is a *point* to them that goes beyond any mere requirement that they be complied with. Very rarely is instruction-following an end in itself. Rather, instructions tend to be means to the realization of ends that are, in the relevant sense, external to them. Flat-pack assembly-instructions are means to the end of pieces of furniture; recipes are means to the end of meals; battlefield orders are means to the end of victories; and so on. And this entails that, except in the rarest of cases – and even in those mostly only by luck – successfully following instructions requires a grasp of the end to which they are directed, of their *point*, so that one sees beyond the instructions, as it were, to their realization. (Just try making sense of, for example, the pictograms that come as instructions with IKEA flat-packs without keeping firmly in mind what the finished product is to be, and indeed what it should look like.)

There are of course exceptions to this – as, for example, when one is instructed to fold a piece of paper into eight, say, and to cut all sorts of intricate little holes in it. Here, there is a point to the instructions that lies beyond them – perhaps that the result, when opened out, should be surprising or delightful – but this is not an end of which one need have any grasp in order successfully to follow them.

It is unlikely, however, that musical scores are helpfully to be thought of in this way. Rather, it seems reasonable to suppose that they are central cases of the kind of sets of instructions which, if they are to be followed successfully, require a grasp of their point. And the natural suggestion is that Toscanini and Furtwängler, in their respective performances of Brahms's symphony, showed that they had indeed grasped one aspect of that point – namely, that the symphony's ending is tragic – an understanding that they may have gained through study of the score itself, through previous experiences of attempting to perform the work, or from hearing the performances of others. That they took the point that they grasped to transcend the authority of (the letter of) the score is shown in the performances of the work that they gave. And that we agree with them about this is shown in our judgement that their performances are brilliant.[10]

---

[10]   It is worth noting, incidentally, that little would have been added to the score had Brahms expressly prescribed there that the work's ending

If the foregoing is correct, we can conclude that instructions whose point lies beyond them, and whose successful implementation requires a grasp of that point, are never indefeasible. And we can note that this is why, to return briefly to Goodman, the demand that a performance comply *completely* with the set of instructions that a score comprises could never be a necessary condition of that performance's being a legitimate instance of the work notated there. For this demand is always open to being flouted by a 'brilliant' performance, by a performance which evinces a grasp of the point of the score that licenses – i.e. renders legitimate – a departure from it.

VII

There are some quite interesting consequences that follow from this, and I'll turn to several of these in a moment. But first it is necessary to address an objection that is sure to be made to the argument that I have just offered.

It will be objected that I have made things very easy for myself by picking an example in which a brilliant performance departs from the score along the dimension of tempo, rather, say, than melodically or harmonically. For, the objection continues, not everything that a score prescribes is prescribed with equal rigidity; and, in particular, prescriptions concerning tempo, as perhaps also dynamics, are not as rigid as prescriptions concerning melody or harmony – i.e. prescriptions concerning the actual notes that are to be played, however loudly and at whatever speed. Which is why – the objection may well conclude – Goodman chose to highlight 'mistakes' and 'wrong notes' rather, merely, than unprescribed accelerations and slowings down.

One possible response to this objection would be to suggest that it argues backwards. From the fact that we are very pleased to regard a performance of Brahms's Fourth, say, as 'brilliant', despite its departure from the score along the dimension of tempo, it seems that we are

---

should be played tragically. For, unless at least some of what he did prescribe lent itself to that end, the instruction would have been empty – which is why, for example, Schubert's so-called 'Tragic Symphony' (his fourth) is impossible to take seriously under that title. (Certain expressive instructions are especially high-risk in this regard, even if, e.g., Elgar's frequent *nobilmentes* constitute a bracing reminder that such risks can, in the event, be worth running.)

to conclude that prescriptions concerning tempo are somehow intrinsically less rigid than prescriptions along other dimensions; and so that the notion of complete compliance with the score does not (really or fully) include complete compliance with the tempo prescribed in it. Which is, surely, just to beg the question.

Moreover, the response might continue, we are *also* very happy to regard a performance that departs from the allegedly more rigid prescriptions concerning melody as 'brilliant', as is shown, for example, by Richter's performance of the Liszt sonata. So what of differences in rigidity now? And if the idea is supposed to be, simply, that Richter's departures are condonable because accidental rather than deliberate, we can easily change the example. Reinvoking a distinction mentioned a moment ago, we can describe Busoni's transcription for piano of the *Chaconne* from Bach's D minor violin partita as an interpretation of it – indeed, as an undeniably brilliant interpretation of it. And yet this interpretation makes melodic prescriptions quite at odds with those to be found in Bach's score: it prescribes notes other than Bach's, and fails to prescribe all of Bach's notes at the moments that Bach prescribes them. But it is 'brilliant' nonetheless because it gets and captures the *point* of the *Chaconne*.

I think that both parts of this response to the objection are correct, as far as they go; but also that they miss a deeper thought that the objection draws upon. This is the idea that, irrespective of what deviations we will tolerate, the *actual notes*, and the *actual* harmonic and rhythmic relations between them, that a score comprises are simply more fundamental to a work's being what it is than are any considerations about how it is to be played – for instance, loudly, softly, increasingly quickly or increasingly slowly, or, indeed, on what instruments.

There is, no doubt, a strong intuitive appeal to this idea – not least because *something* like it may be roughly true of much of the music that many of us listen to. And something like it *is* true, surely, of music in the classical tradition between the early eighteenth and the early twentieth centuries, from which all of my examples have been drawn. So I need to say more.

I noted earlier that, depending on period and style, a score can be prescriptive along a number of different dimensions, and that it can prescribe a greater or lesser amount along each of these. This indicates at once that there is no settled generalization to be made about which dimensions are *intrinsically* more germane or significant than others: their significance in a given score is wholly relative to the period and style of the work notated there. So, for example, in the case of a jazz standard, the most germane dimension will tend to be the harmonic;

which is why suitably acculturated listeners are so much better at spotting them when they are played than are those whose listening habits direct them more automatically to, say, the melodic dimension of the work; for in this style of music prescriptions along the latter are ordinarily to be understood rather flexibly. But note that even here we can only talk of tendencies and of what is ordinarily likely to be the case: there are, as it were, some more or less reasonable stylistic expectations in play; but even these are, in the end, open to revision in light of the peculiarities of particular, individual works, and of the significance, relative to them, of this or that dimension of prescription.

So we can say that, in general, there is a reasonable expectation that in classical music of the relevant period the dimensions of melody, harmony and rhythm will be more significant than that of tempo. And this is, no doubt, why it is relatively easy to find examples of 'brilliant' performances of such music that depart from what the score prescribes along the latter dimension. But – as I suggested a moment ago – it is not as if there are *no* examples of brilliant performances that make other kinds of departures: Busoni's transcription of Bach's *Chaconne* is just one such instance, an instance that will be detected by any suitably acculturated listener.[11] Rather, in this as in all cases, we can talk only of tendencies, of what is generally likely to be true of works of this or that sort. And, of course, the fact remains that the work that I have focussed on – Brahms's Fourth Symphony – *does* contain explicit prescriptions concerning tempo in its score, prescriptions which, even if they are to be regarded as less rigid than some of the others that the score contains, are nonetheless roundly, and even productively, disregarded in the 'brilliant' performances that I have mentioned.

One might in fact be tempted to make a stronger claim in the present context, and say that, because the score contains relatively few prescriptions concerning tempo, as opposed to those concerning rhythm, say, any one of the former should be regarded as *less* defeasible than any one of the latter (if, as Goodman and others assume, the score in some sense 'defines' the work). But this temptation should be resisted. It is true that there is one reasonably robust generalization that lies in this sort of direction – namely, that the less, *overall*, that a score prescribes, the less defeasible are its individual prescriptions

---

[11] Such acculturation is necessary, by the way. I once played recordings of the Bach and the Busoni versions of the *Chaconne*, one after the other, to my kids (both were then under ten), and they were so distracted by the fact that the former was on the violin while the latter was on the piano that they didn't notice the sense in which they were the same.

(consider the limiting case of John Cage's *4'33''*: the playing of any note on the piano *at all* would be sufficient to disqualify a performance as being of that work). But we can't get from there to any useful generalizations concerning individual dimensions of prescription, partly for reasons having to do with a well know informal fallacy, but mostly because, as I have insisted, the significance of this or that dimension in a given score is wholly relative to the period and style of the work notated there, and may even be relative to the work itself.[12]

Thus, to return to the objection, it is true that it is easier to find examples of classical performance that are 'brilliant' despite departing from prescriptions concerning tempo than it is to find them among performances which depart from prescriptions concerning, e.g., melody; and it is true that this is, in part, a function of the reasonable stylistic expectations that an acculturated listener will have in the context of music of this sort. But none of this shows that the idea of complete compliance with a score somehow excludes complete compliance with prescribed *tempi*; nor does it show that the departures from a score of a performer who disregards the latter are somehow different in kind from those of a performer who disregards prescriptions along any other dimension with which a score concerns itself. So the objection fails.

VIII

I have argued, then, that instructions whose point lies beyond them, and whose successful implementation requires a grasp of that point, are never indefeasible. And I have suggested that this shows why, *contra* Goodman, the demand that a performance comply *completely* with the set of instructions that a score comprises could never be a necessary condition of that performance's being a legitimate instance of the work notated there. There is always the possibility that a performance will be given – a 'brilliant' performance – which evinces a grasp of the point of the score in a way that essentially involves, and hence licenses, a departure from it.

I said a moment ago that, if these conclusions are correct, some quite interesting consequences follow. One of these is that the ways in which we can usefully think about musical *content* are circumscribed in respects that some philosophers have missed. So, for example, Andrew Kania has recently warned us of the dangers of equivocating between two senses of 'musical content', according to

[12] For some evidently germane reflections here, see Walton 1970.

one of which we can specify the content of a work in advance of any attempt to grasp or understand its point, according to the other of which we cannot give any such advance specification. He attempts to explain the distinction that he has in mind through an analogy with literature:

> In one sense of 'content' – equivalent to what usually goes by the name of 'meaning' in literary discourse – it is plausible that we could not hope to say what the content of a work is, in advance of 'faithful' (good) interpretations of it... In another sense of content, though..., clearly we *could* know the content in advance of any interpretations of it. Given enough time, I could tell you whether you have a faithful copy of *Finnegan's Wake*, though I have next to no understanding of that work

– just as, he suggests, 'anyone with access to to a copy of [a] score and the ability to read it can tell you to a large extent the content a performance would need to have if it were to be a performance' of a given work.[13]

But the analogy with literature is unhelpful. First, a literary text does not stand in the same relation to a literary work as a score stands in to a musical work. Scores, we have followed Goodman in supposing, are instructions for producing performances of musical works, whereas texts – notwithstanding some heroic argumentation to the contrary by Peter Kivy – are not instructions for producing performances of literary works.[14] So while it is true that one might check word by word that two copies of *Finnegan's Wake* are identical, without an understanding of what those words signify; and while it is perhaps true that there is a sense in which one might be said to be checking thereby that both copies have the same literary content; nothing at all follows from this about the issue of musical content. For the content of a set of instructions is not equivalent to the content of its realization. The content of a score is no more the content of the work notated there, of which performances might be given, than the content of a recipe is identical to the content of the meal prepared in its light, or than the content of a set of flat-pack assembly-instructions is a table, or a day-bed. And this point is evidently unaffected by a properly completed version of Kania's would-be analogy. For it is clearly true that someone without an understanding of a given work could check, note by note, whether two putative scores of it are identical: but this would not be *thereby*

13 Kania 2008: 68.
14 Kivy 2008. For a powerful critique, see Feagin 2008.

to check the musical content of the work for whose realization they provide instructions. However musical content is to be understood, in other words, it cannot be on the assumption that, in terms of content, scores and works are identical.[15]

Another consequence of my argument is that we should perhaps reconsider our willingness to concede to Goodman that complete compliance with the score might at least be a sufficient condition of a performance's counting as a legitimate instance of a work – that, as he has it, 'the most miserable performance without actual mistakes' – i.e. without actual departures from the score – counts as such an instance. I said at the beginning that we were likely to accept this without demur; and perhaps we *should* accept it. But we should also note that a performance might be 'miserable' in Goodman's sense in virtue of competely missing the point of the work performed – by failing to register, for instance, that the work ends in tragedy, by being leaden where light-footedness is called for, by remaining oblivious to the need to be emphatic just *here*, by missing the deep pulse that should animate the work and substituting for it something merely akin to a beat; and so on. We might well think that any performance with *these* shortcomings is not just miserable, because point-missing and aesthetically inert, but is not really an instance of the work at all. And this, in turn, might make us wonder whether ontological and evaluative issues can, after all, be kept as distinct as Goodman and his followers would have us believe.

Perhaps. I'll suggest in a moment that the latter worry is in fact warranted. But as to the former – whether an aesthetically wretched performance of a work can really count as a legitimate instance of it – it seems to me that the proper response is a shrug of the shoulders. Who cares? Count it if you want to – just don't expect me ever to listen to it again. Why should the question whether it is legitimate *as an instance* stir me?

IX

The reason why it might feel as if it should stir me is that the corresponding question at the other end of the evaluative scale certainly

---

[15] Notice that Goodman's own formulation, that a score 'defines' a work, is not guilty of making this assumption: the sort of definition that he has in mind might include the sense in which each of us is defined by our DNA. We are each uniquely identifiable in respect of our DNA – but none of us is *identical* to our DNA.

does have, and has proved to have, real purchase. For, as I noted at the outset, no one at all has been willing to go along with Goodman's thought that 'the most brilliant performance with one wrong note' does not count as a legitimate instance of a work – and this, not for the already good enough reason that it is impossible to make sense of the claim, as I tried to show earlier that it isn't, but for the less philosophical and better, more musical, reason that if *anything* counts as a legitimate instance of, say, Beethoven's Fifth Symphony, then Furtwängler's 1937 performance does. We seem to regard the 'brilliant' performance as a trump card in this context.

I think that we are right to do this, on grounds that I have attempted to defend. I also think that we are right, on much the same grounds, to be more or less indifferent to the question whether the wretched performance should be regarded as a sort of anti-trump card (who cares?). But the next move that has standardly been made – to hunt for identity conditions that allow enough 'wiggle room' to accommodate brilliant performances – strikes me as very problematic; and this is the final consequence that follows from the argument that I have attempted to offer here.

The problem, in a nutshell, is this. Any set of identity conditions is going to have to rule some putative instances of works out, otherwise we'll find ourselves allowing 'Three Blind Mice' to count as a legitimate instance of, say, Beethoven's Fifth. It is, moreover, going to have to rule out the relevant non-instances *a priori*, so that we can disallow this or that deviation from whatever norms the conditions specify in advance of any particular deviating instance. A lot of the time this won't be a problem. Many of the non-instances that are ruled out will be miserable or wretched performances, and no one should much mind or care about the exclusion of these – or indeed have any particular view about them either way. If the odd one has to go to the wall for the sake of a certain theoretical tidiness, then so be it. But every now and again the performance to be disallowed will be a 'brilliant' one; and these, as we have seen, function as trump cards. They show, just as they showed in the Goodman case, that conditions that had been taken to be indefeasibly necessary can, in fact, be no more than sufficient at most. They demand, that is, some extra 'wiggle-room' to be built in. And this means that *any* set of identity conditions, no matter how splendidly accommodating it might be of brilliant performances that we already know about, can only ever be provisional, since it simply cannot have the clout to rule out, *a priori*, the possibility of the next deviant, but brilliant, performance that nobody could have seen coming. We can say, then, that, in this context, the role of brilliant performances is to remind us that our aesthetic expectations, however reasonable, and however ingeniously formulated, are always, in principle, open to disruption. And this, it seems to me, poses a more or less insurmountable obstacle to the identity-project in which Goodman and his followers have been engaged.[16]

University of Southampton
amr3@soton.ac.uk

Bibliography

Davies, Stephen (2001), *Musical Works and Performances: a Philosophical Exploration*, Oxford: Oxford University Press.

Dodd, Julian (2010), 'Confessions of an Unrepentant Timbral Sonicist', *British Journal of Aesthetics* **50**(1), 33–52.

Feagin, Susan (2008), 'Critical Study: Reading and Performing', *British Journal of Aesthetics* **48**(1), 89–97.

Goodman, Nelson (1968), *Languages of Art*, Indianapolis: Hackett.

Hermeren, Goran (1993), 'The Full Voic'd Quire: Types of Interpretations of Music', in M. Krausz, ed., *The Interpretation of Music*, Oxford:Clarendon Press, 9–32.

Kania, Andrew (2008), 'Piece for the End of Time: in Defence of Musical Ontology', *British Journal of Aesthetics* **48**(1), 65–79.

Kivy, Peter (2008), *The Performance of Reading: An Essay in the Philosophy of Literature*, Oxford: Oxford University Press.

Ridley, Aaron (2003), 'Against Musical Ontology', *Journal of Philosophy* **100**, 203–220.

Ridley, Aaron (2004), *The Philosophy of Music: Theme and Variations*, Edinburgh: Edinburgh University Press.

Walton, Kendall (1970), 'Categories of Art', *Philosophical Review* **79**(3), 334–367.

---

[16]   My thanks to the audience at the RIP lecture at which this talk was first given, in November 2010: many of the comments and suggestions made there were very helpful.

Artistic Truth

ANDY HAMILTON

According to Wittgenstein, in the remarks collected as *Culture and Value*, 'People nowadays think, scientists are there to instruct them, poets, musicians etc. to entertain them. That the latter have something to teach them; that never occurs to them.' 18th and early 19th century art-lovers would have taken a very different view. Dr. Johnson assumed that the poets had truths to impart, while Hegel insisted that 'In art we have to do not with any agreeable or useful child's play, but with an unfolding of the truth.' Though it still exerts a submerged influence, the concept of artistic truth has since sustained hammer-blows both from modernist aestheticism, which divorces art from reality, and from postmodern subjectivism about truth. This article aims to resurrect it, seeking a middle way between Dr. Johnson's *didactic concept of art*, and the modernist and postmodernist divorce of art from reality.

It argues that *high art aims at truth*, in something like the way that beliefs are said to aim at truth, that is, it asserts an internal connection with truth. *Each artform aims at truth in its own way or ways*. This relatively modest claim contrasts high art with *art with a small 'a' that aims merely to please*, such as sentimental or sensationalist art. The claim is developed by appealing to a *post-Romantic conception of art*, which says that art is autonomous, and so is its audience in responding to it; artworks present truth-assessable possibilities that should be *freely interpretable*. On this conception, the most valuable art leaves open to the audience how it should be interpreted, and does not preach or broadcast messages, whether religious or political. In contrast, *committed or didactic art* with its fixed, often quite simple meaning – medieval wall-paintings in churches, socialist realism, agitprop cinema – leaves no such freedom.

These then are the options under consideration:

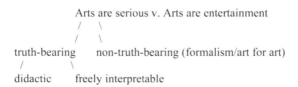

doi:10.1017/S1358246112000185

Andy Hamilton

Given a *non-didactic* conception of artistic truth, art can be autonomous. A broad concept of aestheticism or art for art's sake is compatible with artistic truth, and holds that art is valuable in itself, non-instrumentally. On this view, truth is not a merely useful product of art, but is intrinsic to it.

1. The role of truth in art

Lady Gaga proclaims in her concerts 'I hate the truth!', adding in an interview that 'in fact I hate the truth so much I prefer a giant dose of bullshit any day over the truth'.[1] With less chutzpah but more philosophical sophistication, both Marxists and postmodernists debunk the suggestion that art aims at truth – on the grounds that art is ideological and, perhaps, that truth does not exist. Analytic philosophers are more cautious but equally sceptical, though artistic cognitivism has defenders among them. Gordon Graham, for instance, argues that we value art according to its ability to illuminate human experience, and that beauty and pleasure alone 'cannot explain the value of art at its finest'.[2] Even he does not defend artistic truth, however.

There is an obvious connection between cognitivism and artistic truth. However, except concerning the particular questions of the semantics of fictional discourse, and the impact of factual error on artistic value, truth has been little-debated in Anglo-American philosophical aesthetics. In asking whether the historical inaccuracy of an historical novel affects its aesthetic or artistic value, for instance, it is assumed too hastily that art is defined independent of truth. The focus is on how falsehood detracts from artistic value, not on how truth contributes to it.[3] Against dominant anti-definition or sociological accounts of art, I believe, one can talk at least of salient features, and among these is the property that *high art aims at truth*.

Artists often suggest that this is their intention. James Joyce said that in *Dubliners* his aim was to tell the truth; Picasso, it is said,

---

[1]   Reported for instance at http://www.cleveland.com/ministerofculture/index.ssf/2011/05/lady_gaga_wasnt_born_this_way.html

[2]   Graham (2007), 64. Rowe (2009) considers artistic truth, but mainly in the context of artistic cognitivism; see also Price (1949), Hospers (1970), John (2007).

[3]   For example, Keats's sonnet 'On First Looking into Chapman's Homer' describes Cortez first sighting the Pacific from a peak in Darien. This is erroneous both historically and geographically, but many would argue that its value as poetry is unaffected by the error.

commented that 'Art is a lie that tells the truth'. As Danto argues, art
– by which he means high or fine art, 'Art' with a capital 'A' – must be
about something.[4] Presumably it says, suggests or hints things about
that something – and therefore one can ask whether what it says or
suggests is true.

A rare philosophical proponent of artistic truth is Iris Murdoch,
who argues that art presents us with 'a truthful image of the human
condition in a form which can be steadily contemplated', 'the only
context in which many of us are capable of contemplating it at all'.[5]
However, her claim that practices of looking are educated by engaging
with art rests on unacceptably Platonist assumptions. This article's
more modest thesis carries no suggestion that art is privileged as a
way of knowing; it implies no Romantic conception of poet as seer,
and does not assume a metaphysical or absolute conception of
truth, as those in the humanities who reject artistic truth often
seem to assume. Rather, it advocates a deflationary, anti-metaphys-
ical conception, and elucidates 'Art aims at truth' in terms of
raising or addressing issues which an audience would discuss. Even
this modest conception of artistic truth erodes the dominant philosophical paradigm of art, however.

That art aims at truth does not imply an intellectualist view of art;
unconscious influences are vital in its creation, and art can aim at
truths which the artist does not consciously intend. To say that it
aims at truth is not to appeal only to the author's avowed or conscious
intentions; intentions are manifested primarily through the work.
But there is an essential reference to intentionality; mere illustration
of truths is not sufficient. Artworks can illustrate a truth just as anything else can – a novel, a newspaper article and a radio interview can
all show that racism was endemic in 1930s Britain, for instance – but
that is not what is meant by art's aiming at truth.

Artworks can show how things might be, presenting possibilities
for the audience's consideration. David Harrower's one-act play
Blackbird, for instances, forces us to reconsider our definition of,
and attitude, towards paedophilia – without, as didactic art would,
prescribing some particular response.[6] It challenges us to consider
the question whether a relationship between a man and an under-
age girl could ever have value. In virtue of its form, the play slowly

[4]   Danto (1981).
[5]   Murdoch (1990), 87.
[6]   *Blackbird* is discussed further below; a similar case could be made for
David Mamet's *Oleanna* and the issue of violence against women (Mamet
(1993)).

Andy Hamilton

introduces its audience to the past relationship between the protagonists. There is a compelling dramatic rhythm to the gradual emergence of this information, that concludes with a revelation of the
protagonists' continuing feelings for each other. To fail to consider
the issues concerning paedophilia that the play raises, is to reveal a
very inadequate understanding of it.

To argue that art aims at truth, in the way that I propose, is to offer a
humanistic treatment of art as continuous with other human activities.
It implies a division between art that aims at entertainment, art that
aims at usefulness, and art that aims at truth; and within the latter category, between art that aims at truth and fails, and art that aims at
truth and succeeds. My claim is not that there is a special notion of 'artistic truth', but rather that high art aims at truth in the ordinary sense of
that term. *High art* is not a purely social category, but it is an historically-
conditioned one; it is a possibility fully manifested at a certain stage of
art's historical development, though it may be present in earlier eras.[7]
It is *autonomous art*, created not simply to satisfy a patron, but to
capture authentic aims of the artist. The modernist picture is that
such a possibility, though perhaps standing only a remote prospect
of realisation, opens up when art enters the market-place; it
becomes potentially autonomous at the same time as it becomes a
commodity. Autonomous artworks have ceased to be products for
an occasion, and are liberated from direct social function in service
of court, aristocracy or church; a liberation that music, most socially
retarded of the arts, finally gained only from the later 18th century.

For both modernists and conservatives, autonomous art is consolation for the loss of common culture in an urban, industrialised age.
Scruton for instance argues that high art, far from being an instrument of class oppression, emancipated people from the traditional
common culture: 'high culture…is the most reliable cure for the resulting loneliness. Bourgeois civilisation frees us from the bonds of
common culture, and offers the consolation prize of art'.[8] However,
although Scruton's treatment of art can hardly be described as 'func-
tionalist', he neglects the defining characteristic of autonomous art,
its purposiveness without a purpose – a concept that Adorno borrowed from Kant, transforming it to capture the unique, indirect
social functions that autonomous art has in virtue of its lack of
direct social function.[9] Autonomy, and classic status, involve

[7] A claim defended in Hamilton (2008).
[8] Scruton (1997), 110.
[9] These issues are discussed in Hamilton (2007), Ch. 6, and Hamilton (2008).

232

separation of artworks from the original social circumstances of their production and consumption.[10]

Art that aims only at gratification is art with a small 'a' – diversion or entertainment. Higher art is not merely pleasurable, though it can also entertain, as some works of Dickens and Shakespeare show; the contrast is with *mere* entertainment. The latter description is rather misleading when applied to an important borderline category, even so. To say that *The Artist*, Michel Hazanavicius' recent acclaimed silent film, 'aims at truth', is to overstate its aims; it does not, for instance, show us much about the demise of the silent movie industry that we did not know already. The film is 'knowing' in a postmodern way, cleverly structured and with marvellous set-pieces, but essentially a wonderful entertainment. One could argue the same for Howard Hawks' classic Chandler adaptation *The Big Sleep*, or his comedy *Bringing Up Baby*, though the boundary between high and popular arts is essentially vague. A diet of both high and popular art is ideal, and one that lacks higher art can be argued to be impoverished.

My central claim, therefore, is that high art aims at truth, while other kinds of art aim merely at pleasure, entertainment, fantasy or utility. The claim that high art aims at truth in some way parallels the familiar claim that belief aims at truth. Not all beliefs are true, and not all artworks have truth-content; the claim is normative. Truth is the fundamental dimension of assessment of beliefs, informing our epistemic norms and principles as a goal or theoretical value.[11] For art, truth is *one* fundamental mode of assessingment; one can argue that an artwork fails to achieve truth despite the best efforts of the artist, for instance because their vision is distorted or incomplete.

In each case the claim can be contested; those who treat belief as an informational-state or disposition tend to deny that it aims at truth, while those who regard high art as an essentially self-reflexive or hermetic activity may deny the analogous claim.[12] These alternative pictures should be resisted. There are duplicitous or lying assertions, but not lying beliefs; so belief cannot aim at falsehood. Art is more like the assertion than the belief; even so, if it fails to aim at truth, it is not high art. One could perhaps argue that art, in contrast, can aim at falsehood; perhaps inauthentic or insincere art does this. But

[10]   Hamilton (2009) argues that the concept of 'high culture', despite the intentions of its proponents, seems to draw attention to these circumstances.
[11]   Postmodernists and some pragmatists disagree; see for instance Engel (2005).
[12]   The example of belief is examined in Hamilton (2000).

Andy Hamilton

I would prefer to argue that the main contrast is with art as entertainment, that aims at neither truth nor falsity.

An essential supplementary claim is that *each artform aims at truth in its own way or ways*. This claim is consistent with the possibility of syntheses between artforms, as it is with Greenbergian purism. Painting can aim at truth through lifelikeness or mimesis, while fiction can do so through didacticism; but in both cases, a higher and more sophisticated approach is possible. Art can be said to aim at truth in the following ways:

1. Expression, presentation or consideration of truth or truths
2. Truthful representation
3. Truth to material or materials
4. Authenticity, including authentic performance
5. Historical truth

My focus here is on 1, and to a lesser extent 2 and 3.

The claim of artistic truth should be understood within the context of the historical development of the concept of art. Plato conceived of the aesthetic as sensual – and therefore objectionable – because he seemingly had no conception of art as other than the merely pleasurable, or the instrumentally didactic.[13] By *instrumentally didactic*, I mean art for religion's or politics' sake, where the artwork is treated primarily as a vehicle for the transmission of truth. In such art, there is no *internal relation to truth*, that 'aiming at truth' which is consistent with art for art's sake in its broadest sense, the sense in which art becomes an end in itself.

In fact, in ancient Greek writings concerning activities now regarded as artistic, there is little alternative to the instrumental or diversion model, or the social function model, such as flute-playing at a symposium. I say 'activities now regarded as artistic', because the Greeks had no model of *art* as such, conceived of as manifested across different genres; that is, they had no *system of the arts*. The widely-accepted Kristeller thesis argues that the Western system of the five major arts – painting, sculpture, architecture, music and poetry – did not assume definite shape till the 18th century, even though its ingredients went back to classical times.[14] It is generally agreed that the Greek

---

[13] Plato (1996). The art of the 'rhapsode' is neither didactic nor aims at pleasure; he is nobly inspired.

[14] '...classical antiquity left no systems of elaborate concepts of an aesthetic nature, but merely a number of scattered notions and suggestions that exercised a lasting influence' (Kristeller (1990), 172; discussed in Hamilton (2007), Ch. 1). By 'aesthetic', he must mean 'artistic'.

term *techne* (Latin *ars*) does not distinguish between art and craft, in the modern senses of these terms, but embraced all kinds of human activities which would now be called arts, crafts or sciences.

The evolution of the modern system of the arts accompanied Kant's development of the concept of the aesthetic as a synthesis of the sensory and the intellectual. Other revolutionary developments in the world of the arts during the 18th century included the separation of the value-spheres of ethical and aesthetic, art's growing commodification linked with a developing bourgeois public sphere of taste, and the rise of Romantic ideals of genius and self-expression that helps to constitute a post-Romantic conception of art. I would like to argue that another development of the time was that artistic truth no longer had to be treated in an instrumentally didactic way.

This latter change is important because the account of artistic truth offered here essentially requires freedom of interpretation; that is, that the highest art is *non-didactic*. *Didactic* refers, for instance, to the way that a poem might be 'instructive' in the moralising sense. As Dr. Johnson wrote of Milton: 'Poetry is the art of uniting pleasure with truth, by calling imagination to the help of reason. Epic poetry undertakes to teach the most important truths by the most pleasing precepts, and therefore relates some great event in the most affecting manner.'[15] Johnson did recognise that poetry is an imaginative presentation of truth, differing from direct moral instruction such as a church sermon. Poetry of a lower status could be regarded merely as pleasurable diversion.[16]

The Johnsonian model is applicable to wall-paintings in medieval churches, intended to instruct the unlettered peasantry in Gospel stories; and to socialist realist art or the agitprop films of Michael Moore. A more sophisticated cognitivism underlies the *post-Romantic conception of art*, with its requirement of *free interpretation* by the audience, involving critical debate. According to this conception, high or classic art is neither didactic nor pleasurable diversion; its truth is not reducible to anything as crude as a 'message', and artworks are

---

[15]   From Samuel Johnson (1781). In the 'Preface' to his edition of Shakespeare, he writes: 'The end of all writing is to instruct; the end of all poetry is to instruct by pleasing.'

[16]   Adam Smith comments that poetical licence is allowed, because its purpose is to amuse; the manners of poets 'plainly [show] that it is not their design to be believed', 'Lectures on Rhetoric and Belles Lettres', Lecture XXI, in Smith (1985). For Coleridge, 'A poem is that species of composition, which is opposed to works of science, by proposing for its *immediate* object pleasure, not truth' (Coleridge (1985), Ch. 14); note his stress on 'immediate', however. Wordsworth seemed to place a different emphasis.

concerned, rather, to raise possibilities for consideration. Art is autonomous, and so is its audience in their response.

'Didactic' suggests the settled world-view of Augustan writers such as Samuel Johnson; 'message' implies ideology and persuasion, a battle of ideas characteristic of less consensual times. There is a tendency for proponents of didactic art to deny that art has intrinsic value, and to treat it merely as a vehicle for truth – though Dr. Johnson would not have done so. Oscar Wilde's remark that 'No work of art ever puts forward a view of any kind' can be regarded either as narrow aestheticism, or as a salutary rejection of crudely didactic art in favour of a broader aestheticism that regards art as valuable in itself.[17] Art for art's sake can be interpreted as compatible with art's aiming at truth – if it is regarded as saying that art is valuable in itself, and not merely instrumentally. This is a broad aestheticism, as opposed to the narrow aestheticism of art for art as traditionally conceived. Indeed art for art in the broad sense, and art's aiming at truth, go together; art is not merely the means for projecting a truth, and is valuable in itself. Instrumentally didactic art is not high art, because it is merely a vehicle for transmission of truth; art that does not want to say anything is not high art either, but entertainment or some other variety of lower art.

We must now explore the assumptions of those who reject artistic truth.

2. The rejection of artistic truth

The contemporary separation of art and truth rests on several developments. Later 19th century aestheticism, and the modernism that arose from it, scorned the concept of artistic truth. On this view, an artwork creates its own world, and refers to nothing beyond itself – suggested by Nietzsche's declaration that 'We have art in order not to die of the truth'.[18] But while modernism's tendency was to abolish artistic truth, not all modernists wished to do so – we have

[17] It could also be regarded as flippancy, or as an attempt to avoid implication in illegal activity; Wilde made the remark at his first trial, replying to questioning about a book that allegedly put forward 'sodomitical views'.
[18] Nietzsche (1973), §. 822. On one interpretation, he is arguing that art is a response to the discovery that the world has no truth; beauty is not a reflection of a transcendental realm but a reaction to it. See also Rapaport (1997), 11; Paddison (1993) discusses the modernist introversion of art.

already noted remarks by Joyce and Picasso, and Adorno is a notable exception among art theorists.

However, with postmodernism's incoherent attempt to abolish truth, influenced by Nietzsche and developed by Derrida, artistic truth came under further attack.[19] More interestingly, the Marxist *ideological objection* regards artists as subject to the dominant ideology, and so unable to see the truth about their own society. It undermines truth in all spheres of human activity, and we return to it later.

20th-century Anglo-American philosophy, while rejecting the postmodern onslaught on truth, tends to deny artistic truth, for one or more of the following reasons:

(1)   *Truth is essentially propositional.* Zuidervaart describes a 'tunnel vision imposed by a propositionally inflected theory of truth', but it is an understandable visual impairment.[20] Horwich for instance, in considering the entities to which truth may be attributed, cites utterances, statements and beliefs, and propositions; but not novels, paintings or love.[21] Goodman hesitates to attribute truth to art because its 'carriers...are literal and linguistic', and talks instead of the 'appropriateness' or 'propriety' of a work.[22] Finally, Beardsley holds that, in order to have a truth-value – his interpretation of the claim of artistic truth – an artwork must either contain propositions or suggest and confirm hypotheses about reality, and it does neither.[23]

(2)   *Art is essentially 'aesthetic', emotive or formal in its appeal.* I.A. Richards, for instance, considered art to be a non-propositional language of emotions, a view very commonly applied to music, most notoriously by Deryck Cooke.

(3)   *Artistic truth implies artistic knowledge*, yet the latter is preponderantly banal; literature is replete with 'epigrammatic observations hardly distinguishable from folk sayings'.[24]

This last formulation rests on a key error diagnosed by Adorno – that art says what its words say. It is true that when appreciating autonomous art, we do not simply regard it as a source of useful

[19]   Derrida wrote on the question in his (1987); see also Rapaport (1997).
[20]   Zuidervaart (2004), 151.
[21]   Horwich (1990), 17.
[22]   Zuidervaart (2004), 172, 175.
[23]   Beardsley (1981). See also Young (2001), 70, on the 'propositional' theory of art.
[24]   Stolnitz (1992), 200.

Andy Hamilton

knowledge, nor as a way of stimulating the audience to a course of action, nor to assure them of the soundness of their own beliefs and actions.[25] But this is not sufficient reason to reject artistic cognitivism or the concept of artistic truth; nor is the naive argument (2). Argument (1), as we will see, provides the most fundamental questioning of the concept of artistic truth.

Although the assumption of artistic truth is against the spirit of the age, it residually informs modern responses to literature, for instance; and so Wittgenstein exaggerates when he writes that 'People nowadays think, scientists are there to instruct them, poets, musicians etc. to entertain them'.[26] Toni Morrison's novel *The Bluest Eye*, which describes an incestuous relationship within an African-American family, was criticised for undermining communal solidarity – a response that treats her novel as didactic art with the wrong message, rather than art that yields imaginative or experiential truth. Similarly, J.M. Coetzee's *Disgrace*, which concerns an attack by a black criminal gang on a white father and daughter, has been criticised as racist – presumably for expressing the racist view that most violent crime in South Africa is by blacks on whites. Given that the mere fact of the assault rather than its treatment seems to be what is objected to, the criticism is justified only if black on white violence were a recurrent theme in Coetzee's novels, which it is not.

These examples are instructive, since the criticisms of Morrison or Coetzee assume that art aims at truth didactically, and that it must broadcast the right message – which, it is argued, Coetzee does not do. (I am not saying that a racist novel fails to aim at truth, though that might be argued; just that the objection assumes a didactic model.) That such objections are commonplace, shows that the postmodern questioning of truth has not been fully absorbed – unsurprisingly, given its incoherence - and the very same critics who allege racism would most likely deny truth. This objection is opposed by embattled proponents of artistic freedom, a value integral to the post-Romantic conception of art, that includes the freedom of the artist to shock and outrage.

3. A 'grand narrative' historicist conception of artistic truth

The view of art that I wish to defend, and which contrasts with accounts that reject artistic truth, may be labelled *cognitivist*. Cognitivism about art recognises that it is more than pleasurable

25   See Schiller (1964), and Young (2001).
26   Wittgenstein (1998), 42.

diversion, and that its meaning transcends didactic utility; high art aims not just to give pleasure but to develop understanding – indeed to develop understanding through pleasure. To reiterate, cognitivism *is* represented in Anglo-American aesthetics; but the particular version of cognitivism advocated here, one that finds place for artistic truth, seems not to be.

Cognitivism involving a concept of artistic truth is most readily associated with German Idealist aesthetics. Despite the still common attribution to Kant of an exclusively 'taste' aesthetic, he did recognise broader functions of art, and his formalism does not extend to art itself.[27] But Hegel is the most thoroughgoing artistic cognitivist, arguing emphatically that art's primary role is the disclosure of truth. He held that art is a way of discovering ourselves and the world, not merely a way of beautifying what has already been discovered: 'In art we have to do not with any agreeable or useful child's play, but with an unfolding of the truth.'[28] For Hegel, the content of art is not abstract, but is 'the sensuous appearance [*Scheinen*] of the Idea', that appeals through the senses to the mind or spirit.[29] Hegel's pervasive philosophical impulse is to elevate purely conceptual modes of expression above sensory ones, and since art embodies metaphysical truth through a sensory medium, he is deeply ambivalent towards it. But he allows that as well as being understood conceptually, truth must be experienced sensuously through art, as well as felt and loved through religion.[30]

Hegel's discussion suggests that the concept of high art can be defined in terms other than those social ones – viz., the art of the socially dominant classes – assumed by Marxist critics; high art is autonomous art that aims at, or discloses, truth. However, while orthodox Marxism offers an ideological *critique* of artistic truth, members of the Frankfurt School, notably Adorno, were as much indebted to Hegel's cognitivist affirmation as to the Marxist critique of art. Adorno links truth-content with the 'language-character' that he attributes to all artworks, not just those whose medium is language. Even when its medium is linguistic, what the artwork says is not what its words say, and so music and literature are not so distinct: 'No art can be pinned down as to what it says,

[27] His discussion of *aesthetic ideas* illuminates what I term *imaginative truth*.
[28] Hegel (1975), Vol. II, 1236; see also Adorno (2006), 7.
[29] Hegel (1975), Vol I, 111, and 71.
[30] '...for in inwardness as such, in pure thought, in the world of laws and their universality man cannot endure; he also needs sensuous existence, feeling, the heart, emotion...' (Hegel (1975), Vol I, 97–8).

and yet it speaks'.[31] Progressive art embodies an essential critical function within bourgeois culture, and 'truth-content [is] the task of critique'.[32] For Adorno, artists control only the material, not the content of their work. Austen may have intended her novels as guidance to young women concerning matrimony, but for Adorno, the truth-content of *Pride and Prejudice* is a social truth of which its author may be unaware.

For him, the truth-content of artworks is neither factual nor propositional, but perceptible and structural. He assesses the integration and fracture of its form and content, considering the artwork in its own terms:

> The ceaselessly recurring question that every work incites in whoever traverses it – the "What is it all about?" – goes over into "Is it true?" – the question of the absolute, to which every artwork responds by wresting itself free from the discursive form of answer.[33]

The 'discursive form of answer' is the conceptual or linguistic paraphrase that audiences are always tempted to derive from an artwork, and which Adorno rejects because what the artwork says is not what its words – if it has any – say.

Despite its insights concerning 'what art says', Adornian historicism is a contestable basis on which to defend artistic truth.[34] The more modest, pluralistic conception that I wish to present is consistent with the modernist understanding of art's increasing social autonomy from the 18th century onwards. Unlike Adorno's, however, it does not privilege socially critical art.[35]

4. A more modest conception of artistic truth

A pluralistic conception of artistic truth is found in Gadamer's critique of Hegel – a critique that I think applies also to Adorno's

---

[31]   Adorno, 'Music and Language: A Fragment', in his (1992), 1.
[32]   Adorno (1997), 194.
[33]   Adorno (1997), 168.
[34]   The most substantive recent Adornian treatment is Zuidervaart (2004), who combines it with Heidegger's notion that art discloses truth. He holds that art can be true with respect to the artist's intentions or vision (authenticity); to the audience's interpretative needs (significance); and to the work's internal demands (integrity). ((Zuidervaart (2004), 127–30.)
[35]   A version of modernist theory is defended in Hamilton (2007), (2008) and (2009).

negative, pessimistic development of Hegelian dialectics. Though Hegel recognised 'the truth that lies in every artistic experience [and] is...at the same time mediated with historical consciousness', Gadamer writes, he denied art's historical multiplicity, mistakenly holding that it progresses towards the one, true art:

> Hegel was able to recognise the truth of art only by subordinating it to philosophy's comprehensive knowledge... from the viewpoint of the present's complete self-consciousness...[In making] conceptual truth omnipotent, since the concept supersedes all experience, Hegel's philosophy...disavows the way of truth it has recognised in the experience of art.[36]

For Gadamer, there is knowledge in art, and experience of art contains a claim to truth that is not inferior, but simply different, to that of science: to do justice to 'the truth of aesthetic experience [is to] overcome the radical subjectivisation of the aesthetic that began with Kant'.[37] Gadamer rejects Adorno's view that the highest art is essentially critical – for him, it can be affirmative also – and thus the grand narrative historicism of which that view is a residue.

Like Gadamer, Theodore Meyer Greene regards artistic truth as non-conceptual, though confusingly he also seems to hold that one can regard a work of art as a judgment or assertion – an interpretation of reality – by the artist. He denies that truth is expressed adequately only through a conceptual medium: 'certain aspects of reality can be apprehended and expressed...in and through the artistic media, and...what is thus apprehended and expressed *cannot* be translated into a conceptual medium without vital loss'.[38] He continues:

> The artist expresses his insights and interpretations in the warm and vital language of art, which is as perfectly adapted to the mediation of his normative apprehensions as are scientific prose and mathematics to the formulation of the scientist's impersonalised apprehension of the quantitative aspects of nature's skeletal structure.

---

[36] Gadamer (1975), 85, 87.
[37] Again we see the attribution of an exclusively taste aesthetic to Kant; although he discusses the contrast between free and dependent beauty, Gadamer seems to belong with those who ignore all of the *Critique of Judgment* after the Four Moments. He argues, I think unfairly, that Kant assumes a scientific concept of knowledge that cannot acknowledge artistic truth.
[38] Greene (1940), 427.

Although artists can express propositions whose truth they neither deny nor assert, he holds, 'serious' art is the expression of the artist's sincere convictions.

Greene contrasts the enduring nature of artistic truth with that of science:

> The best of scientific theories are subject to revision as the best artistic insights are not. A great work of art can be true for all time in a way in which no scientific theory can be [because] an individual approach to a given subject-matter is not as subject to correction by other individual approaches...

For Greene, 'Artistic intuitions enjoy a degree of autonomy unrivalled in the scientific enterprise'. The artist's language can be 'as perfectly adapted' as the scientist's – artistic truth is not vague or imprecise by the standards of scientific truth, but aims at a perfect matching of precision and subject-matter.[39]

This last claim seems correct. The poet's or novelist's observation of nature or human psychology on which their work is based, and their search for the right phrase or word, is as exacting as the scientist's precise recording of observations and testing of hypotheses. However, Greene still does not sufficiently separate art from empirical inquiry. He is right that 'a great work of art can be true for all time in a way in which no scientific theory can'. But it is misleading to say that 'a given subject-matter is not as subject to correction by other individual approaches' – for it is not subject at all. A later artwork cannot correct the artistic truths expressed by an earlier one, because – according to a post-Romantic conception - the pursuit of truth in art is an individual and not collective endeavour; indeed it is an endeavour bounded by the work in question. Art does not progress in the same way as science. One can talk of the development of a tradition, and of an artist achieving more fully what they were intending in an earlier work. But while Conrad's *Heart of Darkness* is a fully-realised artistic vision that transforms the stock devices of his earlier exotic romances, it is not a 'correction' of those earlier efforts, which still stand independently.

---

[39] Mortensen, less satisfactorily, refers to 'expression of subjective truth' as one of four features defining the modern system of the arts: 'science or other forms of systematic enquiry...deal with objective facts... We can only get at what a work of art expresses if we actually experience it. It is not possible to repeat or replicate [as it is] possible to substitute one account of the Russian Revolution with another, equally good, account' (Mortensen (1997), 1).

However, it is unusual for an artist to refine their a work through response to the judgments of critics – the collaboration of artist-photographer Jeff Wall and critic Michael Fried is a rare example. When an artwork is released into the world, in the form of publication or exhibition, it acquires a life of its own and cannot normally be retrieved by its creator – though obsessive revisers such as Bruckner have tried to do so. While a scientific theory can be discredited – indeed that is its normal fate – and becomes of purely historical interest, artworks are not discredited unless revealed as fakes; tastes change, and popularity is recognised as ephemeral, but classics endure. The artist has greater creative autonomy than the scientist, though to deny it to the latter entirely, is to subscribe to the unacceptably negative characterisation of scientific culture found in Kant.[40]

Reference has been made to Hegel's elevation of 'conceptual truth' over other modes, and to the suggestion, shared by Gadamer and Greene, that artistic truth is not 'conceptual'. Because 'conceptual' has so many meanings, one could refer instead to 'linguistic' or 'propositional', which are slightly less broad in scope – while recognising that these terms are still badly in need of refinement. "Scientific truth" is often contrasted with artistic truth, but *truth of inquiry* is preferable, since it embraces the humanities as well as the sciences, and this description may also serve in place of 'conceptual'. Critical discourse is 'conceptual', and the role of criticism includes interpreting and assessing the truth that a work aims at. But it is an aid to or expression of our understanding, not a paraphrase of what an artwork says. The truth expressed by an artwork is not a scientific, historical or philosophical truth, but rather, an *experiential or imaginative truth* – art makes truth real to the imagination. Imagination is essential to empirical inquiry too, and art is not the only activity that can express such truths; truths can be conveyed imaginatively through role-playing, psychotherapy and other means.

5. The most persuasive cases: literature, film and drama

We noted earlier Iris Murdoch's persuasive statement of artistic cognitivism:

> [in art] we are presented with a truthful image of the human condition in a form which can be steadily contemplated and indeed it

---

[40]   Kant denies that genius applies to science; Scruton denies that science is part of culture (Scruton (1998)). A useful discussion is Meyer (1974).

is the only context in which many of us are capable of contemplating it at all...Art transcends the selfish obsessive limitations of the personality and can enlarge the sensibility of the consumer.[41]

Murdoch holds that we learn from the characters of Shakespeare or Tolstoy or the paintings of Velásquez or Titian

> ...about the real quality of human nature, when it is envisaged, in the artist's just and compassionate vision, with a clarity which does not belong to the self-centred rush of ordinary life. [The] greatest art ... shows us the world ... with a clarity which startles and delights us simply because we are not used to looking at the real world at all.[42]

These claims are illustrated by David Harrower's one-act play *Blackbird* cited earlier. To reiterate, the play forces us to reconsider our attitude towards paedophilia, but it does not, as didactic art would, prescribe a particular response. It poses the question whether a relationship between a man and an under-age girl could ever have value. In virtue of its form, the play achieves a persuasive effect on its audience, who are slowly initiated into the existence of a past relationship between the protagonists, and into its social unacceptability. There is a compelling dramatic rhythm in the emergence of this information, involving an intense revelation of the protagonists' continuing feelings for each other.

The highest art, such as *Blackbird*, that aims non-didactically at truth, exists at the opposite end of the continuum to didactic art, whether religious or political. One might attempt to elucidate the distinction in terms of Wayne Booth's contrast in *The Rhetoric of Fiction* between showing and telling. Booth argues that authors should not be forbidden from telling, and that it is easy to distinguish those who profess to be showing but are in fact telling.[43] However, showing can be as didactic as telling; there is a continuum in art from didactic to non-didactic, from telling via showing to *presenting possibilities and*

---

[41]   Murdoch (1990), 87.
[42]   Murdoch (1990), discussed and developed in Lamarque (2009), 240, and Lamarque and Haugom Olsen (1994), 154. Note also Wellmer: 'Art does not merely disclose reality, it also opens our eyes. This...transformation of perception is the healing...of an incapacity to perceive and experience reality in the way that we learn to [do] through the medium of aesthetic experience' (Wellmer (1991), 26).
[43]   Booth (1983). Passmore argues that the distinction is vital, and that telling, even in literature, is very confined in its range and only loosely related to seriousness (Passmore (1991), 129).

raising questions.[44] It is the last of these that Harrower's play exemplifies.

The aesthete, narrowly defined, is someone who when asked 'Did this play make you think about attitudes to paedophilia?', might reply 'I hadn't thought about that, I was just marvelling at its compelling formal construction'. Insofar as such an exclusive concern is possible, it amounts to a failure of artistic understanding. (To reiterate, aestheticism or art for art's sake, in the broader sense, regards the aesthetic as an end in itself, without assuming, with Wildean aesthetes, that it is the most valuable end.) Conversely, someone who concerned themselves only with what the play said about paedophilia, treating these as truths of inquiry, would also have an impoverished artistic understanding. To do so would not be a response to the play as art; but to ignore such issues is artistically inadequate also. It could be argued that I have shown not that art aims at truth, but that it aims at critical engagement. However, critical engagement involves a reaction to truth, and asks questions such as 'Is it true that the relationship between an older man and an under-age girl could have value?'

Harrower does not need to have the expertise of the psychiatrist, psychologist or criminologist in this area. He may in fact belong to any one of those professions, but writing a play that focusses on the issue does not require access to any body of disciplinary knowledge. The playwright's knowledge of human motivation is not a disciplinary knowledge like the psychiatrist's or psychologist's (or historian's or philosopher's), but more like an ordinary person's, intensified or magnified.

These areas of expertise concern what I termed *truths of inquiry*. The playwright presents and explores human knowledge of the phenomenon – in *Blackbird*'s case, paedophilia – in an imaginative way. The play makes vivid some of our misapprehensions, in a highly-charged way through its formal presentation. I may emerge from the very intense experience that it affords, wanting to read what the experts have to say, in that way deepening my understanding of paedophilia and social attitudes towards it. The play would not be cited as evidence in a government report, but members of a government commission might be recommended to see it as background to their official responsibility.

---

[44]   For instance, critic Echo Eshun commented on BBC Radio 4's 'Today' programme, on 31/10/11, that video games are not art – by which he meant 'Art' with a capital 'A' – because art 'asks deep questions'. This issue is pursued in the final section.

It is not even clear that the author requires direct acquaintance with their subject-matter. There is a tradition in literature of writing on subjects about which one has no direct experience. *The Lime Twig*, by American writer John Hawkes, a novel about gangsterism on the periphery of English horse-racing and betting, shows no acquaintance with English life, but is higher art than the novels of Dick Francis, who knew a great deal about these subjects. In *The Remains of The Day*, Kazuo Ishiguro recreates English country-house life of the 1930s; Conrad seems to have created the world of *Nostromo* mostly from his reading about Latin America.[45]

However, writers are often advised to write from what they know, and novels written from experience can be especially effective illustrations of Murdoch's claim that '[in art] we are presented with a truthful image of the human condition in a form which can be steadily contemplated'. The *memoir-novel*, or what is sometimes called 'auto-fiction', draws most directly on the author's experience. Solzhenitsyn's *One Day In The Life of Ivan Denisovich* had an explosive impact on Soviet society when it appeared in 1964, during the Khrushchev thaw, because in contrast to Stalin's favoured Socialist Realist morality tales, its genuine realism and truth relayed corroborated facts about the Gulag: 'The sufferings of its heroes were pointless...The Party did not triumph in the end, and communism did not emerge the victor...[Its publisher Tvardovsky said] that the story had "not a drop of falsehood in it"'. Readers who were or had been in the Gulag 'were overjoyed to read something which actually reflected their own feelings and experience. People afraid to breathe a word of their experiences to their closest friends suddenly felt a sense of release'.[46]

One reader wrote to Solzhenitsyn: 'I wept as I read – they were all familiar characters, as if from my own brigade!' The prisoners or 'zeks' in Dubravalag held a group reading, listening 'without breathing':

After they read the last word, there was a deathly silence. Then, after two, three minutes, the room detonated. Everyone had lived the story in his own, painful way...in the cloud of tobacco smoke, they discussed endlessly... And frequently, more and more frequently, they asked: "Why did they publish it?"[47]

---

[45] Baines (1971), 354–58, discusses the likely sources of his knowledge of South America and its politics. One cannot say that *Heart of Darkness* is a greater work than *The Secret Agent*, even though the former is based on direct experience and therefore is arguably more 'realistic' than the latter.

[46] Applebaum (2004), 468, 469.

[47] Leonid Sitko, quoted in Applebaum (2004), 469.

Many Gulag survivors, interviewed in the 1990s, insisted that they had witnessed scenes in books by Solzhenitsyn, Ginzburg or Shalamov, or recognised guards and NKVD interrogators represented there – though records show that this could not have happened:

> ...many victims of Stalinist repression identified so strongly with [these books'] ideological position, which they took to be the key to understanding the truth about the camps, that they suspended their own independent memories and allowed these books to speak for them. [They] frequently lacked a clear conceptual grasp of their own experience [and so substituted] these writers' coherent and clear memories for their own confused and fragmentary recollections.[48]

Figes' final comment is important; art can supply a conceptual framework for their own experience that the individual lacks, something that helps them make sense of it in the way that Murdoch suggests.

There can be misidentification too, however. 'Daddy', the most notorious of Sylvia Plath's *Ariel* lyrics, is a shocking *Grand Guignol* outburst that portrays the writer's seemingly mild-mannered if foolishly obstinate father as a surreal monster. Anne Stevenson comments: 'This distorting wilfulness...became for her poetic truth...The voice [in this poem] is finally that of a revengeful, bitterly hurt child storming against a beloved parent', cursing him for dying.[49] However, the result could be regarded as overwrought or out of control, self-absorbed, striking but not psychologically deep, with little reflection of the universal – even though some teenage readers may identify with it.

Literature's concern with truth therefore exists on a continuum, from the didacticism of Johnson's 'The Vanity of Human Wishes', through the residual moralising of Larkin's 'An Arundel Tomb' with its hint at an 'almost-instinct almost true', to Sylvia Plath's *Ariel* lyrics that seem to have nothing to do with truth. Revelation of the 'child' that Plath remained is not artistic truth in the relevant sense. As we saw, artworks do reveal truth in this way, and it is the task of what Danto called 'deep interpretation' to consider how they do. But this is not the 'aiming at truth' that this article is concerned with, since anything at all – commodified pop music,

---

[48] Figes (2007), 635.
[49] Stevenson (1990), 259, 264. Plath biography is a minefield, and Stevenson is regarded as being on the Ted Hughes side of the debate.

pornography, home movies – can be a source of truth in the sense that by reflecting on it, we arrive at truths otherwise inaccessible.

One could distinguish art concerned with a *common reality* – Johnson, Larkin, Levi, Conrad, Raymond Carver – from art that creates an *alternative reality* that beguiles us: Milton's 'Lycidas', Plath, Peake, Hesse, Woolf, Brian Marley. Larkin and Dickens created works that mirrored our social reality and understanding of it, in a highly personalised way that filters reality through their consciousness and heightens it by their craft. Theirs is not, strictly, an alternative to our social reality; although they present aspects of it that we may deny, or had hitherto failed to understand or recognise, nonetheless their works are strongly rooted in something we all share. Talk of a 'common reality' hopefully allows one to sidestep some of the pitfalls of the debate over literary realism.

In contrast, an alternative reality is presented in the Pastoral tradition in poetry that inspired Milton's 'Lycidas'. This lyrical lament delineates the poet's grief, while portraying Milton and his late friend 'untruthfully' as shepherds. Dr. Johnson condemned its artificiality, complaining that 'in this poem there is no nature, for there is no truth; there is no art, for there is nothing new', its pastoral images 'long ago exhausted'.[50] Later audiences took a different view, holding that the poet's grief is persuasively expressed through pastoral convention. The reality in high art cannot be entirely alternative, however, as in science-fiction – though occasionally, as in Tarkovsky's *Stalker*, or Vonnegut's *Slaughterhouse Five*, science-fiction is high art.

The analogous issue in painting, to which artform we now turn, is illustrated by Watteau's more evanescent Arcadia. As John Golding writes, 'Watteau lived in a world of his own, a dreamworld, one that could exist only in his eye and mind but one that he invites his audience to enjoy, to embrace. *Et in arcadia ego*'.[51] Watteau's rococo *fêtes galantes* express a human reality, otherwise we would have little interest in them; explorers of common and alternative realities can both aim at truth, whilst having different conceptions of its boundaries. Even so, Golding's suggestion that he was the greatest French artist of his century suggests that this was a silver age for French painting. We pursue the implications of this opposition between realism and idealism by considering how the visual arts aim at truth.

[50]   'Life of Milton' in Johnson (1781).
[51]   Golding (2011), 72.

7. Truth in the visual arts, and the ideological objection to artistic truth

Religious art seems to be a paradigm of didactic art. However, in the Middle Ages, church paintings were not just art for religion's as opposed to art's sake. They were religious as much as artistic *arte-facts*: 'all images were...understood to be more than representations or commemorations, bringing the holder into spiritual contact and the semi-presence of the person depicted'.[52] Perhaps something like this is still believed in the modern era – for instance by Mondrian and metaphysical artists – and not just in more tradition-alist cultures. Images of saints and the Virgin in particular became more common in medieval churches after the doctrine of Purgatory was confirmed in 1274; masses for the dead required saintly intercession.

The enduring sense that images bring us into contact with their subject meant that the didactic function of religious art always had an explicit personal dimension. This dimension became amplified, as Clifford Geertz explains:

> Most fifteenth-century Italian paintings were religious paint-ings, and not just in subject matter but in the ends they were de-signed to serve. Pictures were meant to deepen human awareness of the spiritual dimensions of existence...Faced with an arresting image of the Annunciation...the beholder was to [reflect] on the event as he knew it and on his personal relationship to the mys-teries it recorded. "For it is one thing to adore a painting", as a Dominican preacher defending the virtuousness of art put it, "but it is quite another to learn from a painted narrative what to adore".

Geertz argues that the relation between religious ideas and painted images was not simply expositive: '...they were not Sunday school il-lustrations...the religious painter was concerned with inviting his public to concern themselves with first things and last, not with pro-viding them with a recipe or a surrogate for such concern...the relations of his painting to the wider culture was interactive'.[53] Such a model construes artistic truth as inviting contemplation or un-derstanding – as Iris Murdoch's discussion suggests – rather than as the presentation of a choice, or forcing the audience to take a view, as modernists often assume.

[52] Barnwell (2011), 43. See Belting (1994), 308, 351, 362, 410–19.
[53] Geertz (1983), Ch. 5, 104.

Religious art could be more primitively didactic, however, excluding a personal response. The high art of the fifteenth-century Italian Renaissance, where the viewer is already assumed to have received religious teaching or training, contrasts with the often rather crude representations that were once ubiquitous on English medieval church walls – didactic in a way that called for little individual contribution from the viewer. Minimally contributory didacticism is a minor genre in painting, illustrated by Jan Steen's 'The Effects of Intemperance' (1663–5, National Gallery, London) – portraying the ill-effects of alcoholic inebriation – or Holman Hunt's irretrievably moralistic 'The Awakening Conscience' (1853, Tate Britain, London).

Didactic aiming at truth contrasts with the representational truthfulness that art is often assumed to aim at. This is the sense in which paintings and drawings may be true to life; the subject may be more or less accurately represented. Although we admire 'realistic' pictures, we are now inclined to regard them as art with a small 'a', products of skill and craft, employing hard-earned techniques and materials. A true portrayal, in this sense, is no guarantee of artistic value and in some cases – Canaletto for instance – may substitute for insight and imagination. Conversely, portraits and landscapes of great merit may be anything but a true likeness. Among these, clearly, would be the portraits of Francis Bacon, yet he claimed that his paintings 'tell us something true about the world we live in…art is recording… reporting'.[54] Some artists even found a contradiction between didactic and representational truth, however. Burne-Jones commented that his paintings were 'so different to landscape paintings. I don't want to copy *objects*; I want to tell people something'.[55] With modernism's rejection of artistic truth, such didacticism appeared hopelessly conservative.

Although Geertz's richer notion of didactic art allows for a contribution from the audience, who are not merely passive recipients of the truths expressed, the post-Romantic conception of art has the stronger requirement of free interpretation by the audience. That development seems in tension with the patronage system's restriction of artistic autonomy. For instance, Titian in his portrait *Pope Paul III and his Grandsons* is not merely 'reporting' or 'recording', but presenting an artistic vision of the Pope's character. The audience are free, within limits, to interpret the portrait – to judge what kind of

---

[54]   Quoted Passmore (1991), 105. Even – indeed, especially – abstract painters such as Mondrian believed that their work conveyed metaphysical truths.

[55]   Quoted in Dorment (2012), 14.

person or character the Pope is. But in an era of patronage, freedom of both artist and audience are constrained; portraitists could suffer the patron's wrath if they made the subject too fallible-looking.

Modernists such as Attali suggest that, with the decline of the patronage model, the artist becomes free at the same time as their work goes on sale in the capitalist market-place. Proponents of the *ideological objection* to artistic truth, noted earlier, maintain nonetheless that art consistently fails to locate truth. They hold that John Constable's landscapes, whose subjects are the estates of his wealthy friends, unaccountably rather devoid of peasants, are to that extent, 'false'.[56] An analogous and familiar criticism is that Jane Austen's novels neglect the effects of the Industrial Revolution; she herself referred to the 'two inches of ivory' – the very circumscribed social subject-matter – on which she worked.

John Barrell's work on landscape painting and poetry, from the period of transition between patronage and market systems, illustrates the ideological objection. Barrell argues that as the aristocracy became more committed to the economic exploitation of its estates, aristocratic taste developed an interest in more workaday – if not totally realistic – images of rural life.[57] However, he recognises that there were constraints on how the labouring, vagrant and mendicant poor could be portrayed, to be acceptable *décor* for polite drawing rooms; it was only 'discreet hints of actuality provided by tattered clothes, heavy boots and agricultural implements' that marked the English tradition of Gainsborough and Constable from the more artificial Italianate tradition.[58] As a periodical of the time put it:

> ...truth well painted will certainly please the imagination; but it is sometimes convenient not to discover the whole truth, but that part which only is delightful...Thus in writing Pastorals, let the tranquillity of that life appear full and plain, but hide the meanness of it...[59]

---

[56]   Gerhard Richter, no doubt aware of such debates, described his mid-1980s landscapes as 'untruthful' because they glorify nature, whereas nature is 'always against us', and 'knows no meaning, no pity, no sympathy' (Richter (2009), 158).

[57]   For a sharper realism concerning peasant life, one generally has to look to the later 19th century, and the work of Courbet and Millet; however, William Beechey's 'Sir Frances Fordes' Children Giving a Coin to a Beggar Boy' (1793, Tate Britain) portrays a young beggar in very evident poverty and distress.

[58]   Barrell (1980), 6.

[59]   *The Guardian*, no. 22, 6 April 1713, quoted Barrell (1980), 1.

Thus when Gainsborough 'brought together in his landscapes of the 1750s the tradition of French rococo pastoral painting, and the more sternly georgic tradition of the Netherlands painters, this may not have been simply a happy eclecticism, but a combination that enabled him to compose [a reassuring] image of Happy Britannia', a blend of French play and Netherlandish work in rural life.[60]

The implication, based not on direct evidence but rather on a brilliant series of critical intepretations, is that Gainsborough constructs an ideologically-driven image rather than pursuing truth. Marxist critics infer that so-called high art often aims not at truth, but at satisfying the self-image and taste of its patrons or consumers. On this view, art is essentially ideological, having the function of concealing rather than expressing truth.

Such interpretations express what Ricoeur called 'the hermeneutics of suspicion', that interprets all social phenomena by invoking unconscious motivation whether Freudian or Marxist – a 'suspicion' that Ricoeur himself endorses.[61] Barrell's claim is not that Gainsborough composed his 'reassuring image of Happy Britannia' fully intentionally, but rather that he did so in that not fully intentional but still meaningful way in which one is said to act on Freudian unconscious desires. A humanistic as opposed to deterministic Marxism – Lukács rather than Althusser, for instance – would allow that in some sense Gainsborough owned deep-seated commitments to the established order – commitments that could perhaps be avowed after the event – and that this prevented him from aiming at truth in his art.[62]

However, such interpretations are hard to prove, and tend to be as speculative as those of Freudian dream therapy. Maybe Gainsborough just saw rural life as a blend of work and play. His art is affirmative, but still high art, since we judge that although he may make concessions to patrons, he is not aiming simply to be acceptable to them. (One could also argue that since Gainsborough supported progressive bourgeois forces, in ideological terms his art may not be 'false'.) Art that lacked such integrity clearly could not

---

[60] Barrell (1980), 41.
[61] Ricoeur (1970).
[62] Althusser would deny an avowability requirement on the unconscious – see for instance 'Ideology and Ideological State Apparatus' in Althusser (2006); Lukács (1975).

aim at truth, but whether it did lack it would be a matter of critical debate.[63]

In Constable's time, the 'higher styles of landscape' remained those more artificial or idealised ones by Claude or Poussin.[64] That Italianate tradition, like the Pastoral tradition of Virgil in poetry, did not pretend to realism; the kind of truth it aimed at concerned not the everyday world, but an Arcadian realm. Constable or Austen did focus on that everyday world, however, and the most that one could infer from the ideological objection is that they present a partial or parochial truth. They did not aspire to a complete social picture of their society, as does a social scientist, or a realist novelist like Zola. Their concern is psychological depth, not social comprehensiveness, and in that respect their art does aim at truth. High art does not have to aim at 'total' truth.

8. Truth in architecture and music

The most problematic artforms for artistic truth are music and architecture. We noted, and qualified, Greene's comment that what is apprehended and expressed in art '*cannot* be translated into a conceptual medium without vital loss'. This may be felt to be especially true for music and architecture, commonly regarded as non-representational, essentially abstract arts. On this received view, literature and drama are representational and conceptual (or linguistic); painting and sculpture are representational but non-conceptual (non-linguistic); and music and architecture are neither. Some artforms have the capacity to be – or are normally – representational even if they are not always so. Hence abstract painting is non-representational, as perhaps is avantgarde modernist literature such as Joyce's *Finnegan's Wake*.

While artistic truth in imaginative literature might be accepted, its presence in music seems quite obscure. But Adorno suggests how it might be understood. To reiterate, he holds that all artworks, and not just those whose medium is language, possess a 'language-character', which he links with truth-content. By this he means that elements not meaningful in themselves are organised into a meaningful structure:

[63] Much more needs to be said concerning the ideological objection, one that takes account of the critique of ideological explanation found for instance in Graham (1986); see also Geuss (1981).
[64] Barrell (1980), 19.

Andy Hamilton

> Music resembles language in that it is a temporal sequence of articulated sounds which are more than just sounds. They say something, often something human. The better the music, the more forcefully they say it. The succession of sounds is like logic: it can be right or wrong. But what has been said cannot be detached from the music. Music creates no semiotic system.[65]

For Adorno, the truth-content of a Mahler symphony is not captured in literalist programmatic interpretations; nor are Wagner's music-dramas decoded by a process of motif-identification. In contrast, he gives the example of musical affirmation, 'the judicious, even judging affirmation of something that is, however, not expressly stated', such as the first movement recapitulation in Beethoven's 9th Symphony. As we saw, Adorno believes that on the strength of its similarity to language, music constantly poses a riddle, which it never answers – but then, he insists, all art does so.

Before the 18th century, a literary model of music was dominant, and non-vocal music was neglected by theorists. During the 19th century, the non-representational and non-conceptual nature of music became regarded as a sign of its superiority, as it ascended from the lowest to the highest of the arts. (This was not so for architecture). The view that music does not mean anything because it is not about anything – that it is non-conceptual and non-representational and does not even point to any truth – became, and remains, commonplace.

The more humanistic view that connects music and life has always had representatives, however. When Mahler visited Sibelius in 1907, they debated the nature of the symphony:

> I said that I admired its severity of style and the profound logic that created an inner connection between all the motifs... Mahler's opinion was just the reverse. "No, a symphony must be like the world. It must embrace everything".[66]

In seeking extra-musical reference, Mahler belongs with Ives and a few other modernists, in their ambitious attempt to make music reach beyond its apparent muteness, and 'speak'. Sibelius, in contrast, belongs to the tradition of absolute music according to which the form of a work is the working-out of its musical idea, a tradition which achieved its apotheosis in the work of the first and second Viennese Schools, and Brahms, with Schoenberg its most articulate theorist. Yet even that tradition can recognise that music aims at

[65] Adorno (1992), 1.
[66] Quoted in Goss (2009), 346.

truth, construed as the Adornian idea of 'truth to materials' – while like all performing arts, truth in the sense of authenticity to the work is essential.

Architecture is less abstract than music in its expression of function, and more abstract in not being a performing art. The idea of truth to materials is expressed here most famously by Ruskin, who writes that

> The violations of truth, which dishonour poetry and painting, are [mostly] confined to the treatment of their subjects. But in architecture…a less subtle, more contemptible violation of truth is possible; a direct falsity of assertion respecting the nature of material, or the quantity of labour.[67]

He argues that an honest architecture avoids deception, that is, it avoids suggesting 'a mode of structure or support, other than the true one; [such as] pendants of late Gothic roofs'; 'painting of surfaces to represent some other material than that of which they actually consist (as in the marbling of wood), or the deceptive representation of sculptured ornament upon them'; or 'use of cast or machine-made ornaments'.[68] This vocabulary of truth pervaded Victorian attitudes to architecture; for instance, Richard Redgrave wrote that Pugin's works 'deserve commendation for their illustration of truth, and as showing what one man, by earnest and well-directed attention, can achieve in the reformation of taste, and in the training …of other minds to assist in his truthful labours'.[69]

While Ruskin understands truth to materials as 'truth to physical stuff', Adorno regards it as truth to material that is pre-formed and shaped by history. In architecture, 'material' in this historical sense would include the accumulated vocabulary of Georgian door, sash window, pitched roof, or in grander buildings, Doric and Ionic columns, cornices, corbels and turrets. 'Untruth to materials' here would include the steeple that Sir William Chambers provided above the portico of St Martin's-in-the-Fields, ignoring the fact that steeples were never found on Greek temples.

Even in those arts that are least 'language-like', therefore, a case can still be made that high art aims at truth, in the form appropriate to the artistic medium. More work needs to be done, to convince those

---

[67] Ruskin (1980), 124; the quotation is from the opening of 'The Lamp of Truth' in *Seven Lamps of Architecture*.
[68] Ruskin concedes that in some cases, these processes have lost the nature of deceit – for instance, gilding in architecture, as opposed to jewellery, is understood not to be gold.
[69] Quoted in Hill (2007), 473.

expecting something more like propositional truth, that this is indeed artistic truth in an interesting sense – a task that must remain a subject for another occasion.

9. The audience's freedom of interpretation

In this article I have been attempting to develop a more liberal concept of artistic truth than that found in didactic art – one that allows freedom of interpretation by the audience, bestowing on them an autonomy equivalent to that of the artist. This account does not naively ignore the social and historical situation of art, and is consistent with Adorno's stress on the *inexhaustibility of interpretation of high art* – how such art seems continually to invite new interpretation, as each generation understands it in light of its own concerns.

The idea of free interpretation has not been much-explored in the philosophical literature, and an account of it could begin by looking at those genres that undermine or deny it, such as the sentimental or sensationalist. 'Guernica' and *Wozzeck* are intended to shock, but are not merely sensationalist; violent crime fiction such as the novels of Val McDermid, or Hollywood schlock horror, in contrast, exploit a visceral reaction that gives the audience little freedom of response. An instinctive reaction to blood and gore overwhelms critical freedom; as, in a milder way, does the sentimentality indulged by romantic comedy. There is a continuum of cases. Frank Capra's popular classic 'It's a Wonderful Life' elevates a homely didacticism into a paean to the American dream, and is neither kitsch nor the highest cinematic art. Stephen Soderbergh's recent film *Contagion*, in contrast, is slick entertainment that compels attention by trading on hysteria about the danger of an international pandemic; unlike classic art, its impact dissipates with subsequent reflection.

There is political high art that does leave freedom for interpretation – examples are Joseph Conrad's *The Secret Agent* and Heinrich Böll's *The Lost Honour of Katharina Blum*. In Böll's novel, unlike the film based on it by Schlöndorff and von Trotta – still a very impressive interpretation – the message is not driven home, yet is still explicit.[70] It is clear how the author regards, and wants us to regard, the so-called free press, but he shows rather than tells us. Political art like

---

[70] The film, extends the novel's action by including the journalist Tötges' funeral, where his publisher delivers a hypocritical homily condemning his murder as an attack on the freedom of the press.

Böll's does not *force* me to believe that the press is evil – a forthright expression of a view need not be constraining. Didacticism need not imply propaganda art. In the case of Conrad, interpretational freedom – or the novel's range of concern – may lead us to say that it is not *just* political art. It is an artistic decision or capacity, and not a product of confusion, to make a work rich enough to be freely interpretable – although the subject-matter that the artist is tackling may itself be complex and confusing.[71]

Modernist art developed increasingly sophisticated non-didactic strategies for making audiences confront issues. Implicit ambiguities or contradictions force the audience to form a view on the subject, or at least to consider possibilities. For instance, Brecht's plays ask how one can confront a corrupt system in which one is implicated. Even in works that are not music-theatre like *Threepenny Opera*, songs serve to undercut the spoken word. A literal-minded political interpretation – whether by the director or audience – ignores how the playwright presents and simultaneously undermines a view.

Art does many things, apart from aiming at truth. It can fail to achieve truth in many ways; by being false, or by being nonsensical, a category that can include the phenomenon described by Frankfurt as 'bullshit', and embraced by Lady Gaga, as noted earlier.[72] While high art aims at truth, and lesser art aims at entertainment – the latter, though easier to achieve than truth, is not guaranteed – perhaps art can aim at bullshit too. Certainly some artists – Salvador Dalí, Peter Greenaway, Michael Nyman, Lars von Trier, Damien Hirst – aim to impress without caring whether they say anything true, and that is one kind of bullshit.

What I am arguing may seem quite ambitious, indeed over-ambitious. It challenges the deflationary conception which regards artistic truth as referring to a varied collection of virtues partly illuminated by a contrast with narrative or representational truth. On that view, 'artistic truth' is like 'moral victory', a concept parasitic on that of ordinary types of victory; one could not explain it to someone who lacked a grasp of ordinary winning and losing, yet it differs from standard types of winning in that the moral victor loses. This is a picture that I am attempting to undermine. One should question the

---

[71]   Ford Madox Ford's *The Good Soldier*, with its confused narrator, is an interesting example. Powell and Pressburger's *The Life And Death of Colonel Blimp* is another example of political high art; Edgerton (2011) may be simplistic in claiming that it has 'a powerful and clear message', that to fight the Nazis, one must play dirty (156–7).

[72]   Frankfurt (2005); see also Cohen (accessed 2012).

Andy Hamilton

common assumption that there is a 'standard' type of truth, propositional truth.

This article leaves many ends untied, and only gestures at responses to intractable problems such as how music and architecture aim at the truth. Much further work is needed to explain the connection between truth as intended by the artist, and truth as interpreted by the audience; and I have barely scratched the surface of the ideological objection, which may turn out to be several objections. The concept of high art has been left rather open, as has the question of the extent to which its precursors aimed at truth. But I hope at least to have shown that the concept of artistic truth is a richer one than is often supposed, thereby suggesting that the very practice of artistic creation is essentially truth-directed.

Many thanks for comments from: Emma Bennett, Andy Byford, Lucille Cairns, James Clarke, Freya Carr, Arlene Keizer, David Lloyd, David Macarthur, Brian Marley, Max Paddison, Richard Read, Alastair Rennie, Mark Rowe, Barry Smith, Roger Squires, James Steintrager, Rachael Wiseman; and to audiences at the Taste Workshop at the Institute of Philosophy, University of London; the RIP lecture at UCL; and seminars at University of California Irvine, Northumbria University, and Durham University MLAC group.

University of Durham
a.j.hamilton@durham.ac.uk

Bibliography

44
Adorno, Theodor W. (1997), *Aesthetic Theory*, London: Athlone Press.
—. (1992), *Quasi una fantasia: essays on modern music*, London: Verso.
Althusser, L. (2006), *Lenin and Philosophy*, London: Aakar.
Applebaum, Anne (2004), *Gulag: a History of the Soviet Camps*, Harmondsworth, Middlesex: Penguin.
Baines, Jocelyn (1971), *Joseph Conrad; A critical biography*, Harmondsworth, Middlesex: Penguin.
Barnwell, P. (2011), 'Pre-Reformation Parish Churches', in Guillery, P. ed. (2011), 33–48.
Barrell, John (1980), *The Dark Side of the Landscape: the Rural Poor in English Paintings 1730–1840*, Cambridge: Cambridge University Press.

Beardsley, Monroe (1981), *Aesthetics: Problems in the Philosophy of Criticism*, 2nd ed. Indianapolis: Hackett.

Belting, Hans (1994), *Likeness and Presence: a history of the image before the era of art*, Chicago: University of Chicago Press.

Booth, Wayne (1983), *The Rhetoric of Fiction*, Chicago: University of Chicago Press.

Cohen, G.A. (accessed 2012), 'Deeper Into Bullshit', http://philbs. posterous.com/cohen-deeper-into-bullshit

Coleridge, Samuel Taylor (1985), *Biographia Literaria*, ed. J. Engell and W. Jackson Bate, New Jersey: Princeton University Press.

Danto, Arthur (1981), *Transfiguration of the Commonplace*, Cambridge, MA: Harvard University Press.

Derrida, Jacques (1987), *The Truth in Painting*, Chicago: University of Chicago Press.

Dorment, R. (2012), 'Beautiful, Aesthetic, Erotic', *New York Review of Books*, **59**:3, 14–16.

Edgerton, Ds (2011), *Britain's War Machine*, London: Allen Lane.

Engel, P. (2005), 'Truth and the Aim of Belief', In D. Gillies, ed. *Laws and Models in science*, London: King's College, found at http://www.unige.ch/lettres/philo/enseignants/pe/Engel% 202005%20Truth%20and%20the%20aim%20of%20belief.pdf

Figes, Orlando (2007), *The Whisperers: Private Life in Stalin's Russia*, London: Allen Lane.

Frankfurt, Harry (2005), *On Bullshit*, Princeton: Princeton University Press.

Gadamer, Hans-George (1975), *Truth and Method*, Seabury: Seabury.

Geertz, Clifford (1983), *Local Knowledge: Further Essays in Interpretive Anthropology*, London: Fontana.

Geuss, R. (1981), *The Idea of a Critical Theory*, Cambridge: Cambridge University Press.

Goss, Glenda (2009), *Sibelius: A Composer's Life and the Awakening of Finland*, Chicago: University of Chicago Press.

Graham, Gordon (1986), *Politics In Its Place*, Oxford: Clarendon.

—. (2007), *Philosophies of Arts*, 3rd edition, London: Routledge.

Greene, T. (1940), *The Arts and the Art of Criticism*, New Jersey: Princeton University Press.

Guillery, P. ed. (2011), *Built From Below: British Architecture and the Vernacular*, London: Routledge.

Hamilton, Andy (2000), 'The Authority of Avowals and the Concept of Belief', *European Journal of Philosophy*, **8**:1, 20–39.

—. (2007) *Aesthetics and Music*, London: Continuum.

Andy Hamilton

—. (2008), 'Adorno and the Autonomy of Art', in S. Giacchetti ed. *Nostalgia for a Redeemed Future: Critical Theory*, Rome: John Cabot/Delaware University Presses, 251–66.

—. (2009), 'Scruton's Philosophy Of Culture: Elitism, Populism And Classic Art', *British Journal of Aesthetics*, **49**:4, 389–404.

Hegel, F. (1975), *Lectures on Fine Art*, Oxford: Oxford University Press.

Hill, Rosemary (2007), *God's Architect: Pugin and the Building of Romantic Britain*, Harmondsworth, Middlesex: Penguin.

Hospers, John (1970), *Meaning and Truth in the Arts*, Chapel Hill: University of North Carolina Press.

Horwich, Paul (1990), *Truth*, Oxford: Blackwell.

John, Eileen (2007), 'Poetry and Cognition', in *A Sense of the World: Fiction, Narrative and Knowledge* eds. John Gibson, Wolfgang Huemer and Luca Pocci, London: Routledge, 2007.

Johnson, Samuel (1781), *The Lives of the English Poets*, London.

Kristeller, Oscar (1990), 'The Modern System of the Arts', in his *Renaissance Thought and the Arts*, Princeton: Princeton University Press, 163–227.

Lamarque, Peter and Haugom Olsen, Stein (1994), *Truth, Fiction and Literature*, Oxford: Clarendon.

Lamarque, Peter (2009), *The Philosophy of Literature*, Oxford: Blackwell.

Lukács, Georg (1975), *History and Class Consciousness*, London: Merlin.

Mamet, David (1993), *Oleanna*, London: Methuen Drama in association with the Royal Court Theatre.

Mateer, David ed. (2000), *Courts, Patrons and Poets*, New Haven; London: Yale University Press in association with the Open University.

Meyer, Leonard (1974), 'Concerning the Sciences, the Arts – And the Humanities', *Critical Inquiry*, **1**:1, 163–217.

Mortensen, Preben (1997), *Art in the Social Order*, Albany: State University of New York Press.

Murdoch, Iris (1990), *The Sovereignty of Good*, London: Routledge.

Nietzsche, Friedrich (1973), *The Will to Power*, New York: Random House.

Paddison, Max (1993), *Adorno's Aesthetics of Music*, Cambridge: Cambridge University Press.

Passmore, John (1991), *Serious Art*, La Salle, Illinois: Open Court.

Plato (1996), *Plato on Poetry*, ed. Penelope Murray, Cambridge: Cambridge University Press.

Price, K. (1949), 'Is There Artistic Truth?' *The Journal of Philosophy*, **46**:10, 285–291.

Rapaport, Hermann (1997), *Is There Truth in Art?*, New York: Cornell University Press.

Ricoeur, Paul (1970), *Freud and Philosophy: Essay on Interpretation*, Yale: Yale University Press.

Richter, Gerhard (2009), *Writings, Interviews and Letters 1961–2007*, London: Thames and Hudson.

Ruskin, John, (1980), *The Genius of John Ruskin: selections from his writings*, ed. J. Rosenberg, London: Routledge.

Rowe, Mark (2009), 'Literature, Knowledge and the Aesthetic Attitude', *Ratio* **22**:4, 375–97.

Schiller, Jerome (1964), 'An Alternative to Aesthetic Disinterestedness', *Journal of Aesthetics and Art Criticism*, **22**:3, 295–302.

Scruton, Roger (1997), *The Aesthetics of Music*, Oxford: Clarendon.

—. (1998), *An Intelligent Person's Guide to Modern Culture*, London: Duckworth.

Smith, Adam (1985), *Glasgow Edition of the Works and Correspondence of Adam Smith*, Indianapolis: Liberty Fund, Vol. IV.

Stevenson, Anne (1990), *Bitter Fame: A Life of Sylvia Plath*, Harmondsworth, Middlesex: Penguin.

Stolnitz, Jerome (1992), 'On the Cognitive Triviality of Art', *British Journal of Aesthetics*, **32**:3, 191–200.

Wellmer, A. (1991), *The Persistence of Modernity: Essays on Aesthetics, Ethics and Postmodernism*, trans. D. Midgley, Cambridge: Polity Press.

Wittgenstein, Ludwig (1998), *Culture and Value*, Oxford: Blackwell.

Young, James O. (2001), *Art and Knowledge*, London: Routledge.

Zuidervaart, Lambert (2004), *Artistic Truth: Aesthetics, Discourse and Imaginative Disclosure*, Cambridge: Cambridge University Press.

Index of Names

Abell, Catherine 133, 137, 142 n.16
Adorno, Theodor 204, 232, 236–237, 239–240, 253–256
Aeschylus 121
Aglea 11
Alberti, Leon Battista 92–93, 100
Alcibiades 136
Alighieri, Dante 118
Althusser, Louis 252
Andokides painter 147–148
Aphrodite (Venus) 11, 43, 83
Apollo 7
Aquinas, Thomas (Saint) 88, 89
Archer, Jeffrey 16
Aristotle 1–4, 52, 115–119, 130, 180, 190
Arlen, Harold 58
Athene 1
Augustine (Saint) 67, 74, 49, 80, 178 n.6
Austen, Jane 153, 155, 163–169, 173, 201, 240, 251, 253

Babbitt, Milton 56
Bach, Johann Sebastian 36 n.5, 37, 44, 47, 49, 156, 194, 195, 221, 222
Bacon, Francis 250
Barrell, John 251, 252, 253 n.64

Bartók, Béla 195, 204 n.63
Baudelaire, Charles 107
Beethoven, Ludwig van 38, 39–42, 44–46, 156, 170, 189, 192 n.38, 193–195, 197 n.47, 199 n.51, 200, 201 n.58, 209–213, 215, 226, 254,
Benjamin, Walter 86
Berg, Alban 214
Berlin Painter 143
Bernini, Gian Lorenzo 142
Beuckelaer, Joachim 75, 78
Blake, William 106, 117, 123
Böll, Heinrich 256–257
Bookner, Anita 168
Booth, Wayne 244
Borges, Jorge Luis 97165 n29
Botticelli, Sandro 12
Boulez, Pierre 56
Brooke, Rupert 145
Brahms, Johannes 216–220, 222, 254
Brecht, Bertoldt 257
Brutus, Marcus Junius 130
Bryson, Norman 71, 73 n.2
Buber, Martin 198
Budd, Malcolm 185, 33 n.1, 138 n.13

Buddha 6
Burden, Chris 88–89
Burne-Jones, Edward 250
Busoni, Ferruccio 221–222

Caesar, Julius 130
Cage, John 223
Campbell, Don 15
Canaletto (Giovanni Antonio Canal) 250
Canova, Antonio 11
Capra, Frank 256
Carroll, Noël 22 n.17, 100
Celibidache, Sergui 218
Cézanne, Paul 163
Chambers, William 255
Chardin, Jean-Baptiste-Siméon 20, 79, 80, 82
Charles I (King) 142
Chaucer, Geoffrey 179
Chillida, Eduardo 9, 11
Chopin, Frédéric 173, 194
Christ, Jesus 5, 6, 75, 140–141
Cicero 131–132
Clare John 110
Coetzee, J.M. 238
Coleridge, Samuel Taylor 106, 117,

Index of Names

Index of Names

Index of Names

For EU product safety concerns, contact us at Calle de José Abascal, 56–1°, 28003 Madrid, Spain or eugpsr@cambridge.org.

www.ingramcontent.com/pod-product-compliance
Ingram Content Group UK Ltd.
Pitfield, Milton Keynes, MK11 3LW, UK
UKHW020334140625
459647UK00018B/2144